Decoding Luigi Moretti's Architettura Parametrica

Decoding Luigi Moretti's Architettura Parametrica presents an unprecedented critical discussion of one of the earliest theoretical and practical explorations into the integration of scientific thought, mathematical models, and digital tools in architectural design.

Moretti, a renowned professional who engaged in countless intellectual initiatives, developed and refined his architectural vision long before "parametric" became synonymous with computational design. His Architettura Parametrica is an unconventional inquiry of the prospects offered to design practice by digital thinking rather than by digital tools, which were still immature or completely absent at the time. Moretti proposed a unique and still relevant mental landscape that united his fascination with Baroque spatiality, operational research, informal art, optics, cybernetics, ethics, and much more. This research decodes numerous facets of Architettura Parametrica, from the rigid theoretical precepts to the negotiation with design praxis, from the use of equations to aid the research of forms to the speculation on the meaning of architecture through abstract mathematics.

This book offers novel perspectives to scholars interested in the interplay between architectural design practice and theory, mathematics and design methods, digital and architectural culture, and to the growing number of practitioners who are crafting personal narratives within the most disruptive computational techniques.

Giuseppe Canestrino, Architect and PhD, is an adjunct professor and postdoctoral research fellow in Architectural Design at the University of Calabria. He has previously been a guest researcher at Delft University of Technology and a visiting PhD at the Universitat Politècnica de Catalunya. His primary research interest lies in exploring the relationship between digital culture, form-finding, and architectural design also through the investigation of scientific and logical processes for solving design problems. His critical-theoretical research informs his professional practice, in which he engages through participation in design competitions, gaining various victories and honourable mentions. He is the author of *La Concezione Parametrica dell'Architettura* (trad. The Parametric Conception of Architecture, 2024) and his writings have been published in *The Journal of Architecture, The Plan Journal, Nexus Network Journal, Agathòn, Storia Urbana, U+D – Urbanform and Design*, and *Metamorfosi*, among others.

"Giuseppe Canestrino masterfully unveils the forgotten genius of Luigi Moretti at the historical root of parametric architecture, before digital computation. This book is an essential read for architects, scholars, and designers seeking to grasp the theoretical and practical evolution of parametric thinking in architectural design."

Patrik Schumacher, *Zaha Hadid Architects*

"Giuseppe Canestrino's insightful examination positions Luigi Moretti's Architettura Parametrica as a significant milestone in architectural theory and practice. It demonstrates how mathematics, science, and culture were used to establish the groundwork for computational and parametric thinking, essential in contemporary architecture. This is a timely and vital work."

Michael J. Ostwald, *Editor in Chief, Nexus Network Journal, Architecture and Mathematics.*

Decoding Luigi Moretti's Architettura Parametrica

Negotiating Theory and Practice in the Forecasting of Computer-Aided Architectural Design

Giuseppe Canestrino

LONDON AND NEW YORK

First published 2025
by Routledge
4 Park Square, Milton Park, Abingdon, Oxon OX14 4RN

and by Routledge
605 Third Avenue, New York, NY 10158

Routledge is an imprint of the Taylor & Francis Group, an informa business

© 2025 Giuseppe Canestrino

The right of Giuseppe Canestrino to be identified as author of this work has been asserted in accordance with sections 77 and 78 of the Copyright, Designs and Patents Act 1988.

All rights reserved. No part of this book may be reprinted or reproduced or utilised in any form or by any electronic, mechanical, or other means, now known or hereafter invented, including photocopying and recording, or in any information storage or retrieval system, without permission in writing from the publishers.

Trademark notice: Product or corporate names may be trademarks or registered trademarks, and are used only for identification and explanation without intent to infringe.

British Library Cataloguing-in-Publication Data
A catalogue record for this book is available from the British Library

ISBN: 978-1-032-97709-6 (hbk)
ISBN: 978-1-032-97710-2 (pbk)
ISBN: 978-1-003-59500-7 (ebk)

DOI: 10.4324/9781003595007

Typeset in Times New Roman
by KnowledgeWorks Global Ltd.

To Marina, who has always been there.

To Andrea, for whom I will always be there.

Contents

List of figures   *ix*
Note on translation   *xiii*
Image credits acknowledgement   *xiv*

Introduction: Why Moretti matters today   1

1 Moretti within the proto-parametric patchwork:
  Amid international trends and Italian culture   6

  *Italian architectural design culture, between
    anti-scientism and digital transition kick-off 10*

2 Architettura Parametrica: In theory   21

  *The juvenile period and the early insights of Architettura
    Parametrica (1930s–1950) 22*
  *The maturity period and the outline of a personal
    architectural theory (1950–1957) 33*
  *The commitment period and the contaminations of
    an architectural theory (1957–1973) 44*

3 Architettura Parametrica: In practice   66

  *A design exegesis of the Architettura Parametrica
    exhibition projects 67*
  *Formal Analogies with Architettura Parametrica
    in Moretti's oeuvre 95*
  *Methodological analogies with Architettura
    Parametrica in Moretti's oeuvre 105*

4 Foresights and topicality of Architettura Parametrica 124

Continuities and ruptures with contemporary computational design 125
Architettura Parametrica between AI and Parametricism 132

Conclusions 138

Bibliography *142*
Index *152*

List of Figures

2.1 Luigi Moretti, Piazzale delle Adunate, Roma, 1934–1936. Credits: ACSLM, project 59, [A] 36/51/2], [B, C, D, E] 36/42/3; [F, G] 36/42/4; [H, I] 36/42/5; [J] 36/42/8.   29

2.2 Luigi Moretti, Piazzale dell'Impero, Roma, 1937. Credits: ACSLM, project 71, [A, B] 37/77/2; [C] F3130; [D] F3127; [E] F2860.   32

2.3 Luigi Moretti, Studies on the façade of Palazzo Ossoli by Baldassarre Peruzzi. Moretti defines figures I to VI as "relationships between the spaces defined by the frames and their projections". Published in Luigi Moretti, "Valori della modanatura", Spazio a 3, no. 6 (1951–1952): 5–12, 112.   38

3.1 Luigi Moretti, Exhibition of Parametric Architecture and of Mathematical and Operational Research in Town-Planning, Milan, 1960. Representation of equivisibility curves of the W function in: football stadiums M and N, swimming stadiums A and B, Tennis stadium T, and cinema hall C. Credits: Archivio Centrale dello Stato Italiano, Fondo Luigi Moretti [ACSLM, auth. 650/2025], project 162, [M] 60/198/7; [N] 60/198/8; [A] 60/198/11; [B] 60/198/10; [T] 60/198/13; [C] 60/198/15.   68

3.2 Luigi Moretti, selection of models shown at the Architettura Parametrica exhibition. Credits: ACSLM [auth. 650/2025], project 162, [A] F3055; [N-T], Luigi Moretti, "Ricerca matematica in architettura e urbanistica", Moebius, IV no. 1 (1971): 30–53.   69

3.3 Luigi Moretti, plans of the models shown at the Architettura Parametrica exhibition, 1960. Credits: ACLSM [auth. 650/2025], project 162, [N] F3066; [A]: F3053; [C] F3054. [M-T]: Luigi Moretti, "Ricerca matematica in architettura e urbanistica", Moebius, IV no.1 (1971): 30–53.   72

x *List of Figures*

3.4 Overlay between equivisibility curves of the W function and plans of the models shown at the Parametric Architecture exhibition. Football stadiums M and N, swimming stadiums A, tennis stadium T, and cinema hall C. The visibility graph B is superimposed on the only exhibited swimming stadium model. Credits: Composition by the author.   73

3.5 Diagram for calculating the visibility function W in M and N soccer stadiums. The information indicated in bold is provided by Moretti. The information in regular font is added by the author. Credits: Author.   75

3.6 Top: Natural analogies for swimming stadiums with the plant Physalis alkekengi L provided by Moretti in "ricerca matematica in architettura e urbanistica" (1971). Bottom: Diagram for calculating the visibility function swimming stadium B. The information indicated in bold is provided by Moretti. The information in regular font has been added by the author. Credits: Author.   83

3.7 Diagram for calculating the visibility function W in tennis stadium [T] and cinema hall [C]. The information indicated in bold is provided by Moretti. The information in regular font is added by the author. Credits: Author.   89

3.8 Top: Luigi Moretti, model and visibility function of the cinema hall. Bottom: Diagram of the generic polar equation of a circle. Credits: [A] ACSLM [auth. 650/2025], project 162, F3063; [B] Author.   92

3.9 Reconstructions, interpretations, and experiments on Luigi Moretti's visibility functions (W). Football stadiums M and N, swimming stadium B, Tennis stadium T, and cinema hall C. Credits: Author.   94

3.10 Luigi Moretti, preliminary sketches for the Olympic Stadium, Rome, 1937–1940. Note a sketch (G) resembling the elevation of football stadium N. Credits: ACSLM [auth. 650/2025], project 62, [A, E, and G] 37/48/53OR; [B and F] 37/48/54OR; [C] 37/48/31OR; [D] 37/48/30OR.   97

3.11 [A, B, C, and D]: Luigi Moretti, stadium project according to the principles of Architettura Parametrica, 1960. [E]: Luigi Moretti, model for the Olympic Stadium renovation, Rome, 1960. Credits: ACSLM [auth. 650/2025], project 165, [A] 60/200a/3OR, [B] 60/200a/2OR, [C] 60/200a/4OR, [D] 60/200a/7. Project 164, [E] F3078.   98

List of Figures xi

3.12 Luigi Moretti, early explorations and design proposals for the stadiums of the Tehran Olympic Complex, 1966. [A, B, C and D] Stadium for 65,000 spectators. [E and F] Stadium for 100,000 spectators. Credits: ACSLM [auth. 650/2025], project 222, [A] 66/248/11, [B] 66/248/12, [C] 66/248/13, [D] 66/248/124, [E] 66/248/120, [F] 66/248/118. 100

3.13 Luigi Moretti, proposals for the Tehran Olympic Complex masterplan, 1966. Credits: ACSLM [auth. 650/2025], project 222, [A] 66/248/32, [B] 66/248/114, [C] 66/248/1. 102

3.14 Luigi Moretti, juvenile and mature explorations of "architecture for large numbers" morphologies. Top: sketches for the Olympic Stadium project in Rome, 1937–1940. Bottom: sketches for the stadiums of the Olympic complex in Tehran, 1966. Credits: ACSLM [auth. 650/2025], project 62, [A] 37/48/53OR, 37/48/51OR, 37/48/44OR, 37/48/21OR; folder n. 27 [B]. 103

3.15 Luigi Moretti, research on visibility, space and form. Patent "Aviorama" [A, ACSLM, folder n. 40]; Proposal for GIL Theatre in Piacenza, 1933–1935 [B, ACSLM, project 49, 41/131/9]; Visibility and flow studies for Gran Teatro EUR, Rome, 1938–1942 [C and D, ACSLM, project 76, 38/82/4OR]; Visibility studies and an excerpt for a "parametric analysis of the classroom" for the Dance Academy, Rome, 1950–1969 [F and H, ACSLM, project 227, 50/155e/9, 50/115E/8. No archival code for E and G]. Credits: ACSLM [auth. 650/2025]. 104

3.16 Luigi Moretti, Operational scheme of Villa Borghese underground parking, Rome, 1966. Credits: ACSLM [auth. 650/2025], project 226, 65/251/1OR. 107

3.17 Top: Example of an analytical output with strong aesthetic potential compiled as part of the traffic investigation in Rome. With "Istituto di Calcolo delle Probabilità – Centro per la Ricerca Operativa e Sperimentale" of Rome University, desire lines of the city of Rome. Credits: ACSLM [auth. 650/2025], folder n. 50. Bottom: Existing proposal for Farah Park [A] and urban re-design by Luigi Moretti [B], Tehran, 1966. Credits: ACSLM [auth. 650/2025], [A] folder n. 50, [B-C] project 223, 66/249/1, 66/249/2. 111

3.18 Luigi Moretti, geometric-algebraic studies and a proposal for the Chiesa del Concilio Santa Maria Mater Ecclesiae, Rome, 1970. Credits: ACSLM [auth. 650/2025], project 252, [A] 70/275/32or, [B] 70/275/63, [C] 70/275/56. 115

xii *List of Figures*

3.19 Luigi Moretti, combinatorial research inspired by Architettura Parametrica. Top: abacus of variations in fixtures, volumes, facilities in the Corso Italia complex, Milan, 1949 – 1956. Bottom: studies on variations in the façades of the Watergate complex, Washington, 1949 – 1956. Credits: [A] "Ricerche di Architettura. Sulla flessibilità di funzione di un complesso immobiliare urbano", Spazio a 3, no. 6 (—1951–1952). [B] ACSLM [auth. 650/2025], project 174, 61/210/29OR. 117

3.20 Luigi Moretti's projects that hint at the adoption of form-finding techniques: [A] Tabgha Sanctuary proposal, 1967; [B] Viterbo's Baths proposal, 1955–1956; [C] Società Anonima Pellami's canopy, Induno Olona, 1955–1956; [D] Chiesa del Divino Amore proposal, Roma, 1970; [E] Fiuggi Baths, 1963–1970, [F] Tevere's bridge proposal, Rome, 1959. Credits: ACSLM [auth. 650/2025], [A] project 232, F0002; [B] project 252, 53/159/23OR; [C] project 130, F0591; [D] project 251, 70/274/13BIS; [E] project 212, F0231; [F] project 153, 58/180/13, F0028. 119

4.1 [A] Example of D'Arcy Wentworth Thompson's images used by Luigi di Moretti to illustrate his ideas and articles. Moretti used elaborations of Archaeopteryx and Apatornis in "structure comme forme" (1954), in the English and Italian versions of the exhibition catalogue on Architettura Parametrica (1960), and in "Ricerca matematica in architettura e urbanistica" (1971).
[B] Coordinate network of transitions from Archaeopteryx's pelvis to Apatornis' pelvis. Credits: D'Arcy Wentworth Thompson, On growth and form (Cambridge: University Press, 1917), 757, 759, 760. 129

Note on translation

Architettura Parametrica is never translated to emphasise its discontinuities with what is now called Parametric Architecture or Parametric Design.

The titles of the articles *Forma come Struttura* and *Struttura come Forma* remain untranslated to avoid confusion caused by the reversed titles in the English and French editions published in the 1950s and 1960s.

To best capture the nuances of Moretti's thought, his Italian typescripts are referenced when available rather than the English or French translations made at the time.

In line with international studies on Luigi Moretti, translations of his writings by Federico Bucci and Marco Mulazzani are preferred when available.

Image credits acknowledgement

All the images of the *Fondo Luigi Moretti* contained in this book are published courtesy of the Italian Ministry of Culture and of Italy's *Archivio Centrale dello Stato* (authorisation no. 650/2025).

Introduction
Why Moretti matters today

Luigi Moretti (1906–1973), a divisive architect and intellectual, is an example of an accomplished professional who informed his practice with a sustained interest in theoretical and editorial activities. Moretti proposed a continuous cross-pollination between architecture, art, and technical innovation. His oeuvre has been cited and celebrated by key authors of contemporary architectural culture, from Robert Venturi[1] to Peter Eisenman,[2] deemed of interest by prominent critics, such as Kenneth Frampton,[3] and despised by others, such as Bruno Zevi[4] and Manfredo Tafuri.[5] The disdain towards Moretti was inevitably fuelled by his professional ties, first with the leadership of the Italian National Fascist Party,[6] of which he was an open supporter, and later with major Italian real estate groups.[7]

While playing a fundamental role in the design of the *Foro Italico* in Rome,[8] around 1940, he laid the foundations of his personal architectural vision: Architettura Parametrica. His theoretical work pioneered a scientific approach to architecture. Moretti anticipated the integration of digital tools, and advocated for a redefinition of design methodologies, instruments, and goals. Moretti's Architettura Parametrica promoted a renewal of ethical rigour in design. It emphasised the explicit articulation of the hidden relationships among the various parameters that define a design problem. Furthermore, it fostered an interdisciplinary dialogue between architecture and other disciplines such as biology, optics, abstract mathematics, game theory, operational research, psychology, and economics. Moretti's concepts preceded, by several years, studies that introduced a mathematical formalisation of architectural design, such as Christopher Alexander's decomposition of architecture.[9] However, while the 1990s saw the emergence of a cultural tradition around Computer-Aided Architectural Design,[10] Moretti's theories appeared to fade into prolonged obscurity, even within Italy.[11]

Immediately after Moretti's death in 1973, Italian critics continued to recognise the significance of several of his built works,[12] particularly the unparalleled *Casa delle Armi* and *Casa del Girasole*. However, Architettura Parametrica remained in the background, frequently regarded as a fascination, too nascent to significantly impact professional practice. Zevi expressed

DOI: 10.4324/9781003595007-1

criticism regarding Moretti's 1960 *Exhibition of Parametric Architecture and of Mathematical and Operational Research in Town-Planning* remarking: "the parametric method is focused on tools and instrumental goals. But what about its ends? For these, electronic brains are of little use while human brains are needed".[13] Zevi, during a debate in which Moretti also participated, defined the "calculation of shapes in the laboratory of parameters" as a "recourse to magical and abstruse formulas", incapable of addressing the issue of space[14]. Even today, Architettura Parametrica is met with suspicion, particularly regarding its role in the evolution of digital culture and its capacity to anticipate contemporary computational shifts in design. In this panorama, Frampton's appreciation of Architettura Parametrica in 1974 is remarkable. Frampton recognised that Moretti's "essays do not as yet enjoy even a fractional part of the reputation they deserve" while talking about Architettura Parametrica as a dialogue "vis-à-vis [with] the semiological dimension"[15] of architecture.

Moretti's theories did not drive the exploration, from the late 1980s onwards, of the formal, spatial, and methodological possibilities offered by digital software in architecture. In fact, his Architettura Parametrica does not appear among the 26 essays selected by Mario Carpo in his fundamental *The Digital Turn in Architecture 1992–2012*. Other cultural references drove this turn, such as the positions deriving from theories – or, in some cases, the fascinations – of Gilles Deleuze.[16]

We are now witnessing a gradual rediscovery of Moretti's thought, marked by some of the key figures of the *Digital Turn*, such as John Frazer. Frazer argued, with some caution, "that Moretti was probably the first to create three-dimensional architectural form using a complex set of parametric relationships resolved by digital computation".[17] Most notably, Frazer conflates Moretti's Architettura Parametrica with contemporary parametric design – a controversial position to which I will return. Patrick Schumacher, the theorist of contemporary Parametricism, has only recently disclosed the influence of Moretti on Zaha Hadid.[18] In addition, a growing number of scholars, including Mollie Claypool, Roberto Bottazzi, and Daniel Davis, have recognised Moretti's contribution to the origins and development of various intersections between digital technology and architecture.

Contemporary architecture is increasingly influenced by the pervasiveness of digital, computational shifts, and the allure of *scientism*. Therefore, the rediscovery of Architettura Parametrica must be encouraged, not merely to refine historical reconstructions, but rather, because Moretti's theory and work remain highly relevant and can still serve as a guiding framework in today's complex architectural landscape. However, without dedicated monographic studies, the abrupt reintroduction of Architettura Parametrica into architectural discourse risks distorting Moretti's theories and his vision for their application. The immediate association of Architettura Parametrica with Parametricism and Parametric Design has thus suggested a continuity between Moretti's thought and some advanced manifestations of digital in architecture.

These manifestations are heterogeneous and may align with a broader "parametric conception of architecture".[19] Within this conception, architectural design may, with different levels of rigour, "converge with scientific practices, articulate its forms in algorithmic terms, and integrate precise digital tools into its practice".[20] The convenient notion of continuity, suggested by Frazer and previously mentioned, must therefore be critically questioned.

Moretti claimed to have grasped the principles of his theory in the 1940s,[21] a time when he had no access to either computational or electronic tools. In the 1950s, as he promoted Architettura Parametrica, he introduced the term *parameter* not as a variable for generating design alternatives but as a means to uncover the relationships defining a design problem. By 1960, when he outlined possible applications of Architettura Parametrica in both theory and practice, he aimed to establish a renewed balance between architectural form and its functional requirements using operational research techniques. In the 1970s, as digital technology matured sufficiently so as to be able to support algorithmic design, Moretti – by then in poor health – shifted his focus to the cultural and ethical implications of both Architettura Parametrica and the computer.

Therefore, Architettura Parametrica and Parametric Design are distinct concepts, with the latter referring to the practice of linking multiple design attributes to shared parameters, enabling automatic updates whenever parameter values change. Moreover, in numerous writings, Moretti presents Architettura Parametrica as a means of freeing architecture from formal predetermination and predefined stylistic language.[22] This stance is in sharp contrast to the early theories of Parametricism, which define a specific formal repertoire – characterised by smooth splines, NURBS, blobs, and metaballs – to push its agenda.[23] Moretti's Architettura Parametrica, moreover, presents a distinct vision that contrasts with other early encounters between digital technology and architecture. What defines this vision is a fusion of artistic, technical, theoretical, and cultural dimensions, deeply rooted in real architectural practice. In fact, this vision emerged from the expertise of a seasoned architectural practitioner rather than from academia or the eclectic interests of computer scientists fascinated by architecture. Moretti saw Architettura Parametrica as a path to build architecture, not merely as a subject of theoretical speculation.

This complex landscape creates the need to keep questioning the continuity between Moretti's Architettura Parametrica and the contemporary computational shift – not to relegate the former to a new period of obscurity, but rather to revitalise the cultural foundations of the latter. This book pursues this objective, aiming to decode Moretti's Architettura Parametrica from both theoretical and practical perspectives. It explores the diverse theoretical narratives Moretti proposed for Architettura Parametrica, from the rigid frameworks shaped by the integration of operational research into architectural design to more fluid interpretations guided by ethical rather than technical principles. Furthermore, it will examine how Moretti translated Architettura

Parametrica into practice, moving beyond the complex mathematical models presented in the *Exhibition of Architettura Parametrica*, which have been systematically reconstructed in this book for the first time. Additionally, this book seeks to reassess Moretti's cultural legacy in the development of digital in architecture since his writings and experiments anticipated several cornerstones of computational design, including the generation of form through algorithmic procedures; the use of mathematical analyses as fitness functions; the use of optimisation processes via operational research methods; and even an early intuition of the Deleuzean *objectile*. Chapter 1 will reposition Moretti's Architettura Parametrica within the broader evolution of the meaning of "parametric" in architecture, challenging its historical marginalisation – particularly in Italy – and highlighting its impact on both past and future computational design narratives. Chapter 2 will explore the theoretical evolution of Parametric Architecture, tracing its journey from an early, nascent intuition to a fully developed design theory enriched by methodological insights and technical hypotheses. Chapter 3 will investigate the principles of Architettura Parametrica within Moretti's extensive body of professional work, focusing on his renowned mathematical models for "architecture for large numbers" alongside the many instances where he applied his theories through more informal approaches. Chapter 4 will frame Moretti's vision in current and future architectural debate, focusing on what he anticipated, forecasted, and predicted, along with a discussion on future developments of architecture that may be enhanced by the concepts underlying Architettura Parametrica. Thus, Architettura Parametrica will be examined through its dynamic interplay between theoretical speculation and practical demands, demonstrating how Moretti continuously negotiated the values of these inseparable facets of architectural design. Above all, Architettura Parametrica will be approached as a largely uncharted mental landscape for architectural exploration.

Notes

1 Robert Venturi, *Complexity and Contradiction in Architecture*, 2nd ed. (New York: Museum of Modern Art, 1977; first published 1966), 20, 96.
2 Peter Eisenman, "Profiles of Text. Luigi Moretti, Casa 'Il Girasole,' 1947–50", in *Ten Canonical Buildings 1950–2000* (New York: Rizzoli, 2008), 26–48.
3 Cfr. Kenneth Frampton, Introduction to the article: *Luigi Moretti,* "The Values of Profiles. Structures and Sequences of Spaces", *Opposition* 4 (1974): 109–139. Translated by Thomas Stevens.
4 Zevi criticises Moretti repeatedly, while still appreciating some of his architectures, such as the *Casa delle Armi*. His obituary is suggested as a summary: Bruno Zevi, "La scomparsa di Luigi Moretti. Computer inceppato dal dannunzianesimo" [The passing of Luigi Moretti: Computer jammed by D'Annunzianism] *L'Espresso* (29 july 1973). Reprinted in Bruno Zevi, *Cronache di architettura* (Bari: Laterza, 1975), n. 130.
5 Tafuri also reluctantly appreciates some of Moretti's works but despises his "disengagement" and, perhaps, his excessive professional commitment. Cfr. Manfredo Tafuri, *Architettura italiana 1944–1981* (Einaudi: Turin 1982).

Introduction 5

6 Cfr. Paolo Nicoloso, *Gli architetti di Mussolini* (Milan: Franco Angeli, 1999).
7 The relationship between Moretti and the *Società Generale Immobiliare* is noteworthy. It led to the construction of the Watergate Complex in Washington (1961–1970) and the Stock Exchange Tower in Montreal (1961–1971).
8 Cfr. Antonella Greco, Giorgio Muratore, and Francesco Perego, *Foro Italico. Manifesto per un'architettura* (Milan: CLEAR, 1999).
9 Cfr. Christopher Alexander, *Notes on the Synthesis of Form* (Cambridge: Harvard University Press, 1964).
10 Cfr. Mario Carpo, ed., *The Digital Turn in Architecture 1992–2012* (Chichester: Wiley, 2012); Antoine Picon, *Digital Culture in Architecture: An Introduction for the Design Professions* (Basel: Birkhäuser Architecture, 2010); Antonino Saggio, *Thoughts on a Paradigm Shift. The IT Revolution in Architecture* (Rome: Vita Nostra Edizioni, 2020).
11 See Chapter 1.
12 For an essay reflecting on Moretti's figure a few years after his death: Renato Bonelli, *moretti* (Roma: Editalia, 1975).
13 Bruno Zevi, "Cervelli Elettronici? No, macchine calcolatrici" [Electronic brains? No, calculating machines], *L'architettura. Cronache e storia* 62 (1960): 508–509.
14 Bruno Zevi, "*Matematica e architettura. Scienza della costruzioni kaput*" [Mathematics and architecture. Structural mechanics kaput] in *Cronache di Architettura*, n. 552. Cfr. Paolo Portoghesi, Luigi Moretti, Sergio Musmeci, Armando Plebo, and Bruno Zevi, *Structures, Mathèmatiques, Architecture Contemporaine* [Debate transcript], 23 November 1964, in Rome, Archivio Centrale dello Stato – Fondo Luigi Moretti (ACSLM), folder 42. The debate concerns the exhibition of the same name curated in 1963 in Paris (Palais de la Découverte) by Maurice Bayen.
15 Frampton, "Introduction". Thomas Stevens – who translated and wrote an additional introduction – claims Moretti founded the "Società per un'Architettura Parametrica" in 1943; however to date, no archival evidence has been found in the *Fondo Luigi Moretti* kept at the *Archivio Centrale dello Stato Italiano*.
16 Cfr. Mario Carpo, "Introduction. Twenty Years of Digital Design", in *The Digital Turn,* 9–14.
17 John Frazer, "Parametric Computation: History and Future", *Architectural Design* 86, no. 2 (2016): 18–23.
18 Patrick Schumacher, "From Parametric Architecture to Parameters of Social: Interview by Zaira Magliozzi", *AR Magazine* a LV, 125/126 (2021): 440–455.
19 Giuseppe Canestrino, *La concezione parametrica dell'Architettura* [The parametric conception of Architecture] (Siracusa: LetteraVentidue 2024).
20 Canestrino, *La concezione parametrica dell'Architettura*, 13.
21 The evolution of the theory of Architettura Parametrica is discussed in Chapter 2.
22 Luigi Moretti, ""Ricerca matematica in architettura e urbanistica" [Mathematical research in architecture and urbanism", *Moebius* IV, no. 1 (1971): 30–53.
23 Patrik Schumacher, *Parametricism as Style – Parametricist Manifesto*, 2008. https://patrikschumacher.com/parametricism-as-style-parametricist-manifesto. Presented and discussed at the Dark Side Club, 11th Architecture Biennale, Venice 2008.

1 Moretti within the proto-parametric patchwork

Amid international trends and Italian culture

The meaning of "parametric" in architecture is as fluid as it is elusive. It represents a field of possibilities, whose study and conscious practice demand a fundamental premise: recognising a general "parametric conception" of architecture. This conception can be developed through specific methodological, instrumental, and even linguistic references, which often coexist with more empirical design approaches shaped by practice rather than by theory. Within this framework, Moretti's Architettura Parametrica is just one piece of a complex and multifaceted mosaic. Thus, Architettura Parametrica cannot be discussed in isolation from this broader context. More importantly, without this discussion, it is impossible to correct the widespread misconception that conflates different theoretical and operational perspectives in architectural design, such as Patrik Schumacher's Parametricism, computational and parametric design, Moretti's Architettura Parametrica, evolutionary design, and others.

"Parametric" has assumed an all-embracing meaning in architecture. Furthermore, contemporary architectural design culture encourages us to extract a type of *retrospective parametricity* from seemingly divergent experiences. We may recognise parametric structures in Vitruvius's writings, in Baroque space, in form-finding through physical models, and, naturally, in various digital manifestations in architecture – from the pioneering cybernetic applications of the 1960s to recent developments in artificial intelligence. In other words, we continuously reinterpret architectural practice and history along with their intersections with disciplines such as biology and computer science in order to extract metaphors, techniques, methodologies, and design approaches.

Mathematics, form-finding, Moretti's Architettura Parametrica, Baroque spatiality, and advances in CAD form the foundation of the parametric vision discussed by Bottazzi.[1] For Claypool,[2] morphological thought, proto-parametric analogue processes, the cybernetic revolution, early digital explorations, and their transition from the virtual to the physical world shaped the digital landscape in architectural design. I have also explored the origins of the parametric in architecture, proposing three distinct roots[3]: the formalisation

DOI: 10.4324/9781003595007-2

of operational research and pattern languages, emergent or assisted form-finding, and analogue and digital variation. These, along with many others,[4] are not just historical reconstructions but also narratives that either justify or shape personal visions of architectural design. Such narratives can uncover hidden connections between architecture and the many disciplines that drive its evolution. As will be discussed, Moretti passionately sought, debated, and revealed these connections and relationships.

Providing a concise overview of these connections is crucial in defining the cultural and technical domain in which Luigi Moretti operated, both nationally and internationally.

A fundamental premise is that what we now consider "parametric" exhibits significant discontinuities not only with Moretti's Architettura Parametrica but also with the meaning assigned to the term in architecture between the 1950s and the 1970s, the period in which Moretti developed and disseminated his theories. Furthermore, the meaning of "parametric" assumed computational nuances between 1992 and 2012, a period defined by Carpo as the "Digital Turn" in architecture.[5] Today, the parametric in architecture encompasses multiple ideas, ranging from the dynamic update of design solutions to the use of algorithmic tools, and from identifying the parameters that shape a design problem to delegating tasks to computational processes. Further complicating this is the ease with which the term "parametric" is often associated with the intricate forms driven by advanced 3D modelling software, which for years dominated the architectural star system. These evolving concepts frequently diverge from the notion of Architettura Parametrica as developed by Moretti.

To understand Moretti's thinking more intimately, it is necessary to understand both what and who, between the 1960s and the 1970s, were considered close to a general parametric conception of architectural design. A young and bold Charles Jencks, in 1969, wrote *Architecture 2000: Predictions and Methods*[6] in which he proposed that different "architectural species" can evolve simultaneously. Jencks attempted to organise the past and future of architectural theory into "clusters" of traditions (unselfconscious, self-conscious, logical, idealist, intuitive, and activist) that share common traits. Jencks identifies an indefinite "parametric" trend emerging in 1970 as an immediate future for architecture and as part of the "logical" tradition of architectural design. He associates "parametric" closely with Alexander, author of *Notes on the Synthesis of Form*, the seminal text for an "object-oriented" design built on formalised[7] process. Another neighbour of "parametric" is "SCSD" (*Schools Construction System Development*), a particular example of formalisation based on the syntax and on the definition of rules regulating the relationships between its elements. In the dense web of his 1960s references, "parametric" is anticipated by figures such as Pierluigi Nervi, Frei Otto, Riccardo Morandi, Eero Saarinen, Yona Friedman, Jean Prouvé, and Ove Arup, all of whom explored the possibility of researching architectural form with renewed logic and rigour. Taking a step back to the 1950s, we find the emergence of themes central to those who view form-finding as a cultural root of the parametric: suspension structures, space frame, hyperbolic paraboloids, geodesic, and the work of Felix Candela. Systematising these references is not simple; however, it is possible to recognise a general trend: the meaning of "parametric" in architecture referred to the predominance of logical and sequential construction of design solutions over heuristic and intuitive approaches. Moretti stands out remarkably from the landscape described by Jencks. He bases his Architettura Parametrica on foundations far from those suggested by the English architect, except for Guido Figus's form-resistant structures, which he uses to illustrate his famous essay *Struttura come Forma*.[8]

Jencks's evolutionary diagrams are more suggestive than analytical. They also seem highly unstable, as shown by his constant revisions, updates, and corrections.[9] Yet they help illuminate a fundamental point: the original meaning of "parametric" in architecture is detached from the 1960s cybernetic trends, which Jencks instead links to the "idealist" tradition along with trends such as "automated", "custom built", and "system theory". A counterintuitive thesis, yet confirmed today by Mario Carpo, who states that "cybernetic experiments of the 1960s and 1970s, […] did not change architecture at all".[10] Cybernetics did not change architecture because architects were "inspired and excited by the development of the new 'electronic brains', as they were called back then, but throughout the 1960s and 1970s there was next to nothing that architects and designers could actually have done with computers in the daily practice of their trade, if they could have afforded to buy one — which they couldn't".[11] This position at least suggests some interest in the fact that, as early as 1957 – the year Moretti founded the *Institute for Mathematical and Operational Research Applied to Urbanism* (IRMOU) – he both had access to computing tools and used computers to guide the synthesis of architectural forms.

In 1948, Norbert Wiener defined cybernetics in a seminal book as "the entire field of control and communication theory, whether in the machine or in the animal".[12] Moretti was interested in these kinds of studies, given also his citations of Wiener's works in his writings.[13] At the root of the prefix *cyber*, there is neither a digital nor an electronic meaning.[14] The digital sense, instead, did not emerge until Gordon Pask's inspiring work *The Architectural Relevance of Cybernetics*, where, referencing Nicholas Negroponte's work, he proposes that it is "possible to mimic certain aspects of architectural design by artificial intelligence computer programs".[15] Cybernetics had a limited impact on architectural design practice, mainly due to its inability to suggest forms or spatiality of choice. This was despite experiments exploring architectures that could adapt in real-time to functional demands, such as the *Fun Palace* designed by Pask and Cedric Price. Yet, when Pask defined cybernetics as a discipline capable of unifying architecture, sociology, anthropology, ecology, and economics, its proximity to Moretti's definitions of Architettura Parametrica became evident.[16] Above all, when Moretti proposed the concept of "Human Engineering" in the catalogue of the 1960 *Exhibition on Architettura Parametrica*,[17] focusing on designing proper relationships between humans, mechanised systems, and interface devices, the influence of Wiener's cybernetics became evident.

Research on architectural cybernetics – as well as on Architettura Parametrica – reveals an important aspect: early studies on the intersection of computing and architecture were overly optimistic in their goals. In the 1970s, while Nicholas Negroponte presented the idea of using computers as creative collaborators in the architectural design process,[18] engineers, mechanics, and other technical professionals began developing user-friendly CAD software with a more practical aim: enhancing drafting efficiency. A few years later, "the architects' fling with the first age of electronics was quickly obliterated by the postmodern leviathan".[19]

Early computer science provided architects with ideas and theories rather than with tools. Moreover, these tools would have been too complex and clunky for an architect to use without a strong background in computer science. When Moretti used an IBM 610 at the 1960 Architettura Parametrica exhibition, he was already 54 years old. By age 26, he had already designed icons of Italian rationalism, such as the *Casa della GIL* (1933–1938) and the *Casa delle Armi* (1934–1936) in Rome. Archival documents even show that, at just 12 years old, he "began assisting his father [architect Luigi Rolland] in drafting projects, as recorded in an account book dated 1919".[20] After a lifetime of practising architecture at an elite level, Moretti approached digital technology, unlike the young researchers of MIT's Architecture Machine Group. Few of them, like Yona Friedman,[21] would later gain recognition in the international debate as architects rather than computer scientists.

Today, while the meaning of parametric in architecture seems inseparably tied to digital technology, its origins were not necessarily linked to digitisation, software, or even computers. It was not about breaking architectural form into bits but about solving design problems through a logical sequence of actions, reducing heuristic and intuitive aspects.

What has been discussed forms a patchwork of experiences that can be defined as *proto-parametric*, understood as "using analogue means to compute form using parameters".[22] Claypool recently used this term to place Moretti alongside figures like Antoni Gaudí, Frei Otto, and Buckminster Fuller as precursors of contemporary digital thinking in architecture.[23] This definition of proto-parametric raises an important question, namely whether Moretti was truly computing architectural form, or whether it is a widely accepted belief resulting from the lack of in-depth research into his Architettura Parametrica explorations. Before addressing question, it is useful to reflect briefly on the meaning of computation in architecture.

In architecture, most of the various nuances of "computational" refer to processing information through calculations, algorithms, or logical procedures.[24] Computation, therefore, implies creating an explicit link between data (in its various forms) and architectural form through a process that involves a certain degree of automation and, in some way, can solve an entire class of architectural problems. Moretti's theories align with this goal of computation in architecture, as he sought to free architectural design from excessive empiricism. However, as IRMOU collaborators recall, "many of the problems Moretti wished to solve with the new tool [the computer] were, at that time, still too complex in terms of numbers and parameters for feasible execution".[25] Moretti thus aspired to solve certain architectural problems computationally but often had to settle for merely calculating them instead. As discussed in Chapter 3, his use of computers in architectural design did not exhibit the level of automation inherent in the computational approach. Nevertheless, Architettura Parametrica – especially after the founding of IRMOU in 1957 – was deeply influenced by the emerging cultural values of computation, from the ability to reach a solution through a verifiable and reproducible process to the idea of using data to shape architectural forms.

After Moretti's death, this patchwork continued to expand, incorporating influences such as Deleuze's *fold*, the intuition of using animation software to generate architectural forms, the democratisation of scripting through visual programming, and much more. These evolving ideas gradually distanced the meaning of the parametric in architecture from the theories outlined by Moretti. Architettura Parametrica should be studied as a unique phenomenon within the discussed patchwork of precedents. Moretti did not shape his Architettura Parametrica through either a necessary or deliberate exploration of technology. Instead, as will be discussed, he first developed a theoretical vision for design and only subsequently adopted technical methods through a slow and laborious process of interpretation and adaptation. What is most remarkable, however, is that today Architettura Parametrica continues to offer fruitful perspectives for architectural design.

Italian architectural design culture, between anti-scientism and digital transition kick-off

The precedents behind Architettura Parametrica should not be discussed by adapting the outcomes of international research on the broader parametric theme in architecture. Topics fundamental to today's parametric architectural conception, such as form-finding and biological analogies, were marginal in shaping Luigi Moretti's theoretical thought. Instead, his desire to instil a scientific perspective into architectural design fuelled his approach. Understanding the perceived utility of scientific thought in Moretti's society helps explain Architettura Parametrica's reactionary force. His theories, in fact, appear radical when compared with Italian ideologies from the 1930s to the 1970s.

Moretti began defining his Architettura Parametrica around 1940,[26] in his early thirties. This architectural theory was in line with the ideological spirit of a large part of Italy,[27] at the time under the rule of the fascist party. In those years in Italy, "science was seen and used as a useful propaganda tool, serving the regime's self-glorification".[28] In its most extreme forms, "the myth of science spread in Italy through rhetoric that left little room for technicality, favouring instead [...] the imaginary".[29] Italy, in other words, embraced the metaphor of *scientificity* rather than its actual practice. Moretti repeatedly criticised this contradiction, which can be seen as one of the sparks that ignited the need for Architettura Parametrica. The interest in the "myth of science", rather than in the practice of science, led Antonio Gramsci to criticise the "scientific nationalism"[30] resulting from the "breakdown of the unity" of scientific intellectual thought.

Despite Moretti's continuous and personal reinterpretations, it can be argued that this mythologisation of science, to some extent, influenced – and perhaps even created the need for – Architettura Parametrica. Moretti himself stated that Architettura Parametrica is "a mental stance" and not just a technical approach. Notably, Moretti's position aligns with Antonio Gramsci's early recognition of the fragility of scientific culture in Italy. Gramsci wrote: "scientific mentality is weak as a phenomenon of popular culture, but it is also weak among scientists, who possess a scientific mindset only within their technical group. They understand abstraction within their specific field but not as a 'mental stance'".[31] This unique situation helped shape a cornerstone of Architettura Parametrica's agenda: the blend of humanist and technicist visions of architecture.

Architettura Parametrica soon became misaligned with the emerging scientific culture that spread in Italy after World War II. In those years, the thought of prominent figures like Benedetto Croce and Giovanni Gentile gained importance at the expense of scientific culture. Already in 1909, Croce in his *Logic as the science of the pure concept* argued how scientific mentality with its abstractions and mathematisations mutilated the living reality of the world without truly understanding it. In the postwar era, he further argued that "natural sciences and mathematical disciplines have graciously yielded to philosophy the privilege of truth".[32]

In light of this widespread anti-scientific culture, Moretti seems to use some of his reference as a political stance: his decision to illustrate many of his articles with the work of scientists like D'Arcy Thompson,[33] to empathise with the life of mathematician Galois,[34] or to open the exhibition catalogue with a quote from Galileo[35] can be read as political statements. Yet Architettura Parametrica prospers where science and culture meet. It is no coincidence, then, that after quoting Galileo, Moretti gave equal importance on the same page to excerpts from *Orlando Furioso* by Ludovico Ariosto, *The Seven Pillars of Wisdom* by T. E. Lawrence, *The Pisan Cantos* by Ezra Pound, and *American Architecture* by Frank Lloyd Wright.[36]

In this complex context – where anti-scientific culture shaped the nation's ways of thinking – Moretti is perceived and judged in different ways: able to navigate the "components of political-professional power", as Bruno Zevi noted with disdain,[37] yet a perpetual outsider, excluded from the cultural debate that shaped the evolution of Italian architecture. For example, the space Moretti received in texts such as Zevi's *Storia dell'Architettura Moderna* (1955) or Leonardo Benevolo's 1960 volume of the same name is limited to brief mentions, almost journalistic references. Despite the international endorsements mentioned in this book's introduction, Architettura Parametrica is absent in significant monographs addressing architectural theories of the second half of the 20th century. Guillemette Morel Journel provides an overview of the texts where Moretti's work was initially absent and later reassessed.[38] Notably, it was missing from the first edition of Kenneth Frampton's *Modern Architecture: A Critical History* (1980) but included from 2020 onwards. Similarly, it was absent from the early editions of William J.R. Curtis's *Modern Architecture Since 1900* (1981) but included from 1996 onwards. This reassessment, however, did not stem from a newfound appreciation of Moretti's Architettura Parametrica but rather from his other works, such as the remarkable *Casa del Girasole* and *Casa delle Armi*. In *Architecture 2000's* already discussed evolutionary diagram of architecture, Moretti is positioned by Jencks far from the parametric trend, which is conceived as a logical approach to architecture. Instead, Jencks places Moretti within the "self-conscious" and "intuitive" approaches, immersed in a melting pot of architects, occupying an almost central position among the "formalism", "organic", and "pop" trends.[39] In this diagram, Moretti appears alongside renowned figures such as Venturi, Michelucci, Soleri, Moore, and Kahn. However, this 1969 placement captures the marginality of Moretti's theoretical work compared to his much more acclaimed professional practice.

In the Italian context, the absence of references to Luigi Moretti's Architettura Parametrica in books on the intersection of architecture and digital technology in the 1960s and 1970s[40] is striking – perhaps even deliberate. Architettura Parametrica and the experiments of Moretti and IRMOU were absent from the 1969 exhibition *Reality and perspective of computer use in architecture*[41] in Bologna. This absence is surprising, as the event introduced *componenting*, an approach to architectural form driven by digital technology and the inherent tendency of prefabricated forms to be digitised.[42] Nonetheless, Moretti's Architettura Parametrica principles seem coherent with the words of Massimo Foti and Mario Zaffagnini, the exhibition curators: "today's design process, and even more so in the future, must replace the anachronism of the individual gesture where intuition and personal sensitivity guide decisions with information and scientific methods".[43]

Even stranger is the absence of references to Architettura Parametrica in Rome-based architectural studies. *Architettura & Computer*,[44] edited by Maria Zevi, compiles contributions from seminars on *The Computer in Design* held at the Faculty of Architecture in Rome in 1971. There is no reference to Moretti's experiments in this book, despite the presence of writings by Sergio Musmeci and Giulio Roisecco. Both had engaged with Moretti on the themes of Architettura Parametrica.[45] The few who discussed Architettura Parametrica often seemed to misunderstand it. This is the case with Renato Bonelli, who in 1975 stated: "identifying requirements to be translated into variables expressed in quantities while ignoring qualities is a direct and therefore intuitive choice. This contradicts the scientific principles of the method and invalidates its process".[46]

Architettura Parametrica is more than just using computers in architectural design; instead, it is about adopting the methods computers rely on.[47] It is not about embracing the forms that computers can generate but rather their way of thinking. This detachment from form, and thus from space, may have prevented Architettura Parametrica from significantly influencing architectural culture. This argument parallels Carpo's perspective on cybernetic experiments of the 1960s and the 1970s.[48] However, during those years, some Italian architects pursued highly personal and experimental research on how electronic computation could introduce mobility into architectural form. As Franco Purini recalls,[49] this was the case with Maurizio Sacripanti and his proposals for the *Peugeot Skyscraper* competition in Buenos Aires (1961) and the *Cagliari Theatre Competition* (1964–1965). These projects could rival other acclaimed proto-parametric experiments, such as Cedric Price and Gordon Pask's *Fun Palace*, in communicative, formal, and technological innovation.

One of Italy's most eminent architects and academics was reflecting on the role of the computer just as Moretti was writing his famous "testamentary" article on Moebius. In 1971, Ludovico Quaroni described the first computer applications in architecture as "design machines […] still too expensive and, at the same time, too crude, uncertain, and slow".[50] This awareness led Quaroni to see greater value in using computers to explore the possible variations of a design idea through a combinatory approach rather than in actually generating design ideas. Consequently, computers were relegated to automating geometric checks, such as viewing a composition of volumes from different perspectives. Meanwhile, Quaroni hoped that digital technology would eventually become more "docile".[51] In Italy, the hope of using computers to generate rather than merely manage forms was present but faced scepticism. The renewal of scientific rigour in design – essential for fully harnessing the potential of early computers – was met with uncertainty about its relationship with Italy's design culture. Bruno Zevi fully endorsed the computer and, in 1973 – the year of Moretti's death – stated: "Computers stimulate the invention of forms, enriching the lexicon, grammar, and syntax of architecture".[52] When Bruno Zevi spoke about the possibility of walking through digital models to explore their perspectival effects (an aspect Quaroni also found significant), he shifted the focus to space,[53] which was far less central to Anglo-Saxon experiments. At the same time, there were outright rejections of computers in architecture. Also in 1973, Manfredo Tafuri warned about the rise of computing, framing it as part of a broader movement leading to "the first – still Utopian – attempt at capital's complete domination over the universe of development".[54] Tafuri did not engage with the technical potential of computers but criticised the metaphors and themes they inevitably introduced into architectural design.

Maria Zevi, in discussing the relationship between computers and architecture, linked the Beaux-Arts legacy to the tendency of Italian architecture schools to train "artist-creators" rather than technicians.[55] For her, this culture "rejects any scientific approach to art" and architecture.[56] Similarly, Moretti defended computers against attacks from architects operating "in a Beaux-Arts climate" who saw the application of scientific tools as the death of architectural genius.[57] A young Carlo Severati raised an important issue, one not yet fully addressed in the international debate at the time: the influence of computers on shaping architectural languages.[58] He questioned how computers would respond differently depending on a designer's background. Severati reflected on the different roles of the computer for an architect aligned with the organic tradition and one more inclined towards the use of stereometric geometries. This reveals that, in late 1960s Italy, when computers were still technologically underdeveloped, there was already concern about their impact on both architectural practice and culture.

In 1969, discussing the underdevelopment of Italy's professional structure, Foti and Zaffagnini argued that in architecture, "the computer [...] seems to have arrived too soon".[59] Perhaps Italian architecture was lagging behind, but it was neither impervious nor unaware of what was happening abroad. It simply chose a different path, one more aligned with humanist culture. Elena Mortola and Alessandro Giangrande cited pioneers such as Steven Coons – one of the fathers of computer graphics – and topics related to design cognition.[60] They discussed ideas from Marvin Minsky, a pioneer of artificial intelligence, and the possibilities of a "self-improving program".[61] Mortola and Giangrande also discussed figures later recognised in the proto-parametric patchwork, such as Ivan Sutherland, who developed the first drawing software with intrinsic parametric capabilities, and Nicholas Negroponte, whose research explored "an architectural machine" with intelligent behaviour – one capable of self-improvement, as Minsky had speculated.

While Negroponte saw the use of unintelligent computers as leading to the progressive devaluation of the built environment, Italian architectural culture perceived a different risk: the lack of reflection on the relationship between computers and the fundamental principles of architecture. From the Italian perspective, Negroponte's aspirations were "emblematic of the architect's distrust in their own design abilities when faced with increasingly complex problems [...] which manifests in the often unconscious desire to delegate, at least in part, [...] the responsibility of decision-making to others".[62] Sergio Musmeci – now recognised as a key figure in the proto-parametric patchwork, thanks to works like the *Basento* Bridge – seemed to reference Ivan Sutherland's *Sketchpad* and *Lightpen* when describing parametric modelling that linked the deformation of a structure to the geometry of its perimeter.[63] Foti and Zaffagnini's volume *The Electronic Challenge* is filled with references to early parametric precedents: Buckminster Fuller's use of computers for the geodesic dome at Expo 67 in Montreal, Konrad Wachsmann's discretisation of architectural form, and Serge Chermayeff and Christopher Alexander's use of computers to coordinate the interdependent parameters of a design problem.[64] International references extended beyond technical aspects to include cultural influences, such as Marshall McLuhan's *Understanding Media* and algorithmic art, both of which are discussed in Foti and Zaffagnini's *The Electronic Challenge*.

It would be necessary to wait until the end of the "first AI winter" for a renewal of Italian perspectives on the digital realm in architecture. While the *Digital Turn* was emerging internationally, Italian architectural research regained interest in digital technologies. There was a newfound respect for the digital, but it was clear that it had changed: scientific rigour and advanced computer science expertise were no longer needed in order to explore the potential of digital in architecture. Digital thought was no longer used to question architectural principles and to uncover their hidden relationships. Instead, architecture itself began questioning the digital, pushing the limits of what – by the early 2000s – was fundamentally different from the experiments of the 1960s and 1970s previously discussed. Starting in 1996, Antonino Saggio developed the series *The IT Revolution in Architecture*, which, beginning in 1998, published 39 books in Italian, many of which were also translated into English, German, and Chinese. As described by Saggio, "a new group of books that would deal with the relationship between architecture and computing from the structural, cultural and formal perspective. [...] not technical books but books, that would initiate an intellectual debate on the relationship between architecture and computing".[65] This series of books was a pioneering initiative that established a research domain for scholars and practitioners of digital architecture in Italy and beyond. In those years, Franco Purini, reflecting on digital space and its tools, wrote:

> New technologies are foundational spaces, having embryonic content and meaning waiting to be developed. Exploring new technologies means venturing into an unknown territory, rich with potential forms that must be discovered, questioned, defined, and used in new composition.[66]

While the debate on form contrasted those advocating for the dematerialisation of architecture with those seeking to give digital design physicality, space became one of the key topics in discussions about the relevance of digital. Some, like Livio Sacchi, argued that digital technology had unleashed "a culture of space that, perhaps, did not exist before".[67] A more conservative stance came from Massimiliano Fuksas, who firmly stated that "the computer has not changed architectural space in any way".[68] Fuksas pointed to the remarkable spatial achievements of architects like Jørn Utzon and Eero Saarinen, accomplished with "just a pencil and T-square".[69] Purini also discussed how digital tools have driven specific operations on architectural space – such as deformations, compressions, dilations, and torsions – both conceptually and physically.[70] In the early 2000s, there were no in-depth studies of Moretti's Architettura Parametrica, only a few references and citations.[71] Indeed, research into digital architecture and computer science had moved far away from the scientific approach he had originally proposed.

Today, we are facing yet another shift, one that the Italian architectural culture has yet to question. The ability to reach design solutions in a deterministic and reproducible way through computational thinking is now being challenged by new tools that introduce an element of probability into the design process. The many AI-driven tools, some already mature and others still evolving, have revealed that statistical analysis and correlation can contribute to defining an architecture.[72] The evolution of design thinking discussed in this chapter suggests the path forward. There is a pressing need to investigate the spatial and formative dimensions brought by these new tools, ensuring that the cultural debate that has always accompanied digital experimentation in architecture is renewed. In the early 2000s, a rediscovery of Moretti as a practitioner and as a theorist began. This rediscovery was led by architectural historians such as Federico Bucci, Marco Mulazzani,[73] Bruno Reichlin, Letizia Tedeschi,[74] and Cecilia Rostagni.[75]

Today's context, instead, calls for another rediscovery of Moretti's Architettura Parametrica, that this time must unfold from the values and interests of architectural design research and practice.

Notes

1 Cfr. Roberto Bottazzi, *Digital Architecture beyond Computers: Fragments of a Cultural History of Computational Design* (London: Bloomsbury Visual Art, 2018).
2 Mollie Claypool, *The Digital in Architecture: Then, Now and in the Future* (Copenhagen: SPACE10, 2019). https://discovery.ucl.ac.uk/id/eprint/10116421/
3 Giuseppe Canestrino, *La concezione parametrica dell'Architettura* [The parametric conception of Architecture] (Siracusa: LetteraVentidue 2024).
4 The literature on the subject is consistent. For an overview of existing positions: Mario Carpo, "A Short but Believable History of the Digital Turn in Architecture", *e-flux* 03 (2023). https://www.e-flux.com/architecture/chronograms/528659/a-short-but-believable-history-of-the-digital-turn-in-architecture/; Molly Wright Steenson, *Architectural Intelligence: How Designers and Architects Created the Digital Landscape* (Cambridge: MIT Press, 2017); Daniel Cardoso Llach, *Builders of the Vision: Software and the Imagination of Design* (New York, London: Routledge, 2015); Theodora Vardouli, Olga Touloumi, eds., *Computer Architectures. Constructing the Common Ground* (New York, London: Routledge, 2019); Andrew Goodhouse, ed., *When Is the Digital in Architecture?* (Montreal: Canadian Centre for Architecture; Cambridge, MA: MIT Press, 2017); Socrates Yiannoudes, *Architecture in Digital Culture: Machines, Networks and Computation* (New York: Routledge, 2022); Michael Fox and Bradley Bell, *The Evolution of Computation in Architecture* (New York: Routledge, 2024). To view a timeline on the evolution of architectural software: Philip Schneider and Teresa Fankhänel,

"Architectural Software Timeline", in *The Architecture Machine: The Role of Computers in Architecture*, eds. Teresa Fankhänel and Andres Lepik (Basel: Birkhäuser, 2020), 226–237. See also SPACE10's "The Digital in Architecture" timeline realised by Pentagram. https://www.pentagram.com/work/the-digital-in-architecture/story

5 Mario Carpo, ed., *The Digital Turn in Architecture 1992–2012* (Chichester: Wiley, 2012).

6 Charles Jencks, *Architecture 2000: Predictions and Methods* (London: Studio Vista Limited, 1971).

7 Formalised design refers to a structured approach to architectural design, where rules or predefined methodologies guide the generation of form. It ensures consistency, efficiency, and reproducibility in design outcomes. I have discussed one application of Architettura Parametrica as a formalised approach to design: Giuseppe Canestrino, "Luigi Moretti's Formalised Methods and His Use of Mathematics in the Design Process of Architettura Parametrica's Swimming Stadiums", *Nexus Network Journal* 27 (2025 [Published online 2024]): 119–137. https://doi.org/10.1007/s00004-024-00784-x

8 Luigi Moretti, "Struttura come Forma", *Spazio* a 3, no. 6 (1951): 21–30, 110. Reprinted and discussed in Federico Bucci and Marco Mulazzani, eds., *Luigi Moretti: Works and Writings* (New York: Princeton Architectural Press, 2002); Roberto Podda, *Luigi Moretti: Lessons of Spazio* (New York: Routledge, 2024); Annalisa Viati Navone and Guillemette Morel Journel, *Luigi Moretti: Structure et espace* (Paris: Éditions de la Villette, 2024).

9 Cfr. Mark Wigley, "*The Drawing that Ate Architecture*", *Jencks Foundation* (2023). https://www.jencksfoundation.org/explore/text/the-drawing-that-ate-architecture

10 Mario Carpo, "Parametric Notations: The Birth of the Non-Standard", *Architectural Design* 86, no. 2 (2016): 24–29.

11 Mario Carpo, *Beyond Digital: Design and Automation at the End of Modernity* (Cambridge: MIT Press, 2023).

12 Norbert Wiener, *CYBERNETICS or Control and Communication in the Animal and the Machine,* 2nd ed. (Cambridge: MIT Press, 1961; first published 1948), 11.

13 Moretti in his notes for an article on *Civiltà delle Macchine* wrote: "Moreover, I later saw that I am in good company, from Wienner [sic] to François Jacob to all the biologists of the latest generation, aside from [Joseph] Needham and John Haldane. How is the 'human mechanism'?". ACSLM, folder 49. Cfr. Virginio Bettini, Siro Lombardini, Luigi Moretti, and Pietro Prini, "Tecnologia e problema ecologico" [Technology and the ecological problem], *Civiltà delle Macchine* a XX, no. 3–4 (1972): 19–38. See also Cecilia Rostagni, *Luigi Moretti 1907–1973* (Milan: Electa, 2008), 98, note 103.

14 Cfr. Carpo, *Beyond Digital,* 96.

15 Gordon Pask, "The Architectural Relevance of Cybernetics", *Architectural Design* 39, no. 9 (1969): 494–496. More on this: John Frazer, "The Architectural Relevance of Cybernetics", *Systems Research* 10, no. 3 (1993): 43–48.

16 Cfr. Luigi Moretti, "Parametrica Architettura", in *Dizionario Enciclopedico di Architettura e Urbanistica* [Encyclopaedic Dictionary of Architecture and Urban Design], ed. Paolo Portoghesi (Rome: Istituto Editoriale Romano, 1968), 377. This dictionary entry is fully reproduced in Chapter 2, section "Formalised approaches driven by operational research".

17 Luigi Moretti and IRMOU, eds., *Mostra di architettura parametrica e di ricerca matematica e operativa nell'urbanistica* (Milan: Arti Grafiche Crespi, 1960). In the English version, Moretti is listed as the sole author: Luigi Moretti, *Exhibition of Architettura Parametrica and of Mathematical and Operational Research in Town-Planning* (Rome: Istituto nazionale di ricerca matematica e operativa per l'urbanistica, 1960).

18 Nicholas Negroponte, *The Architecture Machine: Toward a More Human Environment* (Cambridge, MIT Press, 1970); Nicholas Negroponte, *Soft Architecture Machines* (Cambridge, MA: MIT Press, 1976).
19 Carpo, "Short but Believable History".
20 Rostagni, *Luigi Moretti*, 8.
21 Friedman conducted research on topics related to Architettura Parametrica: Yona Friedman, *Toward a Scientific Architecture* (Cambridge: MIT Press, 1975).
22 Claypool, *The Digital in Architecture*.
23 Claypool, *The Digital in Architecture*.
24 Among the most recent research on the topic: Fox and Bell, *The Evolution of Computation*. Cfr. note 4.
25 Anna Cuzzer, Giovanni Cordella, Cristoforo Sergio Bertuglia, "Testimonianza. Ricordi dell'IRMOU" [Witness. Memories of the IRMOU], in *Luigi Moretti: Razionalismo e trasgressività tra barocco e informale* [Luigi Moretti: Rationalism and Transgressiveness between Baroque and Informal], eds. Bruno Reichlin and Letizia Tedeschi (Milan: Electa, 2010), 421–427.
26 For a detailed discussion of Moretti's various statements on the origins of Architettura Parametrica, see Chapter 2.
27 Luciano Pellicani and Elio Cadelo, *Contro la modernità: Le radici della cultura antiscientifica in Italia* (Soveria Mannelli: Rubbettino, 2013), 10.
28 Pellicani and Cadelo, *Contro la modernità*, 10.
29 Lorenzo Benadusi, "Il mito della scienza" [The myth of science], in *Scienze e cultura dell'Italia unita* [Science and culture in unified Italy], eds. Francesco Cassata and Claudo Pogliano, 162 (Turin: Einaudi, 2011).
30 Antonio Gramsci, "Note di cultura italiana" [Notes on Italian culture], in *I Quaderni del Carcere* [Prison Notebooks], quaderno 14(I), §38 (1933–1935). https://quadernidelcarcere.wordpress.com/2014/12/07/note-di-cultura-italiana/
31 Antonio Gramsci, "Argomenti di cultura. Logica formale e mentalità scientifica" [Topics of culture. Formal logic and scientific mentality], in *I Quaderni del Carcere*, quaderno 17(IV), §52 (I) (1933–1935). https://quadernidelcarcere.wordpress.com/2015/02/19/argomenti-di-cultura-logica-formale-e-mentalita-scientifica/
32 Benedetto Croce, *Indagini su Hegel e schiarimenti filosofici* [Investigations into Hegel and philosophical clarifications] (Bari: Laterza, 1952), 273.
33 Cfr. Luigi Moretti, "Structure comme forme", *United States Lines Paris Review* 1 (1954); Luigi Moretti, "Ricerca matematica in architettura e urbanistica" [Mathematical research in architecture and urbanism], *Moebius* IV, no.1 (1971): 30–53.
34 See Chapter 2, section "Towards an «Architecture Autre»".
35 Moretti and IRMOU, *Mostra di architettura parametrica;* Moretti, "Ricerca matematica in architettura". The details of the passage cited by Moretti are faithfully copied as he wrote them: GALILEO, *Concerning Two New Sciences – The Second Day* – Ed. Naz., vol. VIII, pp. 169–170.
36 Moretti, "Ricerca matematica in architettura".
37 Bruno Zevi, "Luigi Moretti double-face. Ambizione contro ingegno", in *L'Espresso* (17 February 1957). Reprinted in Bruno Zevi, *Cronache di Architettura* (Bari: Laterza, 1975), n.145.
38 Guillemette Morel Journel, "Lire et faire lire une pensée atypique. Les textes de Luigi Moretti" [Read and let others read an atypical thought. The texts of Luigi Moretti], in Viati Navone and Morel Journel, *Moretti: Structure et espace*, 35–53.
39 Jencks, *Architecture 2000*, 46–47.
40 Cfr. Francesco Maranelli, "The Arrival of the Information Model, 1969. The New International Building Industrialization Frontier and Italy's 'Electronic Challenge'", in *Construction Matters. Proceedings of the 8th International Congress on Construction History*, eds. Stefan Holzer, Silke Langenberg, Clemens Knobling and Orkun Kasap, 48–55 (Zurigo: vdf Hochschulverlag).

41 Massimo Foti and Mario Zaffagnini, *La sfida elettronica: Realtà e prospettive nell'uso del computer in architettura* (Bologna: STEB, 1969).
42 Cfr. Giuseppe Ciribini, "Prefazione", in *Il Componenting: Catalogo della mostra* (Bologna: Edizione E.A. Fiere di Bologna, 1968); Giuseppe Ciribini, "Dal 'performance design' alla strategia dei componenti" [From 'performance design' to component strategy], *Casabella* 33, no. 342 (November 1969): 40–44.
 "Componenting" may also be intended as "component-based approach". Cfr. Maranelli, "arrival of the information model".
43 Foti and Mario Zaffagnini, *La sfida elettronica,* 82.
44 Maria Zevi, ed., *Architettura & Computer* (Rome: Bulzoni Editore, 1972).
45 Roisecco, editor of *Moebius*, publishes a letter from Moretti in anticipation of his 1971 article. Musmeci discusses with Moretti in: Paolo Portoghesi, Luigi Moretti, Sergio Musmeci, Armando Plebo and Bruno Zevi, *Structures, Mathèmatiques, Architecture Contemporaine* [Debate transcript], 23 November 1964, in Rome, AC-SLM, folder 42. The debate concerns the exhibition of the same name curated in 1963 in Paris (Palais de la Découverte) by Maurice Bayen.
46 Renato Bonelli, *moretti* (Roma: Editalia, 1975), 16.
47 See Chapter 4.
48 See note 10.
49 Franco Purini, "A Journey around Digital", *Metamorfosi* no. 9–10 (2021): 12–23.
50 Ludovico Quaroni, "Il computer, mito e speranza dell'architetto" [The computer, myth and hope of the architect], in *Architettura & Computer*, 207–216.
51 Quaroni, "Il computer, mito e speranza dell'architetto", 207–216.
52 Bruno Zevi, *The Modern Language of Architecture*, trans. (Seattle: University of Washington Press, 1978), 43. Originally published as *Il linguaggio moderno dell'architettura* (Turin: Einaudi, 1973).
53 Zevi, *The Modern Language of Architecture*, 43.
54 Manfredo Tafuri, *Utopia, Design, and Capitalist Development* (Cambridge: MIT Press, 1976), 151. Originally published as *Progetto e utopia: Architettura e sviluppo capitalistico* (Bari: Laterza, 1973).
55 Maria Zevi, ed., *Architettura & Computer,* 6.
56 Zevi, *Architettura & Computer,* 6.
57 Moretti, "Ricerca matematica in architettura".
58 Carlo Severati, "Il computer e il ruolo del designer" [The computer and the designer's role], in *Architettura & Computer*, 217–219.
59 Foti and Mario Zaffagnini, *La sfida elettronica*, 12.
60 Alessandro Giangrande and Elena Mortola, "Il computer: Un aiuto nel processo creativo del progettista" [The computer: An aid in the designer's creative process], in *Architettura & Computer*, 67–83.
61 Giangrande and Mortola, "Il computer", 67–83.
62 Giangrande and Mortola, "Il computer", 67–83.
63 Sergio Musmeci, "Il calcolo elettronico e la creazione di nuove forme strutturali" [Electronic calculation and the creation of new structural forms], in *Architettura & Computer*, 147–166.
64 Cfr. Serge Chermayeff and Christopher Alexander, *Community and Privacy: Toward a New Architecture of Humanism* (New York: Doubleday & Company, 1963).
65 Fredy Massad and Alicia Guerrero Yeste, "Talking about the Revolution. Interview to Antonino Saggio", *Il Progetto*, no. 9 (2001). http://www.arc1.uniroma1.it/saggio/rivoluzioneinformatica/Interviste/Btwm/Interview.html. See also http://www.arc1.uniroma1.it/saggio/rivoluzioneinformatica/IndexIT.Html.
66 Franco Purini, "Videointerviste", in *Lo spazio digitale dell'architettura italiana* [The digital space of italian architecture], ed. Maurizio Unali (Rome: Edizioni Kappa, 2006), 75.
67 Livio Sacchi, "Videointerviste", in *Spazio digitale dell'architettura italiana*, 76.

68 Massimiliano Fuksas, "Videointerviste", in *Spazio digitale dell'architettura italiana*, 77.
69 Fuksas, "Videointerviste", 77.
70 Franco Purini, "Videointerviste", in *Spazio digitale dell'architettura italiana,* 78.
71 Francesco De Luca and Marco Nardini, *Dietro le quinte, Tecniche d'avanguardia nella progettazione contemporanea* (Turin: Testo & Immagine, 2003), 12–13. Originally published as *Behind the Scenes: Avant-Garde Techniques of Contemporary Design* (Basel: Birkhäuser, 2002).
72 Giuseppe Canestrino, "Architecture's 'Recording Deluge': The Nexus between Architectural Design, AI, and Data Harvesting", *The Plan Journal* 8, no. 2 (2023): 283–301. https://doi.org/10.15274/tpj.2023.08.02.4
73 The following notes provide references for the major monographs on Moretti. Federico Bucci and Marco Mulazzani, *Luigi Moretti: Opere e scritti* (Milan: Electa, 2000). Republished as *Luigi Moretti: Works and Writings* (New York: Princeton Architectural Press, 2002).
74 Reichlin and Tedeschi, *Luigi Moretti: Razionalismo e trasgressività*.
75 Rostagni, *Luigi Moretti.*

2 Architettura Parametrica
In theory

The future architecture in its unity, that is, urban planning, architecture in the strict sense, and construction, must follow a single method.

For all problems, the parameters defining them, their quantified value, and their interdependence must be precisely listed to solve the systems these parameters pose.

Free formal expression and personal lyrical creativity will be allowed only in spaces left free by the parametric functions or where a precise degree of decision-making freedom is justified.

This method will mean achieving a conscious morality in action, based on a deep respect for others and a responsibility to ensure that architectural facts are fair and accurate. This morality must lead to never proposing new illusory ideas that cannot be realised.[1]

Attempts to interpret the theoretical thought underlying Luigi Moretti's Architettura Parametrica inevitably lead to elliptical narratives. Moretti often proposes ideas and positions in an exploratory, imaginative, and visionary manner, leaving gaps in his theoretical positions. These gaps were filled over time as Moretti repeatedly revisited his ideas. Over four decades, Moretti detailed, refined, and deepened his ideas, moving from intuition to systematisation. This systematisation needs to be reconstructed by looking at the many seemingly disconnected fragments. We could argue that Moretti constructs a retroactive narrative of his positions on architectural design.

In this sense, Architettura Parametrica can be studied as an ongoing evolution of how Moretti intended the meaning, purposes, and methods of architectural design. This chapter, therefore, will often use Moretti's writings, transcriptions, and notes from his mature years to better understand his earlier positions. This chapter aims to discuss Moretti's Architettura Parametrica by capturing three evolutionary phases.

The first period was when, already in the 1930s, Moretti strived to derive the forms of his designs through logical processes, making most of his design decisions explicit and traceable. In this early stage, Moretti's theoretical activity was limited. Thus, the reports, memos, and notes on his drawings recount the desire to identify the parameters that influence the evolution of his projects. A still immature Architettura Parametrica began to emerge from an interest in perception of space and architectural forms, as well as in the desire to make explicit the chain of choices that led Moretti to solve his design problems.

After this juvenile phase, Moretti intensified his theoretical activity, establishing himself as an intellectual as well as an international architect. This was an eclectic phase, in which Moretti absorbed suggestions and breakthroughs from a wide range of disciplines: game theory, mathematical structures, a reassessment of baroque forms, and developments in biology and optics, which gave some of the insight that fuelled his professional practice and editorial activities. At this stage, in the 1950s, Architettura Parametrica was a *forma mentis*, an attitude of scientific seriousness towards the project.

A more structured interest in operational research would give rise to the final phase of Architettura Parametrica, best represented in the seminal exhibition at the 1960 Milan Triennale. Here Architettura Parametrica was not just a mental stance but is equipped with tools, methods, and goals. This was the period when Moretti was most committed to spreading his architectural theory, presenting his ideas at numerous national and international venues. In the writings of this period, as well as in his practical experiments, it is possible to find the principles of contemporary algorithmic design, computational optimisations, and computational thinking. This is also the period when Moretti ventured into the world of informal art, founding the *International Centre for Aesthetic Research* with Michel Tapiè. Moretti became interested in a mosaic of figures who, starting from the scientific world, were able to radiate a new mindset towards architectural design.

This chapter is about the evolution and refinement of a sharp intuition over more than 30 years: bringing architectural design closer to scientific practice without undermining the founding values of architecture itself.

The juvenile period and the early insights of Architettura Parametrica (1930s–1950)

The anthologies of Moretti's essays, such as those compiled by Bucci and Mulazzani[2] or Rostagni,[3] contain few writings from his early years. These early writings address topics unrelated to this research. However, Moretti himself often stated that he began working on Architettura Parametrica in his youth; for example in 1960, he wrote about it for the *Exhibition of Parametric Architecture and of Mathematical and Operational Research in Town-Planning*:

> This outlay that is inspired by the need to apply to the two branches [of] logical and mathematical methods was originated and encouraged by the enunciation of ideas and examples that in 1942 Architect Luigi Moretti

listed under the name of "Parametric Architecture" and that now are being described for the first time.[4]

This timeline was confirmed in 1965 through a questionnaire for *L'Architecture d'Aujourd'hui.*

In Italy, for the first time in the world, architecture and urban planning issues were addressed using new methodologies by a group formed in '42, reconvened in '51, and definitively established in '57 with the creation of IRMOU - *Institute for Mathematical and Operational Research Applied to Urbanism.* [...] Since '42, I have been involved in these issues, and the exhibition held in '60 at the XII Triennale, as previously mentioned, by the [IRMOU] presented the theory and development of my "Architettura Parametrica".[5]

In one of his last and longest writings, Moretti confirmed these dates when asked to discuss modern mathematics, architecture, and urban planning:

You know I've been pursuing this research since 1939–40, exploring these relationships and their full potential to create architecture that embodies the fascinating spirit of our scientifically driven age authentically modern (truly new and revolutionary) not merely modern by historical association.[6]

These references suggest tracing the seed of Architettura Parametrica in the theoretical and practical work of the young but accomplished Moretti, who, at just 26, created a masterpiece of Italian rationalism, the *Casa delle Armi*. The term "seed" is used because, as evidenced by the cited anthologies and research on the *Fondo Luigi Moretti* at the Italian Central State Archive, Moretti's early writings largely lack a focus on mathematics in architectural thought. Except for a brief note in *Giotto Architetto*,[7] where Moretti laments young designers' disregard for mathematics, his early theoretical work appears disconnected from Architettura Parametrica.

Moretti's earlier quotes suggest that it might be helpful to identify potential seeds of Architettura Parametrica. As will be discussed in the next chapter, it seems that several pre-World War II projects may perhaps have hinted at the formal ideas Moretti articulated in his 1960 exhibition.[8] This highlights the opportunity to reflect on works from that period, searching for the parametric seed in both built and unbuilt projects, focusing on their forms, how they challenged established traditions, and, perhaps most importantly, how these forms were sought with an inquisitive, tense, and restless exploration. This task should be based on the idea that an architectural project is a source of "research, theoretical and historical-critical speculation, and [for the] construction of methodological hypotheses".[9] Thus, the seed of Architettura Parametrica will be sought not only in the iconography of certain projects but, above all, in the texts Moretti included in his project boards, such as precise descriptions on executive design drawings and notes, and corrections on working sketches. The proposed approach, therefore, relies on interpreting a variety of fragments – both theoretical and practical – where we find the early signs of some principles (or suggestions) of Architettura Parametrica. This research method differs from that of the following chapters, which are supported by a wealth of writings, speeches, and debates by Moretti on Architettura Parametrica and, more generally, on the relationship between architecture and technical-mathematical culture.

The notebook An architecture of limited parameters

The evocative title of Luigi Moretti's notebook *An architecture of limited parameters* suggests the opportunity to define the theoretical seed of Architettura Parametrica. This notebook, dated between 1925 and 1945, was recently translated and published in open access.[10] The analysis of this notebook reveals the many influences on the young Moretti, from Borromini's architecture to the materials of his Rome, from his interest in fortifications to the Gothic style. These influences anticipate the principles on which he would build some of his most beautiful essays on *Spazio*, such as *Abstract forms in Baroque sculpture* or *Borromini's series of generalised structures*. A first reading of this precious notebook does not clearly reveal the origins of Architettura Parametrica, except in note 195, where Moretti outlines the concept of "chain-like structures" in nature. Here, Moretti proposes that "every aspect of nature has its near and remote causes" in that chain of events "determined by the law of consequence". A "law of consequence" capable of shaping the forms of nature itself, as clarified by the imagery Moretti evokes in this note. If we consider the contents of this notebook as a kind of "allegory of architectural practice", this note suggests the possibility of defining architectural forms through the logical chaining of actions, a concept that is central both in Moretti's mature Architettura Parametrica and in contemporary computational approaches.

This notebook offers some romantic suggestions instead of mature thoughts capable of creating the circularity between theory and design that would emerge in Moretti's later work. To "extract" anticipations of Architettura Parametrica from the notes in this notebook, so rich in tension and potential, would probably be a methodological error. If we follow Viati Navone's thesis that Moretti added the title of the notebook several years after it was written,[11] we can argue that Moretti saw in these notes the seed of his theories. *An architecture of limited parameters* is part of a larger collection of thoughts titled *Notes collected from notebooks loose papers etc. (Year 1925 and following) and transcribed in their original dictions*.[12] In this collection, Moretti discusses tools such as "Galileo's telescope, the reflector telescope at Mount Wilson Observatory, the elementary and electronic microscope" and a "general design for a study of a mechanical brain".[13] These suggestions, following Viati Navone's analysis, reveal that "mechanical physiology, cybernetics and artificial intelligence are disciplines with which Moretti was evidently familiar with perhaps even before his operative research".[14]

Some of the notes in *An architecture of limited parameters* assume a revealing meaning in light of these considerations. Note 2 focuses on the theme of "analysis of the 'successive vision' of architecture and decorations" and the "temporality of vision". Here Moretti critiques how "wide angle camera lenses" suffocate the perception of architecture. Note 208 points to "a drop in power" due to the diminished ability to perceive certain visual phenomena in architecture – such as mouldings, which Moretti explores in a key essay in *Spazio*[15] – "as if the resolutive power of the eye and all of the senses were reduced, degenerated, to more than one third".

This notebook, when read with an understanding of the eventual evolution of mature Architettura Parametrica, invites an exploration of its roots in Moretti's early experiences. In these formative years, design processes and forms were shaped by considerations of optics,[16] the physiological aspects of visual perception, and the articulation of *chain* of thoughts that generate architecture.

It is necessary to clarify that Moretti presents his thoughts through a network of references seemingly distant from architecture. But as Moretti states in *Giotto Architetto*, "everything we have discussed so far is important and useful to me in defining what I consider the point of refraction from which our contemporary architecture began".[17]

In these notes, it emerges that the young Moretti, already in the 1930s and 1940s, had an intuition about what he should focus on and later optimise in his Architettura Parametrica: the perception of architectural forms and the events within them. During these years, the object of optimisation was determined, along with a chosen operational domain, however, the techniques and processes for achieving this optimisation were still unclear.

The seed of Architettura Parametrica in the projects for the Foro Italico: The Olympic Stadium

In a quote from Dino Buzzati's interview with Moretti on the results of his memorable 1960 exhibition, the origins of Architettura Parametrica are traced back to the theme of a stadium designed around the 1940s. Here, according to the interviewer, Moretti reflects on whether the traditional, recognisable forms of stadiums carry an optimal design or if their use is merely repeated out of inertia. Buzzati continues to present Moretti's thoughts:

> Instead of referring to previous models, is it not better to forget them, strip away that force of inertia that dominates all fields of the mind, and start anew?[18]

The stadium referred to in the interview is the Olympic Stadium in Rome, built between 1937 and 1940 at the *Foro Italico* (former *Foro Mussolini*). The stadium's forms, especially some intermediate solutions, foreshadow concepts from the 1960 exhibition, as will be discussed in detail in the next chapter (see Figure 3.10). To trace the roots of Architettura Parametrica, it is essential to refer to notes by Moretti alongside a section sketch. These notes anticipate the positions he would later refine in the following decades. Through these notes, it is possible to discuss how the young Moretti viewed the design practice as a problem to be solved. More specifically, a problem that must first be constructed with great rigour in order to be resolved later.

Moretti created an early textual flowchart of the activities required to define "the best seat and the extremes of dimensions", which is presented in its entirety:

a) Verify absolute visibility:
- Graphically
- Algebraically

Verify visibility of reburied points
- Straight (graphically)
- Oblique (algebraically)

b) Compare curvature as sculpted in plaster and wood models
c) Consider maximum, minimum, and optimal height in the first stand:
- In relation to ball passage (if open, if closed)
- In relation to proportioning to the second ring
- In relation to the existing stand

d) Consider maximum height of the second stand:
- Considering existing roads
- Considering rear passage

e) Determine the average [stand] section and the visibility curvature.[19]

This scheme would be sterile without Moretti's careful analysis of the anthropic, natural, technical, programmatic, spatial, and formal aspects involved in this project. Moretti therefore compiled a list of about 50 items to consider, including VIP stands, athlete movement, loudspeakers, marathon entrance, radial division of seats, vehicular access, numerous facilities serving the stadium, different types of judges, various workers populating the stadium, photographers, film cameras, radio commentary, scoreboard, storage areas, podiums, and much more.[20] He then divided the architectural problem into three subclasses, which, in turn, break down the elementary decisions necessary to construct a design solution. Moretti wrote:

Specific problems:
a) Corridor to the [radio] emission stand
b) Possible relative height based on:
- Corridor
- Doors

c) Sorting corridor:
   - Based on stair plan […]
   - Based on visibility
d) Final corridor
e) Initial corridor

General mechanism problem:
[unintelligible] spacing
a) Inflow and outflow, determination of sorting coefficient
b) Stair section given the coefficient
c) Distribution of stairs
d) Distribution of services:
   - Relative coefficients
   - Locations

Architectural problems:
a) Given the organism, what is the best solution on its own
b) Compare this solution with:
   - General organism
   - Panoramic conditions
Summary and determination of the final typical section.[21]

This list, which is partly a procedure and partly a personal reminder, led to Moretti's final note: "summary and determinations of the definitive typical section"[22] that is one of the most important aspects of stadium design. This mindset aligns with what Moretti expressed in the aforementioned interview with Buzzati,[23] especially when considered alongside the plottings of parametric studies (see Figure 3.1) and the sectional drawings in which Moretti suggested checking the visual cones for potential interference between them.

The Piazzale delle Adunate

The discussion about the Olympic Stadium reveals the essence of early insights into Architettura Parametrica. It also renews interest in earlier projects that share its lexicon, shaped by the "determination", "demonstration", and "analysis" of design problems. These projects could perhaps be described as "unconsciously parametric".

The first of these projects is the *Piazzale delle Adunate* at *Foro Italico* (1934–1936), never built. Its plans, like those of the Olympic Stadium, are accompanied by annotations revealing Moretti's design approach. The pursuit of scientific rigour – or rather the reproducibility of the design process – in the search for the shape of *Piazzale delle Adunate* reflects the efforts of a young Moretti to dispel any doubts about the quality of his proposal in the eyes of a demanding client. A design table containing only text identifies the parameters to consider, divided into two categories: one tied to function and programme, the other to the site.[24] Both categories can guide the evolution of architectural form. Moretti writes for the first category:

> Critical elements given the purpose of the [military] muster complex.
> Determine:
> - Shape of the area spontaneously delimited by the crowd for best visibility of the stage
> - Maximum possible area
> - Best solution for inflow and outflow [...].[25]

Moretti also adds:

> Critical elements given the planimetric constraints.
> Determine:
> - Maximum available area
> - Panoramic constraints that determine possible zones to elevate
> - Possibilities for inflow entrances and outflow exits.[26]

These are the parameters (broadly speaking) for solving this design problem. It can be considered a design problem, continuing the approach of the Olympic Stadium, as Moretti adopts a similar method to the 1960 exhibition,[27] though without mathematical models. Moretti's studies on crowd shape renew the ways the design problem is approached, or rather defined. The way Moretti conducts these studies transforms their results into a sort of anticipation of the project's form. There is a congruence between the results of design analysis and the project's form. It would be wrong to associate this methodology with form-finding; yet, some analogies can be noted: this is a way of formalising a design investigation that naturally leads to forms in equilibrium with the required specifications.

The group of parameters related to planimetric constraints is clearer when compared to a subsequent board dedicated to the "analysis of the general and specific constraints imposed by the chosen and only possible location".[28] This introduces the idea of morphogenesis based on reflections on optimal viewing angles. Moretti specifies the "views to maintain", "views to exclude", possible accesses to the area, and, most importantly, the different relationships with other projects of the *Foro Italico*.

As shown in Figure 2.1, the morphological evolution indicates that for the young Moretti, analysing the design problem is not just a mere routine, but rather a meaningful reflection. Moretti illustrates the spontaneous shape of the crowd (B) and its elongation near entry points close to his project area (C). Showing his fascination with mathematics, Moretti describes these geometries as "close to Gaussian shapes".[29] A synthesis of the previous two schemes (D) informs the initial geometry for the stands (E). This applies only to the crowd facing a speaker. Moretti then studies the case where, in addition to the

Architettura Parametrica: In Theory 29

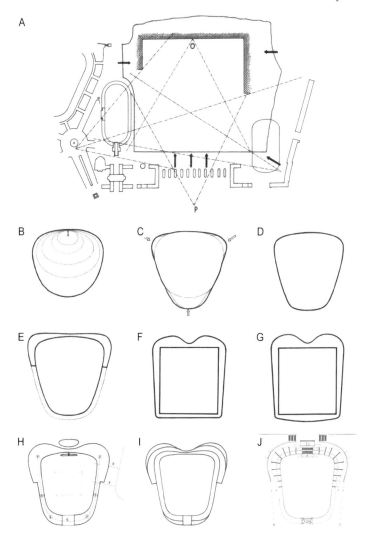

Figure 2.1 Luigi Moretti, Piazzale delle Adunate, Roma, 1934–1936. Credits: AC-SLM, project 59, [A] 36/51/2], [B, C, D, E] 36/42/3; [F, G] 36/42/4; [H, I] 36/42/5; [J] 36/42/8.

speaker, there is a military parade in the square's centre. In schemes (F) and (G), he investigates the crowd's shape in the stands in this specific scenario. The title of this board seems to forecast the concept of the "preforma latissima"[30] that will appear in his later writings[31]: "final composition of the various elements already analysed separately for the various cases".[32] The product is thus a shape moulded by numerous existing planimetric constraints, the hosted programme, and the spontaneous forms a crowd assumes during various events.

The importance of this project in shaping the ideas of Architettura Parametrica – and in the broader methodological dimension underlying architectural design – goes beyond the simple suggestion of form-finding already pointed out. Moretti's diagrams suggest that the form can be divided into areas with the same performance (level curves) which will be central to the 1960 exhibition. Moretti's reference to "Gaussian forms" also anticipates his fascination with mathematics, leading him to Évariste Galois' theories. Finally, this project suggests that a programme of analysis delimits the range of variations of a form. The form can oscillate within this field of possibilities without contradicting the insights gained from the analyses. This anticipates topological thinking in architecture, as defined by Manuel De Landa,[33] and Moretti's concept of "free formal expression",[34] discussed later in this chapter.

The Piazzale dell'Impero

The discussion so far highlights the relationship between form-design and form-analysis in young Moretti's theoretical framework. However, these experiences do not address the physiological dimension of perception, crucial for Architettura Parametrica. Therefore, it is necessary to search among young Moretti's projects for careful consideration of optical issues in analyses and forms. Moretti's masterplan for the entire *Foro Italico*, discussed in a recent article,[35] could be examined, but here the optical issue, shown using "optical telescopes" in the plan, is panoramic rather than physiological. In other projects, like *Piazzale dell'Impero* or *Gran Teatro dell'EUR*,[36] the focus is on the physiological dimension.

Piazzale dell'Impero is a project between urban and architectural scales, fundamental in the compositional mechanisms of the entire *Foro Italico*. In this project, Moretti anticipates various Architettura Parametrica themes, including "chain of difference", initially explored in *An architecture of limited parameters*. With a similar approach to *Piazzale della Adunate*, Moretti strives in a series of compositional diagrams to find a key – through comparative drawing – capable of communicating the reasons behind his design choices, such as the monolith's sizing. This seems like another attempt by a young architect to justify his design. However, from the perspective of this book, Moretti continues to anticipate the traceability of the action behind a design, a concept fundamental to Architettura Parametrica. These are Moretti's captions accompanying his drawings:

> The monolith increases in height, resting perspectively on the central marble spine [Figure 2.2A].
>
> This demonstrates the greater value in size and character that the monolith assumes when placed in an architecturally defined and moderately reduced space [Figure 2.2B]
>
> Elements of minimal height and fine workmanship provide contrast in scale and dimension to the monolith.
>
> Recurrent elements along the avenue are necessary to provide a size comparison even from distant viewpoints.[37]

The issue of the physiological perception of masses and space is revealed in a drawing by Moretti, which declares the logic for determining the main dimensional parameters of the *Piazzale*[38] (see Figure 2.2E). The marble blocks scattered around the square have a width and height that make them clearly visible at an angle of 40°. Their distances are based on a 20° frontal and 40° lateral view. The floor's figurative elements are dimensioned according to the observer's position and a 40° visual cone. This focus on visual perception is central to Moretti's 1960s research and was preceded by early studies on Michelangelo's *Last Judgment* and the *Palazzo dei Conservatori*, recently published in an article by Tommaso Magnifico.[39] In his long career, Moretti will adopt different values for these angles of interest, as analysed by Viati Navone.[40] Beyond the numbers, it's important to understand how an objective and physiological datum can shape architectural form. These analyses must never be superfluous or produce a mass of useless data – as Moretti later emphasised – but must be capable of effectively guiding the project's development.

"Analyze", "demonstrate", "determine". These are the verbs Moretti aligns with in this early explorative and juvenile phase. This suggests a "functionalist" understanding of Architecture by Moretti. However, it's not pure functionalism, as Moretti synthesised his architectural forms within the possibilities offered by his analyses. These analyses should never be superfluous or produce a mass of useless data, as Moretti later emphasised.[41] Instead, the data should be relevant and capable of effectively guiding the design's evolution.

The theoretical systematisation and technical aspects of Architettura Parametrica are largely absent in this early phase. However, the proposed study shows how a series of discrete insights, particularly regarding efficient morphologies in large-scale architecture (stadiums, theatres, squares), will inform Luigi Moretti's formal repertoire. This repertoire, as will be demonstrated, is not only closely related to his 1960 exhibition stadiums but will also be repeatedly attempted to be translated into professional practice.

32 *Decoding Luigi Moretti's Architettura Parametrica*

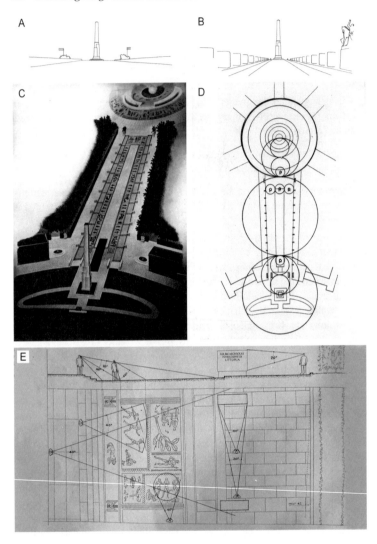

Figure 2.2 Luigi Moretti, Piazzale dell'Impero, Roma, 1937. Credits: ACSLM, project 71, [A, B] 37/77/2; [C] F3130; [D] F3127; [E] F2860.

The maturity period and the outline of a personal architectural theory (1950–1957)

This part of the research is closely linked to the editorial activity of the magazine *Spazio*, directed by Moretti, and two fundamental texts: *Forma come struttura*[42] and *Struttura come forma*. In these texts, Moretti reveals the name of the architectural concept he has been working on for years, both theoretically and practically. Many authors have interpreted and discussed these essays, but Federico Bucci's last book[43] before his untimely death deserves a special mention. Here Bucci read Moretti's discourse as an "architectural theory" with unexpected poetic climaxes. Yet these texts by Moretti remain fruitful and largely unexplored when used to decode his Architettura Parametrica.

If the early years, previously discussed, were marked by a more significant professional engagement than theoretical commitment, we now witness a reversal. During this period, there were fewer intersections between Architettura Parametrica and professional practice, such as the real estate complex in Corso Italia,[44] Milan (1949–1956), possibly due to a stagnation of the latter, as suggested by Zevi.[45] The general mistrust towards Moretti's affirmation as an intellectual and theorist is captured in Zevi's 1957 account of Moretti on the occasion of his receiving the San Luca Architecture Prize. Zevi writes:

> [Moretti] felt strong again and wanted to quickly extend his influence to the cultural field: he founded the magazine *Spazio*, gathering old friends and giving them new vitality. However, it was an immature operation: after seven brilliant and beautifully French-styled issues, the magazine ceased publication. His professional work also faced a crisis, partially mitigated by new initiatives.[46]

This quote remembers the intertwining of politics and architecture underlying Moretti's success, considering his established position as an "architect of the regime" during Mussolini's years. This intertwining was, indeed, leveraged by Moretti. His success is undoubtedly linked to his undeniable architectural talent, but also to the fact that "graduating in '29, Moretti immediately perceived the political-cultural chessboard he had to enter", as noted by Zevi.[47]

The discussion of this phase of Moretti's theoretical thought is divided into two parts. First, Moretti's interactions with mathematics, which provided renewed hypotheses for understanding architectural phenomena, will be discussed. Then, the possible organisations and evolutions of the identified mathematical structures will be examined to identify the peculiar ways of synthesising architectural form driven by Architettura Parametrica. This disarticulation is essential for an in-depth analysis of Moretti's thought, but the mathematical and cultural aspects constantly contaminate each other in his writings. This paragraph argues that, during this phase of Architettura Parametrica's theoretical evolution, mathematics served more as a postural and conceptual inspiration than as a practical tool.

Moretti's mathematical conception of architecture

The mathematics Moretti studied between the end of World War II and the formation of IRMOU in 1957 was largely theoretical and abstract. It provided a vision to decode architecture in both interpretation and practice, not tools for synthesising form. These tools arrived later when Moretti introduced operational research concepts and computers into his theory. During the editorial period of the magazine *Spazio*, Moretti used mathematical terminology to define an architectural hierarchy: *forms* as products of *differences*, *differences* as *chains* when perceived simultaneously, *differences* as *groups* over time, *structure* as the relationship between *differences*, and *global structure* as the union of multiple *structures*.[48] He also introduced new terms into architectural debates to reveal various formative mechanisms: *automorphism, isomorphism, algorithms*, among others.

Before discussing these terms in detail, it's necessary to highlight how Moretti's design lexicon changed: "analyse", "demonstrate", "determine", verbs characterising his youth, were replaced by "differences", "structures", "relationships", "automorphisms", and "isomorphisms". An ontological shift, replacing verbs aimed at practising architecture with concepts aimed at understanding it. This separation was necessary before the synthesis of practice and theory, which Moretti offered in his later years, defined as "the commitment period" in this book.

Discussing the mathematical aspects of this part of Moretti's thought is challenging but essential for a deeper understanding of the concept of "form as structure", as well as "structure as form". As previously, it's useful to identify a clear and mature presentation of Moretti's theoretical and design thinking, and then retrospectively discuss the experiences that anticipated and explored it. This presentation can be found in the opening words of *Forma come struttura*:

> The world of forms reveals itself to us through the differences between one form and another. That is to say, we do not read each form because of some inherent quality it may possess but through the complex of signs, of differences that distinguish it from other contiguous forms, contiguous in space or memory.
>
> Differences are the inevitable, intransgressible flashes of reality and of the forms; they are the forms.[49]

In these words lies the ontological value of Moretti's theory: a shift from the fact itself, i.e., the form, towards the relationships established between the different values of the form, which Moretti calls "differences". This shift requires a new language and a new architectural symbolism to be understood, communicated, and implemented. Moretti himself suggests this symbolism, which will be discussed shortly. Moretti writes:

> Some concepts on form and structure mentioned in this discussion can be noted with the following symbolism:
> - Differences: $d_1, d_2, \ldots d_n \ldots$
> - Chains: $\Sigma i\ \lambda i\ di$ with whole arbitrary coefficients λi
> - Minimal chains: $\Sigma i\ \lambda i(\Delta t)\ di$ with coefficents dependent on the intervals
> - Form: group of differences, as group of chains, where the sum is defined by means of the rules of calculation of the polynomials
> $$F = \left(\Sigma i\ \lambda i\ di\right)$$
> - Automorphism: is defined as the correspondence between differences
> $$di_1 \rightarrow di_2$$
> that induces the correspondence of the automorphism of the group
> $$\Sigma i_1\ \lambda i_1\ di_1 \rightarrow \Sigma i_2\ \lambda i_2\ di_2$$
> - Relationship of order between differences:
> $$di_1 > di_2$$
> Such as can subordinate a relationship of order between chains
> $$\Sigma i_1\ \lambda i_1\ di_1 > \Sigma i_2\ \lambda i_2\ di_2$$
> - Structure: the group of relationship of order
> $$S = \left(di_1 > di_2\right)$$
> - Isomorphism between structures
> $$S = S_1 \sim S_2$$
> - Union of structures:
> $$S = S_1 \cup S_2 \cup \ldots S_i.[50]$$

Through this symbolism, part of Moretti's mathematical thought can be analysed, starting with the concept of *differences*. Two questions arise: why reduce form to a set of *differences*, and what are these *differences*?

Moretti first proposes to "quantize" form, and consequently architecture, by breaking it into finite, discrete elements. This idea, anticipated in *An architecture of limited parameters*, shows his familiarity with the physical concept of "quantum" and his fascination with developments in quantum physics, particularly Heisenberg's "uncertainty principle".[51] Moretti writes between 1925 and 1945:

> The geometric world is quantitative: granular space (Greek atomistics) (granular thinking: quantum of logical thinking) – The quantitative progress of knowledge.[52] We perceive the class, not the particular element.[53]

36   Decoding Luigi Moretti's Architettura Parametrica

This discretisation, referring back to *Spazio*, could lead to a "simplistic vision that sees architecture as a sort of *summa* by way of the juxtaposition of different values".[54] Moretti discretises form not merely to consider "plastic, constructional, and functional values as separate elements in architecture".[55] Using *differences*, rather than individual possible determinations of diverse values, avoids the risk of performing yet another sort of "grammatical analysis of architecture". Moretti's approach aims to capture the complexity of the architecture, not to simplify it. It also serves as a preliminary step to scientifically navigate the various possible solutions to a design problem, or the paths to those solutions. Finally, the "quantization" of form through *differences* and *structures* would permit the definition of "an entirely new aesthetic, and consequently a new criticism, [...] based predominantly on the *structures* of works of art—that is to say, on their identification, on the analysis of their formation and transformation—constituting a rigorous new critical language".[56]

When Moretti elaborates on what a *difference* is, themes central to other writings, such as *The value of moldings*[57] or *Genesis of shapes derived from the human figure*,[58] appear. Moretti explains that in the human face – "the form [of the human figure] that is richest in rapid and sudden difference" – these *differences* refer to colour, quality of material, and chiaroscuro.[59] In architecture, Moretti explains that *differences*, when clustered into *structures*, can refer to static relationships, spaces, plastic relationships, surfaces as geometric entities, light density and more.[60] This analysis shows how Moretti bends mathematics towards a greater interest in values related to the perceptual dimension of architecture, and consequently to architecture as an experiential phenomenon rather than an abstract concept.

Moretti, therefore, looks to abstract mathematics to better understand the concrete nature of architecture, as evidenced by a note in *The value of moldings* in which he analyses the façade of *Palazzo Ossoli* by Baldassarre Peruzzi (see Figure 2.3). Here he proposes a mathematical modelling of the space between the *differences* of a form, whether a facade or a moulding. This note is presented in its entirety as it anticipates a computational approach to space, but also because it has been systematically excluded by other authors[61] who, for reasons different from the objectives of this book, have translated and discussed Moretti's texts.

Note, in general, some behaviours of the relationships between spaces $a_1, a_2, \ldots a_n$ [see fig. 3.3I] enclosed by the main frames[62] of a building facade, and their respective visual angles, $\alpha_2, \ldots, \alpha_n$ [see fig. 3.3II III]

Between the spaces, there are ∞^{n-2} linear relationship. For n = 3, they are $c_1 a_1 + c_2 a_2 + c_3 a_3 = 0$ (e.g. $\frac{a_1}{a_2} = r$, $\frac{a_1}{a_2 + a_3} = R$, etc.), with coefficients: $c_1, c_2, -\frac{(c_1 a_1 + c_2 a_2)}{a_3}$; There are also ∞^{n-2} armonic relationship, such as $\frac{d_1}{a_1} + \frac{d_2}{a_2} + \frac{d_3}{a_3} = 0$ (e.g., for $\frac{1}{a_1} + \frac{1}{a_2} - \frac{2}{a_3} = 0$, a_3 is the harmonic mean of a_1 and a_2); For n ≥ 3 consider cross-ratios and their functions or relationships, important for their invariance in perspective representation; A significant expression of the cross-ratio is $L = \dfrac{(a_1 + a_2)(a_2 + a_3)}{a_1 \, a_3}$.

What is really important, I think, are the relationships of the spaces, not as such, but as determinants of the relationships and ratios of the visual angles under which they are projected. The relationships between the angles $\alpha_1, \alpha_2, \ldots$, or, practically the same up to angles of about 30°, the relationships between the sines or tangents of these angles, are the concrete reality of architectural space [see fig. 3.3II III].

Now, it can be seen that the locus of points where certain relationships of these angles remain invariant is a particular curve of order $2n-2$; For example, for the relationship $tan(\alpha_1) + tan(\alpha_2) - 2\ tan(\alpha_3) = 0$, the curve is as shown in [fig. 3.3IV]. The shaded area indicates a space where, approximately, the relationship is invariant. A harmonic relationship is invariant (Benedicty [sic!]) along a circumference, which becomes a horizontal line if the relationship is also satisfied by the frames. For cross-ratios, it is interesting to note a particular case related to the points of a moulding profile. If these points are arranged on a line, there is total invariance; if on a conic [see fig. 3.3V], there is invariance for all projection points along the same conic.[63]

A complex note, which in its final part goes beyond mathematical modelling to suggest a design stance:

> Finally, it is noted that in practice the architect must identify those types of relationships that vary within a certain anticipated mode in a given visual space. In this visual space, the maximum number of invariance curves of the chosen privileged relationships must be concentrated (fig. ib. VI).[64]

The discussion so far supports the idea that Moretti uses these mathematical metaphors to communicate how he conceives architectural form. In other words, to clarify how it is possible to derive from a single mathematical *structure* (or, in architectural terms, from the complex of relationships underlying a single design idea) a multiplicity of forms, all of which are traceable as determinations of that single mathematical *structure*.

To better understand this point, it is necessary to revisit Moretti's previously discussed symbolism. *Differences*, such as how values like *chiaroscuro* or light vary in space, cluster into *chains* when the perceptual aspect is introduced. A *chain* is an "ensemble of differences, i.e., the form element, perceptible simultaneously".[65] The *chain* is thus a first recomposition of fragmented knowledge, "which in great classical poetry seems to be recognized in the verse, in music has the extension of the 'phrase' or 'cell,' in architecture and painting to the architectural element or tonal group limited by the famous 5° cone of attentive vision".[66] But Moretti recognises that the set of *differences*

38 Decoding Luigi Moretti's Architettura Parametrica

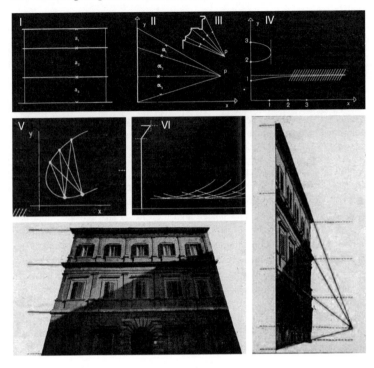

Figure 2.3 Luigi Moretti, Studies on the façade of Palazzo Ossoli by Baldassarre Peruzzi. Moretti defines figures I to VI as "relationships between the spaces defined by the frames and their projections". Published in Luigi Moretti, "Valori della modanatura", Spazio a 3, no. 6 (1951–1952): 5–12, 112.

that can be perceived simultaneously in a *chain* is limited, for example, by the mentioned 5° optical cone. Therefore, the full perception of a complex form occurs by introducing the temporal aspect and *groups of differences*. These are "temporal arrangements of events" related to the perception of *chains* of differences over time, linked, for example, to the "movement of the eye as in architecture and painting".[67]

The *structure* of a non-elementary form is defined by ordering and identifying principles of sequentiality, understood as the arrangement of relationships between *groups of differences* that describe it. Thus, the *structure* of the form is an abstract concept, a set of pure relationships that bear a design value. For Moretti:

> Who clearly understands the structure of a form owns its ultimate meaning, its specific flow beyond the contingent qualities of the form itself.[68]

Moretti goes further, stating that "the creative act of making forms, that is, working in art, is fundamentally the act of communicating, specifying, materializing an unfolding and a certain sequence of unfolding [i.e.] expressing a structure".[69] These words explain that the same *structure* can materialise in an infinite number of forms that do not deny the system of relationships that determined the *structure* itself. Moretti references D'Arcy Thompson's studies on morphogenesis to better explain this concept. He mentions "examples of Diodon and *Orthagoriscus* fish, the pelvic bones of *Archaeopteryx* and *Apatornis*, and many others"[70] using images of these examples without discussing Thompson's theories (see Figure 4.1). As explored in Chapter 4, this approach effectively communicates how a single *structure* can generate multiple forms.

Moretti's mathematical lexicon is completed with the concepts of isomorphism, automorphism, and algorithm. Rather than discussing their mathematical nature, which is covered in other texts, it is useful for this book to discuss the architectural design vision they suggest to Moretti. The concept of isomorphism, although explained in *Forma come Struttura*, is better defined in a 1961 essay on space and light in religious architecture, less focused on mathematical aspects:

> Given that all fundamental values, whether more or less emphasized individually, are closely interdependent, the structure of each of these values, that is the organic set of its modulations, is "isomorphic" to the others and, I would say, projective of that general structure which is the secret heart of the work.[71]

For example, the isomorphism between the *structure* of space, understood as the absence of matter, and that of surfaces indicates that any variation in the former results in a consequence in the latter. Similarly, any determination of the spatial *structure* corresponds to a determination of the *surface* structure. More elusive is Moretti's concept of automorphism, which Bucci briefly defined in one of his last essays as a "transformation that keeps the structure of space unchanged".[72] This concept bears a design stance, suggesting the manipulation of individual differences that shaped a *structure*, rather than remodulating the *structure* itself.

Finally, Moretti uses the term algorithm with a meaning far from the contemporary IT sense. Moretti uses the term algorithm to indicate the processes by which *structures* form and transform.[73] For example, for Moretti, "Greek architecture was an algorithm of structures beaten by the sun; it was a logic of light and shadows of unknown forms where the gods dwelled".[74]

Readers familiar with recent studies on Moretti will notice that Galois is not discussed in this part of the research, unlike other narratives on Moretti's relationship with mathematics proposed by other scholars. Bucci writes that Moretti's definition of *structure* "is influenced by the theories of Évariste Galois (1811–1832), the great French mathematician who died in a duel at the age of twenty, at the center of a series of profound and refined studies". Based on Galois' theory of mathematical groups, or the concept of learning a form "by difference", Moretti defines the *structure* of form as a "set of pure relationships".[75] This concept is temporarily set aside because Moretti's references to Galois, such as in the introduction of the original French version of *Forma come Struttura* and the conclusion of *Ecleticism and Unity of Language,* are cryptic. Therefore, they can be decoded after exploring Moretti's design vision. Galois theories will be discussed in the last part of the chapter, focusing on how mathematics provided Moretti with personal keys to decipher the informal world with Michael Tapiè.

What has been discussed so far is not just one of many mathematisations of architecture, like those by Alexander Klein[76] or Christopher Alexander.[77] Moretti's mathematical perspective can only be understood by grasping the circularity of his thinking. He associates this mathematical thought with the "realm of ideal structures" first discovered in Michelangelo's *Palazzo dei Conservatori* in Rome as "the clearest example, [...] the most rigorous realm of intellectual representation of logically possible structures. [...]" that future architecture must not ignore.[78] This building was studied by the young Moretti, who analysed its "facade and visual angles from the square"[79] anticipating his focus on the physiological aspects of visual perception. The reference to *Palazzo dei Conservatori* also appears in a note in *An architecture of limited parameters* proposing that differences and relationships reveal architecture in non-mathematical terms. Moretti writes:

> The constructive and ideal counterpoint between the pilasters and the secondary orders at Palazzo dei Conservatori is exalted to the limits in an order copied in the structure of Propaganda Fide (it had already migrated to St. John Lateran). This is the difference between the pilasters and the dense slender small columns on the first floor that the total sentiment is like that of a small temple on a mountain.[80]

Mathematics provided Moretti with the foundational framework for his Architettura Parametrica. Once the theory was in place, he turned to operational research for implementation.

Parameters, structure, form, function

Having discussed the symbolism that Moretti proposes to *quantise* architecture, it's necessary to investigate the purpose of this mathematisation. If architecture is a complex of *structures*, i.e., sets of relationships describable in logical-mathematical terms, the design action can temporarily move away from phenomenological determinations to focus on these *structures*. Through this process, Moretti deeply explores the possible genetic directions in thinking, manipulating, and synthesising architectural *structures*. Among these possible genetic directions, Moretti identifies his Architettura Parametrica, first mentioned in *Spazio* in 1951–1952 in the memorable essay *Struttura come Forma*.

This phase of Architettura Parametrica is of particular interest as it is supported by the young Moretti's design experiences discussed earlier, but it has not yet established a close dialogue with operational research and computer science. Thus, Architettura Parametrica, as described in *Spazio*, is an architectural theory lacking the tools, procedures, and methods for systematic translation into design practice. Additionally, the cultural references Moretti would later use to suggest a "mathematical aesthetic" are not yet fully mature. This does not diminish the value of Moretti's theoretical thought but highlights how, during these years, the goal of Architettura Parametrica was to guide design thinking towards a vision with seriousness and ethical rigour.

For these reasons, this paragraph will discuss Architettura Parametrica as a cultural stance for architectural design, postponing the important operational issues. This approach is justified by the way Moretti introduces the name of his theory:

Scientific research, the enumeration of the parameters, and the quantitative mathematical analysis of these parameters are tasks that the new architecture will have to face, in an a priori manner in every case. In this way what I have long solicited and call "parametric architecture" will be born. Its ineluctable geometric character, its rigorous concatenation of forms, the absolute freedom of fantasy that will spring up in places where equations cannot fix their own roots, will give it a crystalline splendor.[81]

To understand Architettura Parametrica, we must begin with the meaning that Moretti assigned to the term "parameter" in those years. This term appears in several articles in *Spazio* and takes on several meanings that need to be harmonised. "Parameter" appears in *Ecleticism and Unity of Language*, the first article in the first issue of *Spazio*, where Moretti uses the term without defining it:

A comprehensive language is born from order and classification in the fundamental and secondary relationships between the infinite parameters of reality.[82]

In a discourse attentive to semantics, languages across the arts, literature, architecture, and criticism, Moretti uses the term "parameter" as a general descriptor of a phenomenon and as functions to be satisfied. Fundamental *parameters* that define a language seem to refer to rules first identified and then shared. Secondary *parameters*, explicitly mentioned by Moretti, include "defence from rain, wind, heat, and cold and the need to move and rest".[83] The major cultural themes of architecture, as well as the more pragmatic questions it must answer, are all grouped under the term *parameters*. Moretti's definition is vague and imprecise but highlights a difference from the long, detailed, and analytical list of *parameters* he outlines for his stadiums in one of his later articles.[84]

Moretti's disarticulation of architecture is not to isolate the themes that define the discipline but to reveal the relationships between them. He is more interested in revealing the connections between parameters than in using them to describe architecture. This leads to his critique of theoretical frameworks that, starting from the "didactic simplicity of firmitas, venustas, and utilitas",[85] have privileged one of architecture's canonical values. This critique seems to anticipate themes of complexity and emergent properties of a system. It also forms the basis of the first agenda of Architettura Parametrica. Given the Vitruvian triad, Moretti believes that:

> [the essence of architecture] arises from the complex relations in which the principal and secondary uses of adjectives, the forces and the modalities that determine and govern them, exist contemporaneously. This complex of relations that constitutes the structure, understood in logical mathematical terms alone and independently from the concrete value of the use of adjectives, constitutes and defines the subject.[86]

This means that architecture is inherently complex, and any attempt to extract and isolate the factors that define it will impoverish its richness and complexity. Architettura Parametrica is therefore fundamentally opposed to the reductive mentality typical of 19th-century thinking, which is still difficult to overcome.[87]

Moretti has a high regard for the Vitruvian thought, which he describes as "subtle, rich, and unifying", despite the distortions by "minor writers and commentators since the 1500s".[88] He firmly believes that architecture exists when every point in space can respond to the needs of reality and representation, technique, function, and expressive facts. This belief gives Architettura Parametrica an almost utopian strength:

> a work is architecture when one of the possible n structures (in a constructive sense) coincides with a form that satisfies a group of required functions and with a form that adheres to a determined expressive course "of the soul of the human work place" that is taken on by the architect.[89]

These goals can be achieved by following various genetic directions, considering a more or less extensive number of design parameters, by necessity or choice. Architettura Parametrica is one of these possible paths. According to Moretti, the genetic direction function → form is exhausted. This direction was theoretically embraced by rationalist architecture and, through Bauhaus, industrial design.[90] Similarly, the direction of form → structure, followed by most organicist masters, is also exhausted for Moretti. His Architettura

Parametrica aims to overcome this by addressing "the discouraging plethora of forms that with the spread of iconographic culture is submerging us, we must instinctively refuse from the beginning as many meaningless forms as possible".[91]

But, as already mentioned, the number and complexity of the parameters must be taken in consideration. Finally, in a preliminary definition of Architettura Parametrica, Moretti writes:

> In fact, if by function we mean the complex of determinative parameters of spaces and their concatenations, no less than of conditions and qualities of materials, the alternative must be clearly indicated.
>
> These parameters may be limited in number and exactly understood, and spaces and materials can be deduced with scientific rigor and therefore the possibilities of oscillation of the forms are minimal. At this point we enter into the field of technique, or better, to the extreme limit of what I call "Parametric Architecture". These parameters may otherwise be numerous and not easily definable, and therefore the function cannot but indicate an approximate form, a latent pre-form that only the successive process of definition of the structure constitutes as a finished figure. Is this not the typical process of structure → form?[92]

A challenging, open definition that leads to ambiguity, as Moretti himself later acknowledges that architecture is "essentially structure", now giving the term the logical-mathematical meaning of "complex of relationships" rather than the physical-Vitruvian meaning. It is suggested, however, that Architettura Parametrica involves accepting this duality, since for Moretti "the creative act of form-making [...] is fundamentally the act of communicating, defining, making tangible an aspect, or a certain sequence of aspects [...] that is, to express a structure".[93]

The cultural foundation of Architettura Parametrica is a reflection on the Vitruvian triad. It stands for a return to the origins, a true and real adherence to Vitruvius' principles, albeit through a genetic direction that postpones the questions of form. The formal problem is postponed just enough to eliminate unnecessary formalism. This is not "functionalism 2.0", where one element of the Vitruvian triad becomes primary. Instead, it is an act of methodological rigour, which humbly asks to investigate the constraints of functions to reach "the mathematical splendor of inevitable[94] forms of parametric architecture".[95] Moretti does not ignore form and its expressiveness, believing that without an expressive intent or drive architecture "remains only a fact of pure construction, or better, of pure technique, subject therefore to the obsolescence of the technique and not the immutability, the immortality of form".[96] In Architettura Parametrica, form and expressiveness are free to move where constraints, relationships between different *structures* (this time with a purely logical-mathematical meaning), as well as the several analyses that define the parameters of a design problem, leave areas of indeterminacy. Moretti writes:

> If these relationships have only very weak bonds of uncertain quantity, the structure imposes only haloes of space wide enough for the architect to almost freely base his game on the other structures. If, instead, this group of relationships has strong bonds or parameters, the structure is defined with mathematical precision and the resulting spatial elements are determined in a strict and unequivocal manner.
>
> Modern architecture, although it raised the banner of functionalism, has until now gathered little from this fertile field. It has conducted only very limited descriptive analysis of the restrictions and has done so with the uncomfortably simplistic attitude of *fin-de-siècle* theoreticians.
>
> The architecture of the future will have to start from this vigorous research on parameters, studies that will separate it completely and substantially from the architecture of the past and from all that we call modern, which will soon be crushed by a new perspective that will reduce it to the level of nineteenth-century architecture.[97]

Architettura Parametrica, in its cultural conceptions expressed in the pages of *Spazio*, is an approach to design that transforms structural, functional, and formal limitations into design accelerators, as confirmed by Moretti's words:

> we want limitations in order to know exactly where to challenge them with the most boundless fantasy.[98]

The commitment period and the contaminations of an architectural theory (1957–1973)

> There are times when old age produces not eternal youth but a sovereign freedom, a pure necessity in which one enjoys a moment of grace between life and death.[99]

Peter Eisenman with Elise Iturbe in *Lateness* recalls this concept by Gilles Deleuze and Felix Guattari to describe the "late style" of an architect: "a phenomenon of personal intransigence, a moment when the artist ceases to heed the norms of the discipline; subjective expression, in the face of death, drives away any formal predeterminations".[100] The latest Moretti's theoretical developments in Architettura Parametrica emphasise this interpretation of the late style on two seemingly divergent tracks of his research.

On the one hand, Architettura Parametrica merges with operational research, providing Moretti with techniques to bridge theory and practice. On the other, Moretti outlines a mosaic of cultural references, both internal and external to architectural design, that supply metaphors and themes for his research. This cultural mosaic is a wealth of influences that Moretti has been shaping since his youth, showing interest in the works of Giotto, Michelangelo, Borromini and Bernini, alongside references to Évariste Galois, Ramon Llull, Galileo Galilei, and others in the pages of *Spazio*. Figures between art and science drew the interest of Moretti. However, driven by his collaboration with Michel Tapié[101] and Art Autre, this mosaic rapidly expanded after 1960, incorporating the latest influences from an informal world where abstract mathematics and avant-garde art coexist. Additionally, there is a fascination with the computer, which will be discussed in Chapter 4.

This paragraph explores these two lines of Moretti's research, convinced that one of the most important values of Architettura Parametrica lies in its tension between technique and art, as well as between formal and informal.

Formalised approaches driven by operational research

The founding of the IRMOU[102] (*Istituto per la Ricerca Matematica e Operativa applicata all'Urbanistica*, translated by Moretti as "Institute for Mathematical and Operational Research Applied to Urbanism") in 1957 catalysed and accelerated the evolution of Architettura Parametrica theories. IRMOU worked on techniques, tools, and problems, providing Moretti with opportunities to test his architectural design theories in practice.

The utopian and lyrical force of *Spazio* is now accompanied by more pragmatic and realistic methodological objectives suggested by IRMOU. The theoretical framework of Architettura Parametrica is now clear and well-defined, built around the technical domain of operational research. Thanks to Moretti's role in IRMOU, the cold and detached approach of operational research is tempered by considerations of ethics and design rigour. This is an unexpected development, given that a few years later, Negroponte would describe operational research methods as "extremely antagonistic to the nature of architecture".[103]

Fundamental, both theoretically and practically, is the delineation of Architettura Parametrica given at the XII Triennale di Milano in 1960. Here, Moretti and IRMOU, in the *Exhibition of Parametric Architecture and Mathematical and Operational Research in Urban Planning*, wrote some of the most fruitful pages of 20th-century architecture for the proposed innovations, the ability to forecast the future development of architectural design, and especially for the unique synthesis of design theory, technique, and practice. The IRMOU seems more involved in certain problems of the Exhibition, such as city subdivision into school zones, basic traffic phenomena, traffic variations with city expansion, traffic structure changes, investment coordination, and an analogue simulator of interdependence phenomena. Moretti seems more involved in the experimental design of six buildings for various events and, above all, in the theoretical pages that precede the experiments. However, theoretical aspects, architectural scale, urban scale, and even territorial scale are closely interconnected in the Exhibition.

Architettura Parametrica, in its union with operational research, shows continuity with Moretti's previous research. This is evidenced by excerpts from the first French version[104] of *Forma come Struttura* that Moretti includes in the catalogue's opening pages. Architettura Parametrica still aims to align architectural project practice with scientific research methods. Unlike in 1954, when the French text of *Forma come Struttura* was published, Moretti now has access to computers and IRMOU's support. The discussion of the catalogue's practical parts is deferred to the next chapter, while this paragraph focuses on its theoretical content.

The "general scheme of the research" of Architettura Parametrica is of extreme interest. The full version of the scheme from the English translation of the catalogue is presented:

"Parametric Architecture" appears like a branch of study tending to insert in the very marrow of present day thought, particularly when it is scientific, the phenomena of architecture and town-planning. To achieve this it is evidently necessary to:

1 refuse empirical decisions or decisions taken because of analogy or through repetition of traditional methods (both ancient and modern);
2 appraise traditional phenomena considering them objective facts, present and, consequently, in relation with the interdependence of their values (technical, expressive, social, etc.);
3 have an exact definition of the themes;
4 objectively observe all conditioning elements (parameters) connected to these phenomena and discover their quantitative values;
5 have the definition of the relations between the quantities depending on the various parameters;
6 consider the indispensability of the contribution of the various abilities and therefore of the various scientific methodologies, according to the criterions of 'Operational Research', in the definition of the conditioning elements and of the relations between their quantities;
7 affirm the liberty of the architect to make his choice and to express himself, provided he does not modify the structural characters of the areas of the phenomenon as determined by the analytical researches;
8 direct the architectural forms towards a maximum and therefore final exactitude of relations in the general structure".[105]

In this scheme, Moretti's cultural positions expressed in *Spazio* reach a compromise with design practice and technique. The preliminary architectural investigations and analysis gain renewed importance, producing not just a programme to follow or a function to satisfy, but defining a domain within which the designer operates. This domain allows architectural forms to oscillate, pulsate and vibrate without contradicting the preliminary architectural investigation. This scheme reintroduces the concept of *structure* with the mathematical-relational meaning Moretti used in *Spazio*. Other mathematical concepts like *differences* and *automorphisms* are excluded from the catalogue. Furthermore, themes like the unity of language, the Baroque, and space sequences are completely absent from the catalogue. These research themes are not pursued by IRMOU and seem to be more related to Moretti who will continue investigating them. In fact, Moretti's eclectic interests permit him to humanise operational research in his design vision.

The Architettura Parametrica's scheme can be seen as a particularisation of the operational research method in architectural design.[106] When Moretti founded IRMOU, operational research was defined in several monographs primarily as a scientific method and "an organized activity with a more or less definite methodology of attacking new problems and finding definite solutions".[107] Operational research, originally developed to optimise the use of military resources, applies mathematics and statistics to model complex problems. These models traditionally address issues highlighted in the catalogue, such as production scheduling, resource distribution and allocation, resource use optimisation, activity planning, and more. There are, therefore, many correspondences between these operations and the design themes that Moretti suggests for his Architettura Parametrica:

Metro stations, hospital and school topologies partially developed by IBM with its 'programs'; general topologies, quantised dimensions and connections of various building types; optimal distribution of services for urban complexes (schools, healthcare, cultural, administrative, commercial, sports, etc.); optimal definition of colours and signage in specific building types, public places, garages, specialised hospitals, etc.; definition of materials to be used in specific themes given technological, economic, and psychological parameters. Obviously, the themes Architettura Parametrica can address with efficient precision are those involving a limited number of parameters.[108]

Reliable, safe, compliant, and consistent decisions supported by objective facts are the products of operational research. Design *structures* with the same qualities are the goals of Architettura Parametrica. This proximity with operational research seems confirmed by the further Architettura Parametrica's methodological synthesis contained in the catalogue: "definition of the theme; singling out the parameters interfering in the theme; definition of the analytical relations between magnitudes depending from the various parameters".[109] This synthesis confirms that Architettura Parametrica, in its union with operational research, shifts the emphasis of design action towards the problem-setting phase. Furthermore, it suggests that, in Moretti's view, a proper design investigation is already a design act. Moretti's writings on innovations brought by scientific instrumentation in urban design confirm this view:

> There are not two separate stages in planning (data collection and determination of processing and interpretation) but rather a unified process.[110]

What has become of form, understood as a possible and physical determination of a *structure*, needs to be investigated. The eight points of the Architettura Parametrica's scheme, along with the applications proposed in the case studies of "architectures for large numbers" that will be analysed later,[111] confirm that a proper design investigation leads to a general direction for the architectural form. The apparent disinterest in the form actually serves to curb its exploration unsupported by scientific facts. This concept is the cornerstone of the latest evolution of Architettura Parametrica: limiting the intuitive, empirical, and somewhat random dimension in architectural design. These aspects are also found in the definition of Architettura Parametrica in Paolo Portoghesi's Dizionario Enciclopedico, to which Moretti contributed[112]:

> Parametrica Architettura: Design method based on logical-mathematical, physical, electronic, biological, psychological, sociological, and economic parameters, proposed by architect Luigi Moretti within the Institute for Mathematical and Operational Research Applied to Urbanism (I.R.M.O.U., founded in 1957 in Rome).
>
> The Architettura Parametrica programme was showcased at the XII Triennale di Milano, curated by L. Moretti with scientific collaboration from B. De Finetti's group, featuring graphs, models, and applications. It aims to transcend empiricism and formalism by using the logical and instrumental possibilities of modern scientific thought. The exhibition exemplified the operational research method applied to architecture and urban planning through themes such as football, swimming, and tennis stadiums, cinema halls (key parameter: visual equiappetibility); habitats; car bodies; traffic studies and variations; urban design and planning.[113]

It is necessary to explain the meaning of the term *parameter* in this phase of the theoretical evolution of Architettura Parametrica. Unlike earlier phases, Moretti provides in *Moebius* a comprehensive list of parameters involved in designing "architecture for large numbers", such as a stadium or cinema hall. This list is much more detailed than what was published for the exhibition over ten years before, demonstrating Moretti's ongoing work on Architettura Parametrica:

> General theme: determination of the optimal space distribution in the areas surrounding a field where phenomena occur, where the term "field" is understood as an area or a portion of space with assigned delimitations.

Architettura Parametrica: In Theory 49

Parameter 1 - In a two- or three-dimensional field, the identification of the various values of the phenomena that occur there and for which information must be provided in the area surrounding the field.

Parameter 1.a - Consideration of the different classes of phenomenon that occur on the field.

Parameter 2 - Quantitative evaluation of the orology of place and climatic factors, and of prevalent photometric conditions to gather information about the global space (the field and its surrounding areas).

Parameter 3. Predicted quantity of information receptors in the space adjacent to the field.

Parameter 4 - Identification of the values of the direct psycho-physiological (sensory) means of reception for gathering information and of the values of the direct subsidiary means (amplification, etc.) In particular, the determination of:

Parameter 4.a - Angle of maximum permissible movement of the median anteroposterior axis of the head with the transversal axis of the pelvis evaluating the frequency of the same movement in relation to the median frequencies of the velocity of movement on the field of the phenomena taking place

Parameter 4.b - Optimal angle for a careful observance for the reception of variations (differences) of a predetermined order that happen on the field

Parameter 4.c - Optimal angle of observation for information of variations of superior entities (vision of the whole difference among groups of differences that were discussed in the preceding 4.b).

Parameter 5 - Determination of the optimal azimuthal angle of observation for the transferal of information from the interior of the field and from the various areas with their values of information that were discussed in 1.a

Parameter 6 - Latitudinal angle, idem.

Parameter 7 - Distribution of spaces adjacent to the field of the receptors according to places (lines, areas, or spaces) of the values of equal information about phenomena that happen on the field

Parameter 8 - Values (limits) of acceptability of the distribution of the spaces of equal information within the exigencies of the concrete support structures of the receptors within the limits of:

Parameter 8.a - Safety (statistical or positional) of the receptors.

Parameter 8.b - Obstruction to the information for each receptor in relation to the presence of the other receptors.

Parameter 8.c - Annexing of the space proper to each receptor evaluated within the time and in the path.

Parameter 8.d - Resignation of the spaces, idem.

Parameter 8.e - Safety of the two preceding issues.

Parameter 8.f. - Acceptability of the physiological effort necessary in order to realize as much as has been stated in 8.b and 8.c.

Parameter 9. - Optimal considerations of all the listed parameters and the economic cost of the concrete structures of support.

The parameters listed above are clearly associated within four groups:

1. Determining factors are the phenomena about which information must be given (P1, 1.a, 2);
2. Determining factors of the quantified characteristics of the receptors of information (P3, 4, 5, and 6);
3. Determining factors of the integration of the two preceding groups (P7 and 8);
4. Determining factors of the integration of the group 3 with the economic field in which P9 occurs.[114]

It is interesting to note that identifying parameters can lead to different degrees of *quantisation* in the design process. Another example of parameter identification, and their varying degrees of *quantisation*, is proposed for an urban-scale problem, specifically related to urbanisation governance:

a General parameters: provide existing and future human aggregates with the best structure adhering to citizens' socio-economic and spiritual needs;

b Parameters mediated by instruments that can resolve the parameters in a).

[...]

1. Parameters concerning a cultural and operational methodology for the theoretical definition and drafting of plans regarding the form and dynamics of existing and future human aggregates;
2. Parameters concerning the instruments to ensure, in practice, the necessary raw material (the territory) for the final formulations of the previous group (the plans).[115]

These parameters refer to both problem-setting and problem-solving activities, but also to both the constraints to be satisfied and the performance to be achieved. This parametrisation of the architectural problem exposes it to a technical drift when the importance of cultural positions is diminished. In addition to the balanced positions between technique and culture expressed in the 1960 exhibition, and the positions showing greater interest in cultural themes in Moretti's solo writings, a third nature of Architettura Parametrica can be identified.

Some of Moretti's explorations in town planning temporarily distanced him from architectural design theories. Thus, in a series of writings, Moretti speaks as an urban (or even territorial) planner, offering another perspective on his Architettura Parametrica. This perspective is captured by some of Moretti's professional activities in collaboration with IRMOU, such as involvement in Rome's master plan and traffic studies,[116] as well as his editorial work for the journal *Informazioni Urbanistiche*,[117] founded and directed by Moretti. In these activities, Architettura Parametrica moves away from synthesising physical forms and offers its tools to provide decision-makers with scientific elements for making political choices in territorial governance. These activities suggest that the more technical aspect of Architettura Parametrica was also implemented for political purposes, legitimising Moretti's presence in working groups like the Rome master plan, and influencing the city's development for decades. Moretti's exploration of urban planning techniques highlights the possibility that the output of Architettura Parametrica is design guidelines rather than physical forms.

To investigate how Moretti's scientific approach to architectural design allows for overcoming unnecessary formalism and basing the design process on objective facts, we need to step away from the exhibition and its catalogue. These concepts, in fact, will be explored in a series of Moretti's solo writings and speeches, which are less burdened by the shadow of IRMOU.

In an informal newspaper interview,[118] Moretti clearly outlines the theoretical and methodological principles of his Architettura Parametrica. For Moretti, an Architect must systematically and repeatedly question design practices driven by inertia, laziness and reluctance to change, rather than proven validity. Moretti does not deny the role of tradition but insists on testing and validating it in order to relieve accumulated burdens by architecture. Besides procedural schemes, Moretti suggests resisting the "seduction of mental habit".[119] Therefore, Architettura Parametrica begins when known design solutions are questioned and new ones are not pursued *ad libitum*.[120] This means that alongside IRMOU's rigid experiments, a more relaxed and informal version of Architettura Parametrica can be adopted without denying its cultural essence, as shown by the numerous experiences discussed in the next chapter.

Previously, it was suggested that Architettura Parametrica is not a sort of "functionalism 2.0" that pushes a revival and renewal of the tradition linked to the modern movement. Instead, Moretti views his Architettura Parametrica as the first true functional conception of Architecture. Moretti writes:

Parametric architecture is nothing but functional architecture. However, the so-called "functional" architecture we've seen in recent decades was functional in name only. In reality, it was always about adaptations, more or less ingenious, of old models. Problems were never addressed in their original and essential terms.[121]

This is a debatable position, theoretically significant yet provocative. The questioning of traditional models leads to "starting from scratch" without preconceived ideas. This results in a renewal of the design resources and efforts invested in an architectural project. A renewal that demands overcoming the concept of the architect as a solitary author working with a few draftsmen. Architettura Parametrica embraces, supports, and promotes the interdisciplinarity that is fundamental in operational research. Moretti pushes a true interdisciplinary that surpasses the sterile "famous sectoral relations",[122] considered by him as excessively vertical studies unable to grasp architecture's complexity. Discussing the nature of the problems that Architettura Parametrica's addresses, Moretti identifies where to find the necessary skills for this heterogeneous design approach:

Pure mathematicians, especially those experts in mathematical logic, statistics, probability, set theory, and group theory, physicists, biologists, mathematical economists, and mathematical sociologists. In this context, the architect must adapt to these new methodologies and equip himself with the necessary tools in order to avoid being a mere executor of operational details or a finisher of larger designs framed by others.[123]

This highlights another cultural aspect of Architettura Parametrica: rejecting analyses and research that introduce a plethora of data and information which do not aid the scientific advancement of the design process.[124] Moretti continues to argue, as he did in *Spazio*, that parameters are important for design, but the relationships revealing unexpected connections between them are even more crucial.[125] Quantifying parameters that fail to reveal these connections and hidden design mechanisms is not only unhelpful but harmful. Architettura Parametrica, therefore, is a dialectical approach that involves constructing the design problem, collecting data for its resolution, and interpreting this data to outline possible design *structures*.

This vision inevitably requires a renewal of architects' education. Moretti strongly argues that an architect's education should "focus on formal logic, mathematical logic, and advanced mathematics (probability, set and group theory, etc.), and on spiral and non-linear reasoning methods enabled by the speed of computers".[126] Architects must navigate various domains related to architecture and urban planning, such as social, economic, psychological, and physiobiological fields. But Moretti also stresses the need for precise knowledge of optics and the psychology of form. He clarifies that architects don't need to have a detailed knowledge of these fields, but should understand how their *structures* are formed and evolve.

In the last words in one of his last articles, and perhaps the last article devoted to Architettura Parametrica,[127] Moretti writes:

> Architettura Parametrica, and this is for me its most important characteristic, proposes, indeed requires, a new rigorous intellectual morality from the architect. It evokes an ethical stance of full and conscious respect for reality, and thus, acting with clear objective justice towards all other.
>
> It rejects resting [on] solutions already developed in classical or modern traditions; it rejects arbitrariness as antisocial; it rejects the personal vanity that results from it; it rejects formalistic carelessness, a direct consequence of the absence of real social commitment (even if this commitment is constantly proclaimed) and the lack of the necessary biological vigour to conquer reality.
>
> Architettura Parametrica ultimately demands humility, which is always a testament to genuine spiritual excellence, and the continuous, arduous, yet joyful patience in action.
>
> Architettura Parametrica opens up a world of new and revolutionary forms for the architecture of the future; for the architect, it offers a behaviour of the highest dignity.[128]

These words, which today read as a testament to Architettura Parametrica, reaffirm the ethical value of eliminating interference between preliminary architectural analysis and formal exploration. More importantly, they clarify that what seems like a challenge to the discipline's foundations is actually an act of humility by the architect: he must forget everything he thought knowing about architecture to start anew with renewed moral and scientific rigour.

Towards an "Architecture Autre"

This paragraph will focus on some of the references from the complex mosaic of cultural influences, both within and outside the world of architecture, that have suggested paths for Moretti to follow, aspects to consider, or simply guided the development of his theories. The paragraph aims to investigate how these references built the foundation for more informal and less rigid applications of Moretti's theories in design practice.

The first and perhaps most crucial influence to discuss is that of Évariste Galois's theories, which shaped the mathematical aspects of Moretti's design theory. Galois's theories permitted Moretti to conceptualise architecture in terms of structures, relationships, differences, and chains. This influence is declared in the introductory note of the French version of *Forma come Struttura*:

> With a contempt similar to that of Wright for the falsely modern "functional" realisations, it is the absence of a truly present-day architecture

that Luigi Moretti reveals. He enables us to glimpse what the architecture of tomorrow might be, founded upon the parameters themselves derived from Galois' so very fruitful notions of groups (the latter, though dating from 1832, have only very recently begun to attain their full development outside the fields of mathematics).[129]

This note should have been written by Moretti mainly because references to Galois in the text are quite implicit. Similarly, the reference to Galois at the end of *Ecleticism and Unity of Language* seems to be a wish for research yet to be done, and thus still immature to guide an architectural theory. Moretti writes in this article: "A European—or even just an Italian—might reflect on the constellation of pure relationships, exposed by that youngster Évariste Galois, that can be seen in the tremor of a leaf on an apple tree or in the wind at night".[130] This quote prompts us to reflect on Galois' theories, which can illuminate the relationships within a design *structure*. It is of undeniable interest that Moretti references Galois both in the first editorial of the first issue of *Spazio* and in what several anthologies indicate as his last article. In this writing, a memorial to architect Giuseppe Vaccaro, Moretti recalls how Galois' last letter opened him to a novel way to understand architecture:

For me personally the habitual way of considering a work is the search for this secret fabric as a link between the various elements of a work, which makes, or attempts to make, the individual forms as interrelated parts in a consciously inseparable fabric. This perhaps derives [...] mainly from Galois' eighteen pages that opened to us the new objective world as a reality of pure interrelations.[131]

The key to Galois' influence on Architettura Parametrica should not be sought by decoding the mathematical aspects of his writings, such as his famous mathematical testament.[132] Instead, one should question the way Moretti interpreted his theories, as Moretti appears inconsistent at times. He, in fact, translate Galois thought from the mathematical to the architectural debate. He undertakes a true "architecturalisation" of Galois's thought, suggesting a focus on the relationships between architectural values rather than on pure architectural phenomena. Moretti elaborates on this as he admits that Galois's theories provided him "a sort of private guardian spirit of mine, to which my mind has continuously turned for thirty years".[133] These positions are also reflected in the transcription of a debate by Moretti:

This breaking of barriers, the rush of a sudden, life-giving, transversal torrent occurred, for the modern world, on that night when Évariste Galois wrote the famous letter to his friend Chevalier, in which he definitively settled some fundamental points of group theory. We know what this theory entails: it has led to the conception of an abstract world, detached from the field of entities to which the operations of a given group refer and from the manner of their representations. In my opinion, this theory still holds hidden and unarticulated implicit philosophical foundations, even though they manifest themselves explosively.

Galois' research, focused on a specific mathematical problem—determining the conditions for the solvability of equations—has, in its developments, in fact, impacted and, in a certain sense, overturned some of the fundamental positions of classical thought. A fact, a world of facts, is no longer defined by the knowledge of the entities themselves that participate in its play and therefore lose all meaning, but only by their relationships. Internal and external-internal relationships define a fact, not the things in themselves that compose it.

The genius of Galois, and of those who later developed his research—up to set theory, topology, and so on—was to conceive the complex of relationships independently of the specific entities that interact within them.[134]

Moretti is interested in Galois's theories because they permit him to understand that architecture is not a sum of facts, but a network of relationships to be grasped, revealed and, according to Architettura Parametrica, designed. Galois' insights revolutionised mathematics' theory of groups.[135] He discussed the possibility of solving some mathematical problems related to the roots of polynomial equations by studying how these roots are connected. This approach studies relationships between entities rather than isolated entities. The Galois letter that Moretti recalls several times is "an extraordinary summary of what [Galois] had achieved and what he might have achieved had he lived to develop and expound more of his mathematical ideas".[136] Here Galois explains that his main question "was concerned with seeing a priori in relations between transcendental quantities or functions, what exchanges one could make, what quantities one could substitute for the given quantities without the relation ceasing to hold".[137] This suggestion, when translated into architecture, has a disruptive design force, as it transforms space and form into entities that can be manipulated without questioning the system of relationships that define them. Where the *structure* of the form cannot be defined, Galois' theories suggest that defining the relationships between other *structures* involved in architecture, from the constructive-static dimension to the role of light, will still allow the unfolding of the form to be understood.

The visions that Moretti uses to define and implement his Architettura Parametrica are not limited to Galois' suggestion. Since the main aim of this book is to discuss the process of negotiation between theory and practice in Moretti's Architettura Parametrica, it is useful to discuss the experiences that brought Moretti closer to Michel Tapié and the field of *Art Autre*, whose meaning is closely related to *Informal Art*. This experience systematises some of Moretti's cultural references with those of Tapié, which were already recognised by scholars like Rostagni,[138] Tedeschi,[139] and Imperiale.[140] These references are already found in the issue of *United States Lines Paris Review*, which also featured the first French draft of *Forma come Struttura*. Here, in the conclusion of an article on *Art 'Autre'*, Tapié writes:

> It seems nonsense to talk of Aesthetics [...] if we think of Plato, St. Thomas, Paccioli, Boileau, Spinoza, etc... but not if we think of Heisenberg's Uncertainty [principle], of Galois' Groups, of Cantor's Transfinite, of the continuity of the Topology of sets, of the Abstract Spaces (I advise the reconsideration of this wonderful word to art critics accustomed always to giving it a sense of restrictive puritanism), of the Real Numbers, of psychogenesis, of Modern Logistics, of all which permits us to reconsider the notions capable of supporting the rigorous operation of an "Other" Aesthetic.[141]

Moretti in the sixties is seriously interested in the world of informal art, introducing his personal mathematical, spatial, and informal interpretations into it. Rather than reconstructing this intriguing history, it is more useful to continue decoding Architettura Parametrica by discussing, as was done for Galois, some of the design metaphors suggested to Moretti by this complex patchwork of references. Several references cited by Tapié recur in various writings of Moretti. If we add to this the writings where he and Tapié collaborated in different forms, it is evident that Moretti these references were deeply rooted in his cultural background. For example, a note about Heisenberg's uncertainty principle was in the notebook *An architecture of limited parameters* written between 1925 and 1945. From what has been discussed so far, it is clear that the reference to Heisenberg has a design value as it provides a scientific counterpoint to Moretti's way of working in architectural practice: moving, with scientific rigour, in uncertainty, between halos of indeterminacy and probability. The intertwining of *Art Autre* with Moretti's theoretical thinking, and more specifically with Architettura Parametrica, seems sealed when Moretti defines the latter as "Architecture Autre".[142]

In 1960, Moretti and Michel Tapié founded the ICAR, the *International Centre for Aesthetic Research*, in Turin.[143] This dynamic study group aimed to break with figurative tradition by interpreting and practising art in the light of modern scientific thought. Moretti and Tapié's *Le Baroque Gènèralisè: Manifeste du Baroque Ensembliste*[144] reveals their intention to redefine the figurative tradition through a mathematical lexicon. The artists they promote and exhibit are organised into groups that intersect and overlap. The "Ensemble ordonné des artistes sélectionnés en février 1965: l'élément ommun est le baroque généralisé" is, for example, based on the following groups: "intuitionnisme artistique; structures ensemblistes; baroquisme stylistique; formalisation axiomatique".[145] These groups aim to reveal relationships rather than categorise artists. They do not seek to simplify but to highlight complexity.

This approach mimics a recurring theme in Moretti's design praxis[146]: proposing multiple design solutions and grouping them to uncover hidden or implicit relationships. Similarly, Moretti's selection of projects for his solo exhibition in Madrid[147] and the illustrations in his notable book, *50 Immagini di Architetture di Luigi Moretti* (with a valuable preface by Giuseppe Ungaretti and recently largely reprinted in a volume by Bucci[148]), aim to emphasise the complexity of his architecture. In this book, the complexity of Moretti's architecture does not emerge through individual determinations, i.e., projects, but through the implicit or explicit relationships these projects establish among themselves.

The *Manifeste* by Moretti and Tapié offers interesting insights into the nature of the mathematics of Architettura Parametrica. This manifesto was published on the occasion of the inauguration of the ICAR museum *Barocco di Insiemi* and aims to mark:

> The beginning of new research, entirely centred on "ensemblisme" and "baroquisme" [...] both from a structural and ethical perspective; because the artistic phenomenon, that is, the creation of structures, can only exist by surpassing itself.[149]

Moretti had already stated that architectural design is essentially the creation of *structures*.[150] But now this principle is extended with Tapié to all arts. The content of the *Manifeste* suggests that the mathematics Moretti is interested in can be divided into two branches: a more operational mathematics that provides tools and techniques for his formalised architectural approaches, and an abstract mathematics that provides metaphors for more informal applications. Examples of the introduction into architectural design of the first type of mathematics, such as the use of parametric equations, conics, and linear optimisation, will be discussed in the next chapter. Returning to abstract mathematics, such as Galois' theories, Moretti does not use these concepts to solve architectural problems; instead, he relies on techniques like elementary algebra. Abstract mathematics has a more theoretical role in Moretti's vision of architectural design: it provides metaphors and indicates research directions. Moretti is more interested in how abstract mathematics "overflows" and impacts aesthetics, ethics, and philosophy in general. Or, using Tapié's words, Moretti is interested in what "radiates outside the framework of strict abstract mathematics".[151] From this point of view, the essays *Forma come Struttura* and *Struttura come Forma*, and thus the positions of Architettura Parametrica, are products of an irradiation of abstract mathematics towards architecture.

Tapié writes that "Luigi Moretti defines aesthetics as the study of the intersection of two groups, one 'artistic', the work of art, and the other 'biological', the art enthusiast".[152] This position reaffirms that Moretti was more interested in the perception of the fact than in the fact itself, in other words, in the relationship between the art and the art observer. This position was anticipated by his numerous studies on the perception of architecture, as discussed in the previous paragraphs. Moretti's studies on Baroque *structures* align with this interest. He defines the Baroque *structure* as "a spatial structure with an exaggerated time dimension"[153] and, as such, it requires a process of successive learning to be fully understood. More precisely, a Baroque *structure* can only be understood when studied over time from multiple perspectives, addressing various themes, moving from the subsystems that compose it to the general structure, and then back to the subsystems. This means, in contemporary terms, that a Baroque structure, as defined by Moretti, is a complex system with emergent properties that requires multiple observations to be understood. Moretti presents these ideas in *Annotazioni sul barocco*,[154] an essay organised into 24 points that focus on the relationship between an observer and a baroque *structure*. A similar theme was already explored by him through a mathematical interpretation of Baldassarre Peruzzi's *Palazzo Ossoli*[155] (see Figure 2.3). In almost every point of *Annotazioni sul barocco*, Moretti proposes a mathematical formalisation of the concepts expressed in the text. He calls this mathematisation "notes for a formal transcription". This operation is similar to the one he employed at the end of the essay *Forma come Struttura*, although the mathematical modelling is now much more complex and refined. Furthermore, in the essay *Strutture d'Insiemi*[156] included in the appendix to the *Manifeste*, Moretti uses another mathematical formalism as a tool to fix verbally expressed concepts. An excerpt of the mathematical formalism used in *Annotazioni sul barocco* is provided below:

$$S \equiv \bigcup_{i=1}^{n} s_i$$

S: Acquisition of the form (of the set)

s_i: Acquisition of the subsystems spatially and structurally different subsets

$$t = t\left(n; s_1, s_2, s_3, \ldots, s_n\right)$$
$$t = t\left(1; s_i\right)$$
$$t\left(n; s_1, s_2, s_3, \ldots, s_n\right) > t\left(1; s_i\right)$$

t: mechanical time for acquiring s, function of n (number of elements) and the characteristics of each element.

s_i: unique element repeated [...].[157]

This mathematical symbolism corresponds to the first three textual points of Moretti's essay, which are:

1. THE CHALLENGING REDUCTION TO A GEOMETRIC PATTERN—OR OF REPETITION—, THE RICHNESS AND COMPLEXITY OF THE FACTS COAGULATED WITHIN THE FABRIC OF THE WORK, THE NECESSITY, THEREFORE, TO TRAVERSE THEM ALL TO PRODUCE A CLEAR READING, TO FULLY CONSUME THEM, ARE THE CHARACTERISTICS OF A BAROQUE STRUCTURE AS OPPOSED TO A NON-BAROQUE ONE.

2. A BAROQUE STRUCTURE IS A SPATIAL STRUCTURE WITH AN EXAGGERATED TIME DIMENSION.

3. IN A BAROQUE STRUCTURE, THE COORDINATE OF TIME IS INTRODUCED AS A SUPPORT FOR REPRESENTATION AND AS A NECESSARY CONSEQUENCE FOR ITS CONSUMPTION, WITH A DOMINANT DIMENSION. IN CONTRAST, NON-BAROQUE STRUCTURES LACK TEMPORAL SUPPORTS IN THEIR REPRESENTATIONS, AND THE READING TIMES ARE SHORTENED.[158]

To a mathematician, Moretti's formalism might seem mild and not rigorous, but to an architectural design scholar, it is disruptive. It forces the acquisition of important mathematical skills, which do not immediately translate into design tools and techniques. These skills suggest professional rigour, but also an aesthetic to pursue. There are no physical forms in this abstract mathematics, yet its value lies in the awareness that structural and mathematical conception of form opens up a seemingly limitless morphological world.[159] This morphological world is one where no solutions are implicitly more valid than others, where there are no paths traced by others to be followed. A morphological world that now needs to be discussed in its practical applications, the forms it has suggested in design and the methods it has introduced.

Notes

1 Luigi Moretti, *Il significato attuale della dizione architettura* [The current meaning of the term architecture], debate transcript, Accademia di San Luca, 16 April 1964. Republished in *Moretti visto da Moretti* (Rome: Palombi, 2007).
2 Cfr. Federico Bucci and Marco Mulazzani, *Luigi Moretti: Opere e scritti* (Milan: Electa, 2000). Republished as *Luigi Moretti: Works and Writings* (New York: Princeton Architectural Press, 2002).
3 Cfr. Cecilia Rostagni, *Luigi Moretti 1907–1973* (Milan: Electa, 2008).
4 Luigi Moretti, *Exhibition of Parametric Architecture and of Mathematical and Operational Research in Town-Planning* (Rome: Istituto Nazionale di Ricerca Matematica e Operativa per l'Urbanistica, 1960), 5. The accredited authorship of the Italian version differs: Luigi Moretti and IRMOU, eds., *Mostra di architettura*

parametrica e di ricerca matematica e operativa nell'urbanistica (Milan: Arti Grafiche Crespi, 1960).
5 Italian preliminary typescript for the article: Luigi Moretti, "Architecture 1965: Évolution ou Révolution. Réponses au Questionnaire", *L'Architecture d'Aujourd'hui*, no. 119 (1965): 48–51. For the typescript: Rome, Archivio Centrale dello Stato – Fondo Luigi Moretti (ACSLM), folder 44.
6 Luigi Moretti, "Ricerca matematica in architettura e urbanistica" [Mathematical research in architecture and urbanism], *Moebius* IV, no.1 (1971): 30–53. Republished in Bucci and Mulazzani, *Luigi Moretti: Works and Writings*; Roberto Podda, *Luigi Moretti: Lessons of Spazio* (New York: Routledge, 2024).
7 Luigi Moretti, "Giotto Architetto", *Quadrivio* no. 9 (7 March 1937). Republished by Bucci and Mulazzani and in Annalisa Viati Navone and Guillemette Morel Journel, *Luigi Moretti: Structure et espace* (Paris: Éditions de la Villette, 2024).
8 See Chapter 3, section "Formal analogies".
9 Roberta Lucente, *Il progetto come fonte, come metodo, come prassi* [The project as source, as method, as practice] (Rome: Aracne, 2014), 21. Lucente examines this position also through an exegetical reading of Moretti's *Casa delle Armi*.
10 Luigi Moretti, *Architettura a parametri limitati*, 1925–1945. Published in Tommaso Magnifico et al., eds., *Luigi Moretti: The Form, Structure and Poetic of Modernity*, *AR Magazine* a LV, no. 125–126 (special issue, 2021): 70–89. https://www.architetiroma.it/ar-web/ar-magazine-125-126/
11 Annalisa Viati Navone, "THE BAROQUE UNDER THE LIGHT OF THE TACCUINO. An Intellectual Trajectory Constructed a Posteriori", *AR Magazine* a LV, no. 125–126 (2021): 220–237.
12 Viati Navone, "THE BAROQUE UNDER THE LIGHT OF THE TACCUINO", 220–237. This complete collection of notes is preserved in the Moretti-Magnifico Archive (AMM).
13 Viati Navone, "THE BAROQUE UNDER THE LIGHT OF THE TACCUINO", 220–237.
14 Viati Navone, "THE BAROQUE UNDER THE LIGHT OF THE TACCUINO", 220–237. The proximity between Moretti and Cybernetics has been discussed in Chapter 1.
15 Luigi Moretti, "Valori della modanatura", *Spazio* a 3, no. 6 (1951–1952): 5–12, 112. Republished by Bucci and Mulazzani, Viati Navone and Morel Journel, and Podda.
16 This topic will be further explored in this book. The paragraph "the 'parameters' of vision" by Reichlin is recommended. See Bruno Reichlin, "Figure della spazialità", in *Luigi Moretti: Razionalismo e trasgressività tra barocco e informale* [Luigi Moretti: Rationalism and Transgressiveness between Baroque and Informal], eds. Bruno Reichlin and Letizia Tedeschi (Milan: Electa, 2010), 19–59.
17 Moretti, "Giotto Architetto".
18 Dino Buzzati, "Grideremo 'GOL!' da un'ala di farfalla. Che cos'è l'Architettura Parametrica" [We will shout 'GOL!' from a butterfly wing. What is Parametric Architecture], Corriere della Sera, 19 October 1960, 5.
19 ACSLM, "Progetto dello stadio olimpico ed esecuzione fino al secondo anello delle gradinate", project 62, 37/48/5OR.
20 ACSLM, p. 62, 4/48/1OR; 4/48/2OR; 4/48/3OR.
21 ACSLM, p. 62, 37/48/5OR.
22 ACSLM, p. 62, 37/48/5OR.
23 Buzzati, "Grideremo 'GOL!'".
24 ACSLM, "Piazzale delle adunate al Foro Mussolini", project 59, 36/42/1.
25 ACSLM, "Piazzale delle adunate al Foro Mussolini", project 59, 36/42/1.
26 ACSLM"Piazzale delle adunate al Foro Mussolini", project 59, 36/42/1.

Architettura Parametrica: In Theory 61

27 See Chapter 2, section "Formalised approaches" and Chapter 3, section "A design exegesis".
28 ACSLM, p. 59, 36/42/2.
29 ACSLM, p. 59, 36/42/3.
30 May be translated as "broad preliminary form".
31 Luigi Moretti, "Struttura come Forma", *Spazio* a 3, no. 6 (1951-1952): 21–30, 110. Republished by Bucci and Mulazzani, Viati Navone and Morel Journel, and Podda.
32 ACSLM, p. 59, 36/42/5.
33 Manuel De Landa, "Deleuze and the Use of the Genetic Algorithm in Architecture", *AD – Architectural Design* 72, no. 1 (2002): 9–13.
34 See also note 1.
35 Maria Grazia D'Amelio and Tommaso Magnifico, "Luigi Moretti's project for the Foro Mussolini", *AR Magazine* a LV, no. 125–126 (2021): 184–205.
36 For further insights into this project that support the theses of this book: Luca Ribichini, Tommaso Magnifico, and Flavio Mangione, "The Imperial Theatre by Luigi Moretti: The Importance of Drawing in the Concept of Space", *Disegnare Idee Immagini* 46, no. 1 (2013): 30–41. As written in note 8 of this article, the Moretti-Magnifico Archive includes folders titled: "Calculation of distribution in space—elevation visibility curve; Verification of step visibility for oblique views; Planimetric distribution of equal visibility curves for performances on a plane and performances in space within a defined surface".
37 ACSLM, "Piazzale dell'Impero al Foro Mussolini", project 71, 37/77/2.
38 ACSLM, p. 71, F.2860. The drawing is published in Plinio Marconi, "Il Piazzale dell'Impero al Foro Mussolini in Roma", *Architettura* 20, no. 9–10 (September–October 1941): 347–359.
39 Tommaso Magnifico, "Luigi Moretti. Being in the Clearing of the World", *AR Magazine* no. 125–126 (2021): 46–67.
40 Cfr. note 31 in Annalisa Viati Navone, "'Un nuovo linguaggio per il pensiero architettonico'. Ricerca operativa e architettura parametrica" ["A new language for architectural thought". Operations research and parametric architecture], in *Luigi Moretti: Razionalismo e trasgressività,* 408–419.
41 Cfr. Luigi Moretti, "Strumentazione scientifica per l'urbanistica" [debate transcript], *Giornata di studio sul tema Cultura e realizzazioni urbanistiche: convergenze e divergenze,* Fondazione Aldo della Rocca (Rome: CNR, 16 December 1965). Republished in Gabriele Esposito De Vita, ed., *Luigi Moretti e la Fondazione della Rocca. Urbanistica e Ricerca Operativa* (Rome: GB Editoria, 2009).
42 Luigi Moretti, "Forma come Struttura", *Spazio*, estratti, 1957. Already published as "Structure comme forme", *United States Lines Paris Review* 1 (1954). Republished as "Form as Structure", *Arena* (June 1967). Republished by Bucci and Mulazzani, and Viati Navone and Morel Journel.
43 Federico Bucci, *FORM, STRUCTURE, SPACE. Notes on Luigi Moretti's Architectural Theory* (Matosinhos: AMAG, 2021).
44 "Ricerche di Architettura. Sulla flessibilità di funzione di un complesso immobiliare urbano", Spazio no. 6 (1951–1952). This article, signed "S.", could be attributed to Moretti according to *Moretti visto da Moretti*, 153. See also Chapter 3, section "Methodological Analogies".
45 Bruno Zevi, "Luigi Moretti double-face. Ambizione contro ingegno", in *L'Espresso* (17 February 1957). Reprinted in Bruno Zevi, *Cronache di Architettura* (Bari: Laterza, 1975), n. 145.
46 Zevi, "Luigi Moretti double-face. Ambizione contro ingegno".
47 Zevi, "Luigi Moretti double-face. Ambizione contro ingegno".
48 Moretti exposes this terminology in the final part of *Forma come Struttura*.
49 Moretti, "*Forma come Struttura*".

50 Moretti, *"Forma come Struttura"*. Compared to Bucci and Mulazzani's translation, some symbolism has been corrected.
51 Moretti, *Architettura a parametri limitati*, 147.
52 A different translation from the text published in *AR Magazine* is proposed.
53 Moretti, *Architettura a parametri limitati*, 147.
54 Moretti, "Struttura come Forma".
55 Moretti, "Struttura come Forma".
56 Moretti, "Forma come Struttura".
57 Moretti, "Valori della modanatura".
58 Luigi Moretti, "Genesi di forme dalla figura umana", *Spazio* a 1,no. 2 (1950): 5. Republished in Bucci and Mulazzani, Viati Navone and Morel Journel, and Podda.
59 Moretti, "Forma come Struttura".
60 Moretti, "Forma come Struttura".
61 The anthologies by Bucci and Mulazzani, Viati Navone and Morel Journel, and Podda do not translate this note.
62 The meanings of "frames" [cornici] and "molding" [modanature] are closely related in this Moretti's article.
63 Moretti, "Valori della modanatura".
64 Moretti, "Valori della modanatura".
65 Moretti, "Forma come Struttura".
66 Moretti, "Forma come Struttura".
67 Moretti, "Forma come Struttura".
68 Moretti, "Forma come Struttura".
69 Moretti, "Forma come Struttura".
70 Moretti, "Forma come Struttura". Cfr. D'Arcy Wentworth Thompson, *On Growth and Form* (Cambridge: University Press, 1917).
71 Luigi Moretti, "Spazi-luce nell'architettura religiosa" [Light-spaces in religious architecture], *Atti della IX Settimana di Arte Sacra* (Rome: Tipografia Poliglotta Vaticana, 1961).
72 Federico Bucci, "Automorfismi e 'unità di linguaggio': la teoria architettonica di Luigi Moretti" [Automorphisms and "Unity of Language": The Architectural Theory of Luigi Moretti], *Studi e ricerche di storia dell'architettura* 10 (2021): 108–122.
73 Moretti's article that most closely aligns with the proposed meaning is *Forma come Struttura*.
74 Luigi Moretti, "Strutture e sequenzi di spazi", *Spazio* no. 7 (1952–1953): 9–20, 107–108. Republished by Bucci and Mulazzani, Viati Navone and Morel Journel, and Podda. Bucci discusses the meaning of "algorithm" for Moretti in "Painted Words", in *Luigi Moretti: Works and Writings,* 136–155.
75 Bucci, "Automorfismi e 'unità di linguaggio'".
76 Cfr. Matilde Baffa Rivolta and Augusto Rossari, eds., *Alexander Klein: Lo Studio Delle Piante E la Progettazione Degli Spazi Negli Alloggi Minimi, Scritti E Progetti Dal 1906 Al 1957* (Milan: Mazzotta, 1975).
77 Cfr. Christopher Alexander, *Notes on the Synthesis of Form* (Cambridge: Harvard University Press, 1964).
78 Moretti, "Forma come Struttura".
79 See the images published in Magnifico, "Luigi Moretti. Being".
80 Moretti, *Architettura a parametri limitati*, 128.
81 Moretti, "Forma come struttura".
82 Luigi Moretti, "Eclettismo e unità di Linguaggio", *Spazio* a 1, no. 1 (1950): 5–7. Republished by Bucci and Mulazzani, Viati Navone and Morel Journel, and Podda.
83 Moretti, "Eclettismo e unità di Linguaggio", 5–7.

84 Moretti, "Ricerca matematica in architettura". The list of parameters will be discussed in the section "Formalised approaches".
85 Moretti, "Struttura come Forma".
86 Moretti, "Struttura come Forma".
87 Moretti, "Forma come Struttura".
88 Moretti, "Struttura come Forma".
89 Moretti, "Struttura come Forma".
90 Moretti, "Struttura come Forma".
91 Moretti, "Struttura come Forma".
92 Moretti, "Struttura come Forma".
93 Moretti, "Forma come Struttura".
94 A slightly different translation from that of Bucci and Mulazzani is proposed.
95 Moretti, "Struttura come forma".
96 Moretti, "Struttura come Forma".
97 Moretti, "Forma come struttura".
98 Moretti, "Struttura come forma".
99 Gilles Deleuze and Félix Guattari, *What Is Philosophy?* (London: Verso, 1994), 2–3.
100 Peter Eisenman with Elisa Iturbe, *Lateness* (Princeton: Princeton University Press, 2020), 11.
101 Michel Tapié (1909–1987) was a French art critic, curator, and theorist known for promoting *Art Informel* and postwar avant-garde movements.
102 Rostagni writes about IRMOU in *Moretti 1907–1973*, 98 note 108: "The scientific committee includes: Leandro Canestrelli (psychologist), Vittorio Castellano (statistician), Anna Cuzzer (physicist), Raffaele D'Addario (statistician), Mario de Benedicty (mathematician), Ezio De Felice (mathematician and architect), Bruno De Finetti (professor of financial mathematics), Aroldo De Rivoli (physicist), Franco Lepri (physicist), Giuseppe Pompily (professor of geometry), Vittorio Somenzi (physicist), and Cristoforo Bertuglia, Giuseppe Brenci, Giovanni Cordella, Dario Furst, Giuseppe Vaccaro, and Tiziano Zelaschi". Cfr. Anna Cuzzer, Giovanni Cordella, Cristoforo Sergio Bertuglia, "Testimonianza. Ricordi dell'IRMOU" [Witness. Memories of the IRMOU], in *Luigi Moretti: Razionalismo e trasgressività*.
103 Nicholas Negroponte, *Soft Architecture Machines* (Cambridge, MA: MIT Press, 1976), 189.
104 Moretti, "Structure comme forme".
105 The texts extracted from the English version of the catalogue are proposed. For a full translation from the Italian text: Roberta Lucente and Giuseppe Canestrino, "Distance between Theory and Practice in a Project by Luigi Moretti, Parametric Architecture's First Theorist", *The Journal of Architecture* 28, no. 5 (2023): 749–777. https://doi.org/10.1080/13602365.2023.2251029
106 Viati Navone, "Ricerca operativa e architettura parametrica".
107 Philip M. Morse, *Methods of Operations Research* (London: Chapman and Hall, 1951), 1.
108 Moretti, "Ricerca matematica in architettura".
109 Moretti, *Exhibition of Parametric Architecture*, 11–12.
110 Luigi Moretti, "Alcune considerazione sulla programmazione scientifica nel campo dell'urbanistica" [Some consideration of scientific programming in urban design], *Relazione al 3° convegno INARCH su "I problemi dello sviluppo di Roma"* (20 February 1965).
111 See Chapter 3, section "A design exegesis".
112 For the correspondence between Paolo Portoghesi and Moretti, see ACSLM, folder 39.
113 "Parametrica Architettura", in *Dizionario Enciclopedico di Architettura e Urbanistica* [Encyclopaedic Dictionary of Architecture and Urban Design], ed. Paolo Portoghesi (Rome: Istituto Editoriale Romano, 1968), 377.

114 Moretti, "Ricerca matematica in architettura".
115 Luigi Moretti "Finalità e mezzi della Riforma Urbanistica" [Purposes and tools of the urban planning agenda], debate trascript (23 April 1963). Published in *i quaderni del* π no. 6 (1964).
116 See Chapter 4, section "Methodological Analogies".
117 The journal released 20 issues between January 1960 and August 1961. The editorial of the first issue states that "the many disciplines and countless real-world situations involved in planning require urbanists to gather accurate information, particularly in related fields that may not fall within their direct expertise".
118 Buzzati, "Grideremo 'GOL!'".
119 Buzzati, "Grideremo 'GOL!'".
120 Moretti uses the Italian term "a braccio". Moretti, "Strumentazione scientifica per l'urbanistica".
121 Buzzati, "Grideremo 'GOL!'".
122 Moretti, "programmazione scientifica".
123 Moretti, "Architecture 1965", italian typescript.
124 Moretti, "Strumentazione scientifica".
125 Moretti, "programmazione scientifica".
126 Moretti, "Architecture 1965", italian typescript.
127 This statement is supported by anthologies of Moretti's writings, such as those compiled by Rostagni, Bucci, and Mulazzani.
128 Moretti, "Ricerca matematica in architettura". A slightly different translation from that of Bucci and Mulazzani is proposed.
129 Moretti, "Structure comme forme".
130 Moretti, "Eclettismo e unità di Linguaggio".
131 Luigi Moretti, "Ultime testimonianze di Giuseppe Vaccaro", *L'architettura. Cronache e storia* a XVIII, no. 3 (1972): 146–161.
132 Évariste Galois, *Testamentary Letter to Auguste Chevalier*, 29 May 1832, Bibliothèque nationale de France, Département des manuscrits, NAF 3414, fol. 48r–49v.
133 Luigi Moretti, "Forma come Struttura", debate trascript, *exhibition Le Corbusier e le nuove tecniche del costruire*, (Rome: Galleria Nazionale d'Arte Moderna, 20 April 1969). Cfr. Rostagni, *Moretti 1907–1973*, 97, note 70.
134 Giulio Carlo Argan, Luigi Moretti, Raffaello Morghen, Adalberto Pazzine, "Coincidenze e Relazioni delle Espressioni Culturali" [debate trascript], *Civiltà delle Macchine*, a. XIII, no. 4 (1965): 37–47.
135 Cfr. Peter M. Neumann, *The Mathematical Writings of Évariste Galois* (Zurich: European Mathematical Society, 2011).
136 Neumann, *The Mathematical Writings of Évariste Galois*, VII.
137 Galois, *Testamentary Letter.*
138 Rostagni, *Moretti 1907–1973*, 92–95.
139 Letizia Tedeschi, "Algoritmie spaziali. Gli artisti, la rivista 'Spazio' e Luigi Moretti (1950-1953)", in *Luigi Moretti: Razionalismo e trasgressività*, 136–177.
140 Alice Imperiale, "An 'Other' Aesthetic: Moretti's Parametric Architecture", *LOG* 44 (2018): 71–82.
141 Michel Tapié, "Devenir d'un art 'autre'", *United States Lines Paris Review* (July 1954).
142 Paolo Portoghesi, Luigi Moretti, Sergio Musmeci, Armando Plebo and Bruno Zevi, *Structures, Mathèmatiques, Architecture Contemporaine* [Debate transcript], 23 November 1964. ACSLM, folder 42.
143 Cfr. Chiara Maraghini Garrone, *TABULA RASA. La storia dell'ICAR di Michel Tapié de Céleyran* (Turin: Paola Caramella Editore, 2020).
144 Luigi Moretti, Michel Tapié, *Le baroque Generalise. Manifeste du Baroque Ensebliste* (Turin: Edizioni del Dioscuro, 1965).

145 Cfr. Michel Tapié, "D'un ordre autre dans le baroque ensembliste", Opera Aperta, a. I n. 3–4 (1965): 97–99.
146 Cfr. The many solutions proposed for the Watergate and Via Decima complexes, for Corso Italia, Fiuggi's Baths, and many other projects.
147 Cfr. *Moretti visto da Moretti.*
148 Bucci, *FORM, STRUCTURE, SPACE.*
149 Moretti and Tapié, *Le baroque Generalise.* See the introduction note by Ada Minola, president of the ICAR.
150 See note 69.
151 Michel Tapié, "Overture", in *Le baroque Generalise.*
152 Tapié, "D'un ordre autre dans le baroque ensembliste".
153 Luigi Moretti, "Annotazioni sul barocco", in *Le baroque Generalise.*
154 Moretti, "Annotazioni sul barocco".
155 See section "Moretti's mathematical conception of architecture".
156 Luigi Moretti, *Strutture di Insiemi*, 1962. Reprinted in *Opera Aperta*, a. I n. 3–4 (1965): 100–104. Reprinted by Viati Navone and Morel Journal.
157 Moretti, *Strutture di Insiemi*, 1962, 100–104.
158 Moretti, "Annotazioni sul barocco". The text is capitalised faithfully to the original Italian version.
159 Luigi Moretti, "Ouverture", in *Le baroque Generalise.*

3 Architettura Parametrica
In practice

In a series of conferences, debate transcripts, and articles, Moretti claimed to have repeatedly attempted to apply the theoretical framework of Architettura Parametrica to his projects.[1] These statements are often tempered with a note of caution, as he acknowledged that in his architectural works, he had only incorporated some of the "basic principles" of his research.[2] Moretti's admission that he never fully translated his design theories into practice has led to general scepticism about the validity and usefulness of the theoretical framework of his Architettura Parametrica.[3] However, the multiple and previously discussed nuances of Architettura Parametrica – ranging from intuitive methods to informal approaches and rigid operational research tools – encourage the search for the various "basic principles" underlying Moretti's theories in his extensive body of work.

This chapter explores whether the different theoretical modulation of Architettura Parametrica can be linked to corresponding practical modulation. To do this, the practical dimensions of Architettura Parametrica, understood as a negotiation process between an architectural theory and its necessary translation into project praxis, are questioned.

This research is hindered by the extremely limited sources where Moretti associates Architettura Parametrica with design procedures, not just theoretical and cultural positions. Moretti explicitly applies the methods and techniques of Architettura Parametrica only in the projects of the 1960 *Exhibition of Parametric Architecture and of Mathematical and Operational Research in Town-Planning:* two football stadiums, two swimming stadiums, a tennis stadium, and a cinema hall. Moreover, mathematical models that lead to the synthesis of architectural forms are available only for these projects.[4] Starting from the procedures described in the exhibition catalogue, the mathematical models with which Moretti synthesises the forms of his stadiums will be thoroughly analysed in order to discuss the methodological implications arising from such an architectural design approach.

Subsequently, formal analogies with these large-scale architectures will be sought in Moretti's extensive professional work, considering both built and unbuilt projects. In particular, forms influenced by the synthetic knowledge

DOI: 10.4324/9781003595007-4

Moretti derived from his research on stadium visibility, rather than simply replicating the organic forms he exhibited, will be identified. This reveals how, since the 1930s, Moretti sought to reiterate a series of insights aimed at optimising stadium forms – insights that were scientifically validated only in the 1960 exhibition and which have been continually revisited thereafter. Finally, experiences in which the mindset of Architettura Parametrica led not to architectural form, but to different methodological principles and techniques in architectural design, will be explored.

This chapter, therefore, discusses three possible narratives through which Moretti translated the theories of Architettura Parametrica into design practice: the synthesis of technique and form described in the 1960 exhibition, the apparent predominance of formal intuition over the rigour of technical analyses, and finally, the adoption of techniques that do not lead to formal predetermination.

A design exegesis of the Architettura Parametrica exhibition projects

In the notorious 1960 XII Milan Triennale exhibition, Moretti explored "architectures for large numbers", proposing an innovative design method that shaped architectural form through analytical optimisation of visual quality. Before examining these methods, it is important to consider why Moretti chose this theme to demonstrate the potential of Architettura Parametrica. In *Forma come Struttura*, Moretti declared his fascination with themes where the spatial structure of architecture is subject to numerous constraints, as he explained: "We feel the need to challenge something that has an objective order, a law to bend if possible, to be in dialogue with another and gain their assent".[5] This indicates that when Moretti referred to architecture for large numbers – a theme discussed in the previous chapter – he did not only mean the idea of a crowd that shapes architectural form, a concept he had already addressed in 1934–1936 with the *Piazzale delle Adunate* (see Figure 2.1).[6] "Large numbers" also represent the multitude of parameters that influence, constrain, and limit architectural design. Moretti wrote:

> Especially for themes where parameter investigations focus on statistical analyses and the behaviour of large numbers, exceptional results can be achieved. For example, in a stadium where the spatial curves of the stands depend on 14 defined parameters, existing stadiums will, in the future, appear—as they indeed are—as no more than interesting works of craftsmanship.[7]

Building on these premises, Moretti required an architectural theme that balanced showcasing the potential of Architettura Parametrica with conducting mathematical analyses that were streamlined and easily manageable.

68 *Decoding Luigi Moretti's Architettura Parametrica*

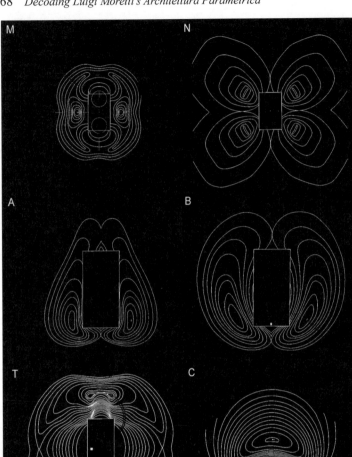

Figure 3.1 Luigi Moretti, Exhibition of Parametric Architecture and of Mathematical and Operational Research in Town-Planning, Milan, 1960. Representation of equivisibility curves of the W function in: football stadiums M and N, swimming stadiums A and B, Tennis stadium T, and cinema hall C. Credits: Archivio Centrale dello Stato Italiano, Fondo Luigi Moretti [ACSLM, auth. 650/2025], project 162, [M] 60/198/7; [N] 60/198/8; [A] 60/198/11; [B] 60/198/10; [T] 60/198/13; [C] 60/198/15.

Architettura Parametrica: In Practice 69

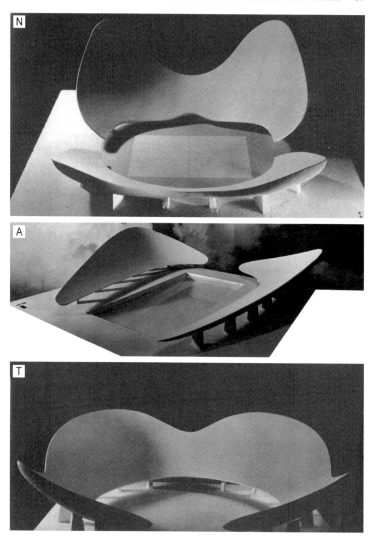

Figure 3.2 Luigi Moretti, selection of models shown at the Architettura Parametrica exhibition. Credits: ACSLM [auth. 650/2025], project 162, [A] F3055; [N-T], Luigi Moretti, "Ricerca matematica in architettura e urbanistica", Moebius, IV no. 1 (1971): 30–53.

Among the numerous parameters cited in the well-known *Moebius* article (fully reported in Chapter 2), visibility emerged as a particularly accessible area of investigation. This accessibility was tied to Moretti's extensive work on the subject, beginning with the *Foro Italico* projects, which provided him with specific scientific tools to tackle these designs. In addition, Moretti probably sought a theme that was not heavily rooted in rigid architectural traditions, allowing him to overcome the inertia often associated with conventional design approaches more easily.

We can also consider which themes were unsuitable for Moretti and IRMOU research. Due to technical limitations, which will be discussed shortly, Moretti required a theme with a dominant morphogenetic parameter – one capable of overshadowing the influence of other parameters in shaping architectural form. Indeed, Moretti's optimisation process is fundamentally monoparametric. An interesting viewpoint emerged in a discussion where Bruno Zevi asked Moretti why, in his opinion, Architettura Parametrica was more suited to social housing than to villas. Moretti replied:

> It is not true that a method works for social housing but not for a wealthy man's villa; however, there is a question of parameters. In an economic house, the parameters are countable because, for example, the constraint—the parameter of the economy—dominates a series of dependent parameters. The design of a single villa, at most, lacks this constraint or has it only as a broad condition, while many other parameters, entirely subjective and specific to a particular client, come into play.[8]

From this reasoning, a key scenario emerged to construct six design problems: a large number of spectators observing a dynamic event over a period of time. Within this framework, a stadium and a cinema hall can be addressed using similar hypotheses, techniques and tools. Moretti sensed that these themes offered "a law to bend"[9] with the scientific rigour of his Architettura Parametrica.

Moretti identified a consistent family of problems to demonstrate the potential of Architettura Parametrica. This consistency is evident in how he presents each project, their initial assumptions, and their mathematical and geometric modelling. Moretti's process did not return the final form; instead, it provided a graph of "visual equiappetibility" curves, which served as a fitness function, measuring the visuospatial quality of each point in space for a given event. Architectural form is thus designed considering this graph, which corresponds to a visibility function that Moretti referred to as W.

Moretti defined an architectural problem rather than an architectural type, highlighting his focus on formal topologies over architectural typologies. The mathematical modelling for calculating W varied significantly between projects, with adjustments in the calculation processes, in the parameters involved, and in the methods used to derive them. This demonstrates that

Moretti's exploration of Architettura Parametrica in the exhibition is a collection of methods and techniques for structuring design mathematically, rather than a rigid model to be adopted uncritically.

The design analysis of these architectures is hindered by gaps in the reconstructions Moretti provides in the exhibition catalogue. He did not explain how the equations were constructed and often did not describe the purpose of the mathematical and geometric structures involved. Additionally, Moretti did not clarify the process of translating visibility analysis results – presented as 2D plots – into the 3D forms of his architectures. These gaps undermine the scientific rigour of his approach, as they affect the method's replicability. However, they are valuable as they suggest a degree of indeterminacy in the results of visibility analyses. As will be shown, Moretti did not always propose morphologies for his stadiums that fully align with his analyses (compare Figures 3.4 and 3.9); yet, he never fundamentally questioned the validity of these results.

This suggests that Moretti's forms, in this particular application of Architettura Parametrica, did not stem from a sterile interpretation of shapes dictated by visibility analysis results. Instead, Moretti avoided the risk of technical automatism. The form was guided by equations; yet, these equations – with their errors, imprecisions, inconsistencies, and ambiguities – became flexible tools in Moretti's hands. This reflects a genuine negotiation between theoretical aspirations and practical needs.

The exhibition architectures will be explored through their mathematical models, aiming to uncover how Moretti designed them and, above all, the inconsistencies that reveal the humanity of Architettura Parametrica. The research will adopt Moretti's perspective, accepting the limitations of the IBM 610 he used instead of modern computing tools, which studies have shown can easily interpret those equations with tools that Moretti was not able to access.[10] Contemporary tools surpass Moretti's constraints, risking an incomplete understanding of his design thinking. The IBM 610, as used in Moretti's applications, could tabulate functions numerically but was unable to solve complex design problems. The proposed research is not an *Archaeology of the Digital*,[11] as there is no software to recover or explore, rather it is just a brief textual description by Moretti in the exhibition catalogue. Instead, Moretti's equations will be approached through "algorithmic reenactment", a research method recently proposed by Alexander Galloway.[12] Moretti's equations will be treated as "computational artefacts" to translate, rewrite, debug, and reconstruct, focusing on form, space, and design methods rather than programming.[13] According to Galloway, "algorithmic reenactment" offers both greater technical awareness and new cultural and methodological insights. Borrowing Ernst's framework on "digital memory", this research will explore Moretti's equations to examine the "technological conditions of the sayable and thinkable in culture, an excavation of evidence of how techniques direct human or nonhuman utterances—without reducing techniques to mere apparatuses".[14]

72 *Decoding Luigi Moretti's Architettura Parametrica*

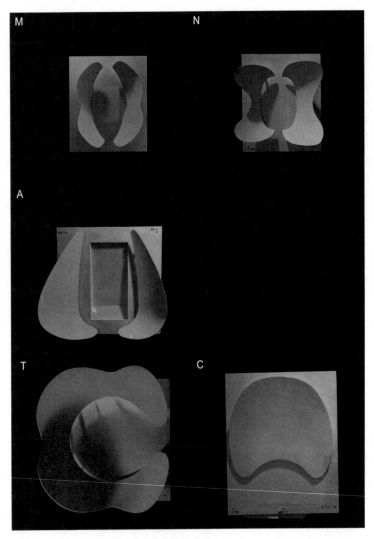

Figure 3.3 Luigi Moretti, plans of the models shown at the Architettura Parametrica exhibition, 1960. Credits: ACLSM [auth. 650/2025], project 162, [N] F3066; [A]: F3053; [C] F3054. [M-T]: Luigi Moretti, "Ricerca matematica in architettura e urbanistica", Moebius, IV no.1 (1971): 30–53.

Architettura Parametrica: In Practice 73

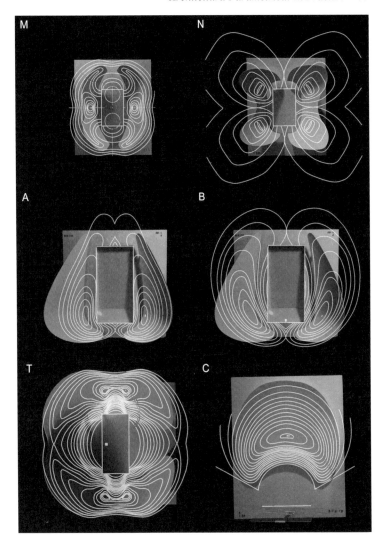

Figure 3.4 Overlay between equivisibility curves of the W function and plans of the models shown at the Parametric Architecture exhibition. Football stadiums M and N, swimming stadiums A, tennis stadium T, and cinema hall C. The visibility graph B is superimposed on the only exhibited swimming stadium model. Credits: Composition by the author.

74 Decoding Luigi Moretti's Architettura Parametrica

Football stadium M

For the football stadium, Moretti recognises that this design theme requires the:

> definition of a large number of parameters, divided into three classes: parameters relative to the object of information (the game), relative to the type of information (direct visual), relative to the features of the specific class of information regarding the subject (the viewer).[15]

This seems to be the prelude to a multi-objective design process, able to consider aspects pertaining to the different subjects and objects involved in this design theme. However, in the first practical example presented in the Architettura Parametrica exhibition catalogue, stadium M, he assumes several simplifying assumptions for "clarity of exposition":

a) Visibility of the entire football field

b) Areas of greatest interest identified in the two circles of centers C1 and C2, located on the longitudinal axis of the field, at a distance of 15 m. from the shorter sides and 50 m. in diameter, with a diameter of 50 m.

c) For each of the said areas of interest, visibility is a function of the distance from the centers of the areas, zero at the center, maximum when the area is viewed under an angle of 35°, and tending to 0 when the distance to the field tends to ∞.[16]

The reasons for the pursuit of this "clarity of expression" could be numerous and not necessarily solely related to Moretti's technical limitations. If we acknowledge the catalogue's communicative role, the purpose of which is to bring as many designers as possible closer to the world of Architettura Parametrica, it seems that Moretti wants to begin his presentation with an easy-to-understand example. Therefore, Moretti proposed to measure the quality of space through the use of a single "visibility function W". W is formed by the sum of two contributions that measure the visual quality with respect to centres of interest C_1 and C_2 (see Figure 3.5M). To calculate the visibility function W, the catalogue provides the following equation:

$$W = d_1^k e^{-kd_1} + d_2^k e^{-kd_2}. \qquad (3.1)$$

From these assumptions, using the geometric indications provided for the areas of greatest interest C_1 and C_2, the measurements of the soccer field considered by Moretti were derived graphically: the soccer field presents a length of 120 metres and a width of 74 metres. Moretti does not explain the process that led him to hypothesise the positions of points C_1 and C_2. The choice

Architettura Parametrica: In Practice 75

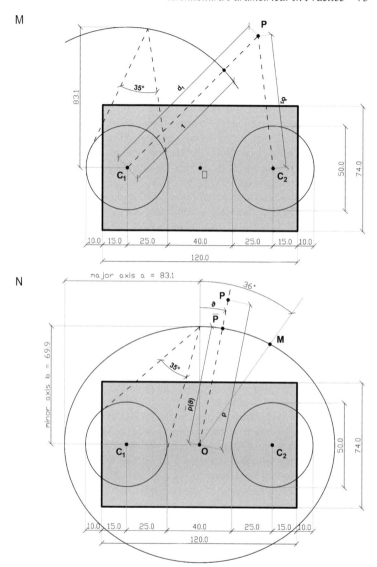

Figure 3.5 Diagram for calculating the visibility function W in M and N soccer stadiums. The information indicated in bold is provided by Moretti. The information in regular font is added by the author. Credits: Author.

76 Decoding Luigi Moretti's Architettura Parametrica

of these areas of interest may be traced back to the results of an analysis, explained in the pages of *Moebius*.[17] Here Moretti proposed a survey using photogrammetric instruments to map the positions of different players and the ball on the soccer field over time. Moretti divided a football pitch into 294 zones and recorded the position of all players and the ball at intervals of 2–4 seconds. A coefficient of interest is then applied to the collected data, ranging from 1 for the long sides of the pitch to 3.5 for the penalty areas. By repeating the operation for many events and for many years (Moretti proposed 5 years), it is possible to derive the amount of visual information emitted by each point in the field analytically. This is an investigation whose application would also be recommended by Moretti for the preliminary studies for the design of swimming stadiums A and B.[18]

Moretti's directions can be easily verified in a parametric modelling software, merely by replicating the elementary actions underlying his equations. This research, however, does not just seek to verify Moretti's equations but aims to understand their logical-compositional mechanisms in order to understand how Moretti could first design and then use them. To do so, a preliminary discussion of the mathematical nature of Moretti's equations is necessary. It can be argued that equation (3.1) was not derived rigorously but, instead, was "constructed" through the composition of an elementary set of mathematical functions. These elementary functions seem to be chosen for their ability to shape a limited number of insights simply and intuitively. The parameter d, which returns the distance between a point P and centres of interest, is used so that visibility W is equal to 0 when P is placed on a centre of interest and tends to infinity as the point P moves further away. The second part of the equation is responsible for returning a maximum when the areas of interest are viewed under a 35° angle. In fact, the function $d_1^k e^{-kd_1}$ has a maximum for $d=1$. Moretti proposes to normalise the distance d from the centre C with respect to the circle that sees the areas of interest under an angle equal to 35° (see Figure 3.5M). Therefore, it becomes clear that equation (3.1) translates, into mathematical terms, the identification of the maximum visual quality at those points from which the area of interest is seen under an angle equal to 35°. Moretti's explanations for stadium M end by assigning the value 10 to the k parameter.

The following is a speculation of the process employed by Moretti and the IRMOU to design the formula of stadium M. Also, to deeply understand how these equations, intended as innovative design tools, can be used, the analytical operations necessary for the derivation in the explicit form of the total visibility function W are briefly given. The importance of expressing W in explicit form, i.e., dependent on the generic x_p and y_p coordinates of a point in space, is related to the need to have an equation that can be easily calculated and mapped, even with the rudimentary tools available to Moretti. For this first stadium, the proposed operation appears almost trivial. However, this is a propaedeutic operation to understand the design process underlying the subsequent stadiums, which present significantly more complex mathematical structures.

The first step is to calculate the measure of the radius of the circle with respect to which the normalisation is performed. Moretti does not explain this passage, but states that for the calculation of W it is "implied that the unit of measurement of distances is taken to be that from which one of the areas of interest is viewed under the optimal angle (35°)". Identifying with r the radius of the circle of interest, this normalised distance d' can be calculated as follows:

$$d' = \frac{r}{\sin\left(\frac{35°}{2}\right)} = 83{,}137 \ m. \tag{3.2}$$

Assuming a Cartesian coordinate system with origin in the centre of the field, the distance of a generic point P from the centres of interest can be calculated, for the centre C_1, using the well-known formula:

$$d(P; C_1) = \sqrt{(x_p - x_{c1})^2 + (y_p - y_{c1})^2}. \tag{3.3}$$

To apply the normalisation, it is sufficient to divide equation (3.3) by (3.2). The operations conducted thus make it possible to express W in explicit terms, thereby replicating the design process used by Moretti and IRMOU.[19] In order to demonstrate how the proposed reconstruction permits calculation of the visual quality as the succession of a series of analytical operations manageable even by the rudimentary instruments available to Moretti, only for this stage the explicit formulation of W that associates a measure of visual quality with each point P defined by the coordinates $(x_p; y_p)$ is reported:

$$W = \left(\sqrt{\{(x_p - x_{c1})^2 + (y_p - y_{c1})^2\}}\right)^k e^{\left\{-k\sqrt{\{(x_p - x_{c1})^2 + (y_p - y_{c1})^2\}}\right\}}$$
$$+ \left(\sqrt{\{(x_p - x_{c2})^2 + (y_p - y_{c2})^2\}}\right)^k e^{\left\{-k\sqrt{\{(x_p - x_{c2})^2 + (y_p - y_{c2})^2\}}\right\}}. \tag{3.4}$$

By comparing the visibility curves calculated by Moretti (Figure 3.1M) and the visibility curves calculated analytically (Figure 3.9M), important differences emerge. These differences can also be traced in previous research that, using different methods, digitalised Moretti's equations for stadium M.[20] However, these researches did not explicitly acknowledge these divergences. It is interesting to note that Moretti's operations on the form of his stadium

78 *Decoding Luigi Moretti's Architettura Parametrica*

appear to be supported by the results of his analyses. However, the values of the W function found with the proposed reconstruction disprove the forms of the Moretti stages and, ironically, appear consistent with the forms of a traditional stage.

Football stadium N

For stadium N, Moretti proposes a series of textual insights from which to derive another visibility function:

a) along each radius through O the visibility, which is zero in O, grows to a maximum, then decreases until it becomes zero at infinity

b) the place of the maximums is an ellipse, which has as its foci 2 points C1 and C2 located on the major axis of the field 15 meters in front of each of the goals. This ellipse pass through the point located on the transverse axis from which the two circles, with centres at C1 and C2 respectively and radius 25 meters (zone of interest), are seen under an angle of 35°;

c) as ϑ changes, the maxima on each radius change, reaching a maximum value when ϑ is 36°.[21]

The formula for the visibility function proposed by Moretti is the following:

$$W = x^{k(y)} e^{-k(y)x}. \tag{3.5}$$

With:

$$k(y) = 3.5y^2 - 2.5y + 1.5, \tag{3.6}$$

$$x = \frac{\rho}{\rho(\vartheta)}, \tag{3.7}$$

$$y = \frac{2\vartheta}{\pi}. \tag{3.8}$$

This formulation of W implies that stadium N adds a viewing angle parameter to the formulation of stadium M. This angle allows the visual quality to be calculated as a single contribution, although two zones of interest continue to be considered for the identification of the curve of maximum visibility. This stadium, therefore, places particular emphasis on an optimal curve, in this case an ellipse, on which the phenomenon is best observed. The use of an optimal visibility curve would also be at the core of the A and B swimming stadiums.

The ellipse of the stadium N has its two foci in the centres of the two zones of interest, C_1 and C_2, which are positioned in a similar way to stadium M. Moretti stated that visibility is a function of the angle ϑ between the transversal axis and the conjunction between the spectator and the centre of the field. Finally, he proposed to locate the absolute visibility maximum for $\vartheta = 36°$.

Attempting to reconstruct the possible process adopted to design these equations poses new challenges compared to stadium M. An initial novel feature is undoubtedly the greater complexity of the W formula, within which contributions are nested that, as will be shown, assume different roles in the management of visual quality values.

Firstly, it can be recognised that equation (3.5) has a conceptual composition similar to equation (3.1), in that it is based on the combination of a parameter that takes into account distance and a parameter that takes into account the angle of vision. This W formula is too complex to understand its functioning intuitively, nor how it was designed. To untangle this complexity, a divide and conquer approach can be implemented, starting by reasoning on the actual role played by the k, x and y parameters by looking at their trends, with particular reference to their maxima or minima. The polynomial equation of k returns a minimum of almost 1 for $y = \frac{5}{14}$. By substituting this value into the equation of y, the angle of view that maximises the function k is obtained. This angle, ϑ_{MAX}, is relatively close to $36°$ that is the value which Moretti defines as "optimal":

$$\frac{5}{14} = \frac{2\vartheta}{\pi} \rightarrow \vartheta_{MAX} = \frac{5\pi}{28} \cong 32.14°. \tag{3.9}$$

Therefore, the first inconsistency with the textual instructions results in a shift of the four axes of optimal diagonal visibility, as shown in Figure 3.9N. However, a more interesting aspect is to verify whether W returns maxima for $x = 1$, that is, when the viewer is on the aforementioned optimal ellipse. This can be verified analytically by deriving W with respect to x. The derivative obtained has a zero for $x = 1$ which results in a visibility on the optimal ellipse.

This elucidates the mathematics underlying the visibility function; however, it does not permit speculation on how the equation was designed. To answer this problem, we must first divide the problem of optimisation concerning angle ϑ from that concerning distance x. Isolating the latter problem gives the equation:

$$W_x = xe^{-x}. \tag{3.10}$$

This is a well-known equation for every calculus student. W_x is zero for $x = 0$, has a global maximum for $x = 1$, tends to zero for $x \rightarrow \infty$. It is, therefore, an equation that perfectly mathematises Moretti's insights, with particular reference to the first point of his instructions.

In this particular case, therefore, rather than "equation design", it is appropriate to speak of "equation composition", since the well-known exponential structure has been bent to Moretti's insight.

To derive the visibility function W (equation 3.5) explicitly, it is first necessary to clarify the roles of the various parameters involved. Moretti calls ρ the distance between a point P and the centre of the field O, while also he calls $\bar{\rho}(\vartheta)$ the distance between the centre of the field O and the intersection of the ellipse with the line passing through P and O (see Figure 3.5N). The equation x (equation [3.7]) therefore, has the role of normalising the distance with respect to the optimal ellipse. Given Moretti's instruction, the radius r of the circle of interest is equal to 25 m and the distance c between the centre and a focus of the optimal ellipse is equal to 45 m. The major axis a and minor axis b of the optimal ellipse can be calculated as follows:

$$d' = \frac{r}{\sin\left(\frac{35°}{2}\right)} = \frac{25 \ m}{\sin\left(\frac{35°}{2}\right)} = 83,137 \ m, \tag{3.11}$$

$$b = \sqrt{d'^2 - c^2} = 69,90 \ m, \tag{3.12}$$

$$a = \sqrt{b^2 + c^2} = 83.137 \ m. \tag{3.13}$$

It is evident that d' and a are equal. A possible way to calculate the W equation may rely on the use of well-known mathematical formulas for distances between points and between ellipses and points. According to this approach, it is necessary to introduce the formula for the intersection of an ellipse and a line to calculate $\bar{\rho}(\vartheta)$. Assuming a Cartesian coordinate system centred at point O, we can derive the coordinates of point $\bar{P}$:

$$\bar{x}_p = \pm \frac{(a\ b)}{\sqrt{a^2 y_p^2 + b^2 x_p^2}} x_0, \tag{3.14}$$

$$\bar{y}_p = \pm \frac{(a\ b)}{\sqrt{a^2 y_p^2 + b^2 x_p^2}} y_0. \tag{3.15}$$

In the equations above, y_p and x_p represent the Cartesian coordinates of a generic point P. Equations (3.14) and (3.15) return Cartesian coordinates only, so the distances required to calculate equation (3.7) must be obtained. These can be calculated with the well-known formula:

$$\rho = \sqrt{(x_p - x_0)^2 + (y_p - y_0)^2}, \qquad (3.16)$$

$$\bar{\rho}(\vartheta) = \sqrt{(\bar{x}_p - x_0)^2 + (\bar{y}_p - y_0)^2}. \qquad (3.17)$$

To calculate y (8), the value of the angle ϑ must be made explicit in analytical form. It is possible to calculate this angle using the arctangent formula:

$$\vartheta = \left| \operatorname{atan}\left(\frac{x_p - x_0}{y_p - y_0} \right) \right|. \qquad (3.18)$$

The operations performed allow us to express equation (3.5) in explicit terms, thus replicating the design process used by Moretti and IRMOU. The visibility curves calculated by Moretti (Figure 3.3N) and those derived analytically (Figure 3.9N) show some differences that do not undermine the validity of Moretti's insights. Notably, at ϑ_{MAX} (36°), Moretti's visibility function appears flatter than the analytical calculation. The equations proposed for stadium N have been modified over time. For example, the numerator and denominator of function y (equation [3.8]) were swapped in the captions of an article on Architettura Parametrica published shortly before the exhibition[22] and the catalogue draft.[23] This draft, held at the Central Archive of the Italian State, shows corrections to equations and texts in Moretti's handwriting, confirming his direct involvement in the exhibition's operational aspects

Swimming stadiums A and B

Compared to a football stadium, a swimming stadium differs not only in the size of the sports area and the number of spectators but, according to Moretti, also in the distribution of visual quality. For him, the pool hosts asymmetric activities and therefore the visual quality map has only one axis of symmetry, unlike the two found in football stadiums M and N. Those are the insights from which to derive the visibility function W of the swimming stadiums A and B:

a) Visibility of the entire pool.

b) Visual appeal: higher for zones A_1 and B_1 where departures, arrivals, dives, and water polo fields are located; lower for zones A_2 and B_2 where the swimming turns take place.

82   Decoding Luigi Moretti's Architettura Parametrica

c) No high-speed athletes' movements in water and consequent possibility of considering a visual field, physiologically sustainable, of up to 120°.

d) On the radius R from the centre P_0 of the zone of greater appeal, visibility increases from zero up to a maximum (which is dependent from ϑ that is angle formed by R with the longitudinal axis of the pool) then decreases and tends to zero when the distance from P_0 tends to infinite.

e) The maximum on a ray, $M(\vartheta)$, is minimum for $\vartheta = 0$, increases until $\vartheta \leq \frac{\pi}{2}$, then decreases until it resumes for $\vartheta = \pi$ the same value as for $\vartheta = 0$.

f) For each radius, an ellipse having the foci in the centres of the two zones of interest was assumed (for the stadium B) as the location of the maximum. In stadium A, a curve accounting for the prominence of interest of zone A_1 was preferred.[24]

Moretti's swimming stadiums continue to apply the approach used for stadiums M and N. However, he assumes that visual information is more dense at the starting and finishing points than at the turning line. As Moretti explains, designing a swimming stadium requires recognising that different areas of the pool offer varying levels of visual appeal. Point F of the provided instructions indicates that clear guidelines were given for identifying points of maximum interest in stadium B, while such guidelines are missing for determining the curve on which the points of maximum interest lie in stadium A. Additionally, while the catalogue mentions six stadiums, there seem to be only five exhibition models. One of the two swimming stadiums is missing. Or, at least, the catalogue does not provide any further instructions for calculating the visibility of stadium A beyond those already given. This omission must be highlighted as it undermines the replicability of Moretti's research.

Moretti presented the following formula to assess W in stadium B:

$$W = e^{y(1-y)-k(y)(x-\log(x))}. \tag{3.19}$$

With:

$$k(y) = 4y^2 - 4y + 2, \tag{3.20}$$

$$x = \frac{\rho}{\overline{\rho}(\vartheta)}, \tag{3.21}$$

$$y = \frac{\vartheta}{\pi}. \tag{3.22}$$

Architettura Parametrica: In Practice   83

The meaning of some of the parameters (see Figure 3.6) involved in those equations is explained in the catalogue:

ρ is the distance of the generic plane point (in which visibility is evaluated) from the centre P_0.

$\bar{\rho}(\vartheta)$ is the distance of the centre P_0 from the point $\bar{P}$ which is the intersection between the radius considered and the main visibility curve.

ϑ is the angle between the considered radius and the longitudinal axis of the swimming pool".[25]

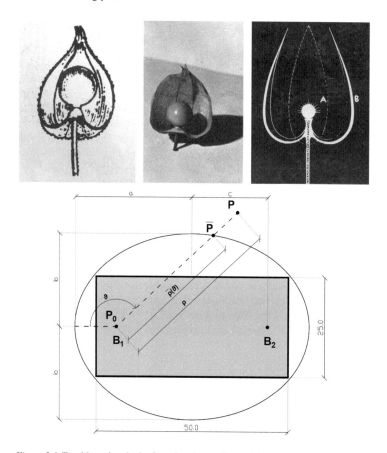

Figure 3.6 Top: Natural analogies for swimming stadiums with the plant Physalis alkekengi L provided by Moretti in "Ricerca matematica in architettura e urbanistica" (1971). Bottom: Diagram for calculating the visibility function swimming stadium B. The information indicated in bold is provided by Moretti. The information in regular font has been added by the author. Credits: Author.

In order to understand how Moretti was able to construct these equations, an analysis of their mathematical aspects is needed. The mathematical model of these equations is linked to the genesis of the architectural form and therefore reveals some clear design principles. All angles and distances are calculated in relation to the B_1 focus of the optimal visibility ellipse. Distances are normalised against the optimal ellipse using a method similar to that of stadium N, while the viewing angle ϑ is measured along the stadium's longitudinal axis. This means that the mathematical model is not indifferent to what it is measuring, but is designed to measure it in an agile and efficient way. By analysing the various terms involved in the definition of W, it begins to emerge that it is an assembly of design insights. The function $k(y)$ (equation [3.20]) reaches its minimum at $y = \frac{1}{2}$, a value that, when substituted into y (equation [3.22]) yields the optimal viewing angle ϑ of 90°. Likewise, it can be observed that $e^{y(1-y)}$ attains a maximum at $y = 1$, reinforcing the significance of visual quality at the ideal 90° angle. Additionally, the expression $(x - \log(x))$ achieves its maximum when $x = 1$. Considering the nature of x (equation [3.21]), this implies that visual quality improves for points along the optimal ellipse. Notably, the x function serves to normalise distances from the primary focal point to the ellipse of optimal visibility. This aspect is crucial as it highlights the significance of the curve of optimal visibility, which is an ellipse for stadium B and an analytically and graphically undefined curve for stadium A.

Following these qualitative observations, the mathematical aspects of the problem can be approached with greater awareness. While determining the visibility function for various spatial points seems relatively straightforward, computing the values of x, ρ, and $\bar{\rho}(\vartheta)$ within a Cartesian coordinate system presents greater complexity. However, certain strategies found in equations from other exhibition architectures suggest that Moretti framed the problem in a way that aligns with calculations in a polar coordinate system. Beyond the use of polar notation for $\bar{\rho}(\vartheta)$, Moretti positions the primary focal point B_1 at one of an ellipse's two foci, from which distances are measured. This supports the hypothesis that Moretti determined $\bar{\rho}(\vartheta)$, using a polar coordinate system centred at B_1, applying the following well-established equations of the ellipse's polar form:

$$\bar{\rho}(\vartheta) = \frac{a(1-e^2)}{1 \pm e \cos\vartheta}. \tag{3.23}$$

With:

$$e = \sqrt{1 - \frac{b^2}{a^2}}. \tag{3.24}$$

In these equations, a and b represent the major and minor semiaxes of the optimal ellipse, while e denotes its eccentricity. To apply these equations, the angle ϑ must be determined for each point P, which can be achieved using the arctangent function. The distance ρ is then computed as the direct distance between a fixed reference point and a generic point. One unresolved aspect in Moretti's work concerns the dimensions of the pool, and, therefore, the values of ellipses a, b, and c. Consequently, it is assumed that the pool corresponds to an Olympic-sized pool measuring 50 metres by 25 metres. This assumption allows for the graphical determination of the ellipse's major and minor semi-axes, calculated as approximately 30.7 m and 23.3 m, respectively.

The visibility function W of stadium B, derived from the reconstructed analytical process (see Figure 3.9B), does not contradict Moretti's intuitions. However, it is important to note that morphologies of the functions diverge. The sole 3D model of the swimming stadium displayed by Moretti in the exhibition resembles stadium A rather than B (see Figure 3.4A). This model presents an asymmetrical configuration, where one stand closely aligns with the visibility function mapping for stadium A, while the other replicates the first's morphology but is adapted to accommodate a larger audience. This demonstrates how Moretti developed his stadium designs by first analysing results and then applying a series of functional and aesthetic refinements. Moreover, it demonstrates what Moretti means by topological thinking. The shapes of stadium A oscillate between visibility isocurves, generating optimised forms for different audience sizes. Still, a parameter can be identified to justify this asymmetry between the stands: sunlight, which, in an open-air pool, may impair visibility from one of them.

Before moving on to the next projects, it is necessary to discuss some attempts to reconstruct the design process behind stadium A. A caption in the *Moebius'* article,[26] suggests a natural analogy behind the analyses of the two swimming stadiums. This caption states that the plant *Physalis alkekengi L.* "exhibits a pattern of similarity with the forms obtained for the visibility curves of the pools, where (A) (see top right of Figure 3.6) approximately represents the centroid of the most relevant information values of the phenomena occurring in the field". Based on these images, despite the awareness that this may be a mere conjecture, similar curves to the shape of this plant were sought in the numerous books potentially available to Moretti, particularly those offering curve catalogues, with special attention to curves expressed in polar forms. After exploring books such as *A Book of Curves*[27] and testing various curves – especially from the cardioid family – without achieving results close to Moretti's stadium A visibility plot, it was concluded that, like the tennis stadium, this function was shaped more by formal and visual intuition than by the actual calculation.

Tennis stadium

The tennis stadium is particularly interesting as it represents a kind of *aporia* in Architettura Parametrica. Moretti's indications lead to a mathematical dead end, an incalculability of the visibility function. He gives some insight into

86 Decoding Luigi Moretti's Architettura Parametrica

the design processes of the tennis stadium that goes beyond the mathematical model. Moretti explains that the basis of his design for this stadium is the desire, given the rapid movement of the ball, to minimise spectators' head movements. He writes:

> For tennis stadiums, the usual formalism reaches pinnacles at the outermost limits of stupidity. The cartoons of thirty years ago that presented "Mickey mouse, spectator at a tennis match," which turns his head almost 180 degrees every half inch or even less, should have been enough to teach architects. They should at least have learned by personal experience. Such is the power of the viscosity of tradition and the biological lack of vital force when affronting reality with engaged attention.[28]

Consequently, Moretti proposed a shape for this stadium that allowed spectators to enjoy a total view of the playing field. He proposes the following assumptions for the tennis stadium:

a) visibility of the whole court;

b) greater visual appetence for a certain region of the court;

c) high speed of the game (trajectory of the ball) and in consequence maximum angle physiologically compatible for the field of vision 100°

d) visual appetence in relation to the distance from the center of the court and to the angle from which the zone of interest is seen.[29]

The formula for the visibility function proposed by Moretti is the following:

$$W = x^k e^{-kx} e^{-hd}. \tag{3.25}$$

With:

$$k = 4.5, \tag{3.26}$$

$$h = 1. \tag{3.27}$$

While the textual indications clarify the stadium's design philosophy, Moretti's diagrams lack detail and explanations on the parameters involved in calculating W. Many geometric parameters discussed below are not stated by Moretti but are hypothesised and introduced to make his design method replicable. Furthermore, other publications by Moretti in which the equations for the tennis stadium are proposed also do not provide any more information than the catalogue, while the draft of the catalogue does not give any useful correction for the tennis stadium.

Analysing the function W (equation [3.25]), it can be recognised that total visibility is "the product of two functions, one dependent from the angle at which the area of interest is viewed and the other from distance from the centre of the field (d)",[30] as explained by Moretti. The contribution of the angle appears to be traceable to the term x^k, but Moretti gave no textual indication for its calculation. If we look at the geometry of the problem proposed by Moretti (see Figure 3.7T), we can assume that x can be traced back to the distance between the centre of the circle that forms an angle to the arc of 100° with respect to the two edges of the field and the centre of a second circle that depends on the position of the point under consideration P. More precisely, this is the circle passing through points A, B and the generic point P. However, this approach is particularly problematic, as this circle rapidly degenerates as P approaches the line passing through A and B, causing various difficulties in the analytical calculation of W. Additionally, the described function W seems to be made to calculate visibility along the field's long side, making little sense for the short side. This requires calculating W for only half the field and mirroring the results, which is not mathematically elegant. Another critical and revealing aspect of the stadium's incompleteness is a graphical normalisation – assigning 1 to the length of the segment $\left(\overline{O_{35°}O_{100°}}\right)$ – without analytical confirmation. Finally, it can be verified graphically that the angle that Moretti indicates as 100° has a quite different value of about 117°.

However, it is possible to force the calculation of the visibility function W, acknowledging the noted gaps. The intention is to force this construction to reflect on Moretti's design methods, rather than on the accuracy of the final results, which will clearly be unreliable. The most challenging value to compute is x. In order to determine point O_p, the generic angle ϑ of point P can be calculated using the well-known dot product:

$$\vartheta = \cos^{-1}\left(\frac{\vec{PA} \cdot \vec{PB}}{|PA||PB|}\right). \tag{3.28}$$

It is evident from the known relationships between the inscribed angle and the central angle that $\widehat{AO_pM}$ equals the previously calculated ϑ. Therefore, the segment $\overline{O_pM}$ can be easily calculated as follows:

$$\overline{O_pM} = \overline{AM}\cot(\vartheta). \tag{3.29}$$

Now x can be calculated as the simple sum of two terms:

$$x = \overline{O_pM} + \overline{O_{100°}M}. \tag{3.30}$$

A final parameter of W is the distance of point P from the field's centre, easily calculated using the well-known distance formula between two points:

$$d = \sqrt{(x_p - x_0)^2 + (y_p - y_0)^2}. \tag{3.31}$$

By applying the proposed equations sequentially, to each point P with coordinates $(x_p; y_p)$ it is possible to assign a value for the visibility function W however, a methodological note is necessary. In previous stadiums, the function W and their defining parameters appeared to be shaped by deliberate mathematical intuition, such as the opportunity to use a polar coordinate transformation. This is not the case for the tennis stadium. The reconstruction proposed in this book is just one possible way to calculate W using the tools available to Moretti. Several alternative approaches could have been employed, such as a polar coordinate-based method using equation (3.38), which will be discussed later for the cinema hall.

Comparing the analytically obtained W values with those proposed by Moretti reveals that the visibility curve morphologies are similar along the field's long side but differ significantly on the short side. This supports the earlier observation of W's ineffectiveness in calculating visibility for the short side. This geometric-analytical reconstruction suggests that also the W function for the tennis stadium was calculated more intuitively than analytically. In fact, the W function curves drawn by Moretti do not appear consistent with the type of function involved (linear, power, and exponential), as they exhibit "so many oscillations, with so many inflection points, that seems drawn by someone whose pulse trembles".[31]

Despite the discussed aspects representing significant gaps or mathematical distortions, an even more critical issue, from this book's perspective, is the inconsistency between the theory and practice of Architettura Parametrica, revealed by how this stadium's shape was derived from the W function results. In this case, Moretti appears to have excessively interpreted the "halos of indeterminacy" left by rigid analyses, an aspect discussed multiple times in Chapter 2. Overlaying Moretti's W function results with the tennis stadium's plan (Figure 3.4T) reveals the removal of stands on one long side is not supported by the analysis results. Furthermore, the near-circular shape of the inner perimeter of the stands has only marginal correspondence in Moretti's W function graphs. However, a deep understanding of Architettura Parametrica permits to argue that the form of the tennis stadium contradicts those analyses to achieve a spatial quality that pure technique alone could not provide.

Cinema hall

The last model presented at the Architettura Parametrica exhibition refers to a movie theatre for which Moretti calculates the visual appetence with respect

Architettura Parametrica: In Practice 89

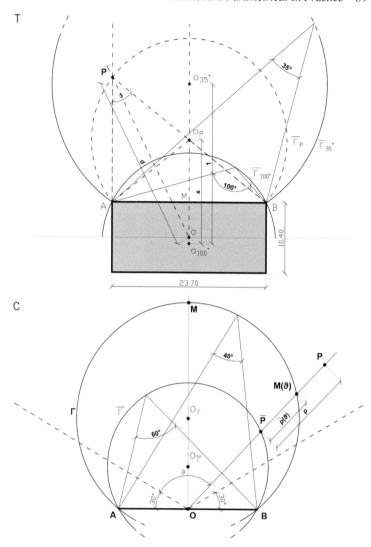

Figure 3.7 Diagram for calculating the visibility function W in tennis stadium [T] and cinema hall [C]. The information indicated in bold is provided by Moretti. The information in regular font is added by the author. Credits: Author.

90 Decoding Luigi Moretti's Architettura Parametrica

to the "plane normal to the screen passing through its major axis".[32] Moretti assumed the following hypotheses:

a) visibility, along a radius passing through the center O of the AB screen, is nil along the circumference which sees the screen at an angle of 60° and inside the same circumference, because in this region the portion of screen that can be seen without having to move the head becomes too small; along the radius visibility increases till it attains its maximum along the circumference Γ which sees AB at a 40° angle, it then decreases until it becomes nil at infinity;

b) on circumference Γ visibility is maximum at M, which is the intersection of Γ with the line perpendicular to the screen in O; it decreases at both sides of OM down to the point where it is nil on the radiuses passing by O (in the plane under consideration) forming an angle of 30° with the screen, because at that angle which is less than 30° we may assume the deformation of the pictures on the screen is too great on account of the perspective.[33]

Subsequently, Moretti proposed a function that "translates this property in the simplest way":

$$W = 4y(1-y)x^k e^{-k\,y}. \tag{3.32}$$

With:

$$x = \frac{\rho}{\bar{\rho}(\vartheta)}, \tag{3.33}$$

$$y = \frac{3\vartheta}{2\pi}. \tag{3.34}$$

To satisfy his hypotheses, Moretti designed an equation that has a minimum at a viewing angle of 40° and a maximum at a viewing angle of 60°. In addition, he had to maximise visibility when the viewer is perpendicular to the centre of the screen. If we look at the product $4y(1-y)$, however, we can recognise that this part of the equation returns a maximum for the viewer perpendicular to the screen and a minimum for the viewer at a viewing angle of 30°: it has a maximum at $y = \frac{1}{2}$ which, when substituted into (equation [3.34]), returns precisely the position perpendicular to the centre of the screen. The equation x (equation [3.33]), however, returns a maximum when the spectator is placed on the circumference Γ (see Figure 3.7C).

A hypothesis is proposed for the possible design process adopted by Moretti, and the analytical operations required to derive the total visibility function W in explicit form are briefly outlined. It should be noted that the reconstructions are dimensionless as Moretti did not provide any measurements for this cinema. From how the cinema problem has been geometrised, it is evident that Moretti used different lengths normalised to circumferences, therefore making it easier to derive these distances from the polar equation of the circumference. It therefore seems obvious to assume a polar coordinate system with origin in the centre of the screen O. Consequently, for each point P it is necessary to calculate ϑ. Subsequently, $\bar{\rho}(\vartheta)$ and ρ can be derived through the differences between the polar coordinates and the distances to the centre O. The radii of the circumferences Γ and $\bar{\Gamma}$ are calculated using the well-known chord proprieties:

$$AB = 2r\sin\alpha. \tag{3.35}$$

While the distances between the centres of Γ and $\bar{\Gamma}$ and the centre of the reference system can be calculated simply through Pythagorean theorem:

$$r_0 = \sqrt{r^2 - \overline{OA}^2}. \tag{3.36}$$

The values of angles ϑ are calculated from a Cartesian coordinate system with the origin in the centre of the screen by using the arctangent2[34]:

$$\vartheta = \operatorname{atan2}(y_p; x_p). \tag{3.37}$$

It is now necessary to recall the generic polar equation for a circumference since it has been assumed that the reference system is not centred in the centre of the circle. A generic circumference identified by the polar coordinates $(r_0; \gamma)$ and of radius a is described by the equation[35]:

$$r^2 - 2rr_0\cos(\varphi - \gamma) + r_0^2 = a^2. \tag{3.38}$$

The terms of which are identified in Figure 3.8.
By expressing r explicitly in equation (3.38), we obtain:

$$r = r_0\cos(\varphi - \gamma) + \sqrt{a^2 - r_0^2\sin^2(\varphi - \gamma)}. \tag{3.39}$$

Equation (3.39) may be further simplified, as for circumferences Γ and $\bar{\Gamma}$ we have $\gamma = 90°$ since their centres lie on the perpendicular from the centre of the screen. It is now necessary to proceed with the calculation of all the distances required to calculate the lengths $\bar{\rho}(\vartheta)$ and ρ. The distance $\overline{OP}$ is easily calculated as follows:

$$\overline{OP} = \sqrt{(x_p - x_0)^2 + (y_p + y_0)^2}. \tag{3.40}$$

92 *Decoding Luigi Moretti's Architettura Parametrica*

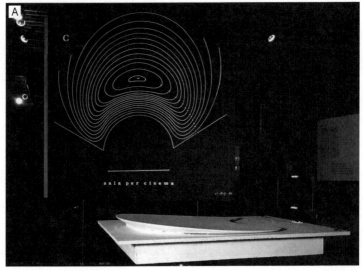

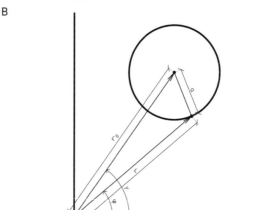

Figure 3.8 Top: Luigi Moretti, model and visibility function of the cinema hall. Bottom: Diagram of the generic polar equation of a circle. Credits: [A] ACSLM [auth. 650/2025], project 162, F3063; [B] Author.

The distances $\overline{OP}$ and $\overline{OM(\vartheta)}$ are calculated by introducing the correct values of the parameters r_0, γ and a for the circumferences Γ and $\overline{\Gamma}$ into equation (3.39):

$$\overline{OP} = 6{,}81\cos\left(\varphi - \frac{\pi}{2}\right) + \sqrt{13{,}85^2 - 6{,}81^2 \sin^2\left(\varphi - \frac{\pi}{2}\right)}, \qquad (3.41)$$

$$\overline{OM(\vartheta)} = 14{,}30\cos\left(\varphi - \frac{\pi}{2}\right) + \sqrt{18{,}66^2 - 14{,}30^2 \sin^2\left(\varphi - \frac{\pi}{2}\right)}. \qquad (3.42)$$

It is now possible to calculate $\bar{\rho}(\vartheta)$ and ρ through simple differences between the equations derived. In particular, ρ is equal to the difference between equations (3.40) and (3.41) while $\bar{\rho}(\vartheta)$ is equal to the difference between equations (3.42) and (3.41).

The operations conducted offer a viable way to derive equation (3.32) in explicit terms, through a process as close as possible to the possibilities of Moretti and IRMOU. It is pointed out that the catalogue gives no indication for the calculation of the parameter k. Consequently, we assume k = 4, 5 as in the previous case of the tennis stadium. The analytically calculated visibility curves (Figure 3.9C) can be considered consistent and congruent with the results obtained by Moretti (Figure 3.1C).

A short note on Moretti's mathematical compositions

In a typewritten draft held in the Italian Central State Archive, Moretti, before recalling an anecdote about the 1960 exhibition, wrote: "Every technology has an asymptotic limit beyond which further progress becomes futile, even insane. This limit is inherent in the technology itself; it marks its death".[36] This note suggests that the inconsistencies, gaps, and errors found in the exegesis of his equations may not stem solely from Moretti's shortcomings. Rather, they may reflect his awareness of having reached a technological limit. Surpassing this threshold would have reduced the exhibition's experiments to pure technique, stripping them of their architectural significance.

Moretti infused his theory of Architettura Parametrica with an almost utopian charge, making it almost unattainable. Designing a stadium while rigorously accounting for the full list of parameters he presents in *Moebius*[37] seems almost impossible. Even more challenging is attempting this with the limited computational power available to Moretti. It is no coincidence that the "architectures for large numbers" in the exhibition are shaped by a single functional parameter linked to visibility. This continues to suggest that applying Architettura Parametrica requires a trade-off between theory and practice. The exhibition highlights different kinds of these trade-offs: the qualitative calculation

94 *Decoding Luigi Moretti's Architettura Parametrica*

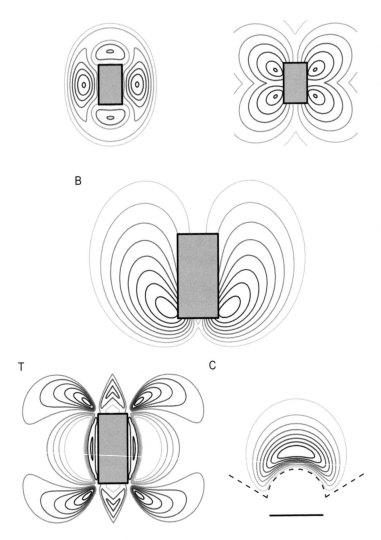

Figure 3.9 Reconstructions, interpretations, and experiments on Luigi Moretti's visibility functions (W). Football stadiums M and N, swimming stadium B, Tennis stadium T, and cinema hall C. Credits: Author.

of function W in swimming stadium A, subtle adjustments in the form of swimming stadium B, the alignment of visibility and form in the cinema hall, and the incalculability of the tennis stadium to name a few. Yet Moretti's theoretical writings confirm that, with due caution, this approach can still fit within the methodological framework of Architettura Parametrica. He writes:

> To proceed intellectually in Parametric Architecture it can be said that a double dose of intuition and fantasy are required; one dose for predicting, identifying, and imposing the quantifiable parameters and their relationships; another to organically complete the globalization of the forms closing the gaps that leave the nonquantifiable parameters.[38]

Architettura Parametrica fostered trust in scientific thought. Yet Moretti, as a designer, understood that full scientificity is an ideal to strive for rather than a true objective. He did not subordinate design practice to science; rather, he made science serve design. This may explain why, as will soon be discussed, the stadium morphologies presented in the exhibition were already anticipated in Moretti's projects from the 1930s. This suggests that he employed mathematics strategically, using it to search for novel scientifically accurate forms – perhaps with some bias – but also to validate his formal intuitions retrospectively. In some cases shown at the exhibition, it seems that Moretti applied mathematics to confer epistemological certainty on the shapes he had already envisioned.

To the best of my knowledge, Moretti's equations waited over half a century before starting to be rigorously studied. Perhaps this is because, as Christopher Alexander notes, logic and mathematics are viewed with suspicion by many designers. In *Notes on the Synthesis of Form*, he writes: "The introduction of mathematics into design is likely to make designers nervous".[39] This book, and in particular the research done on Moretti's equations, aims to challenge this prejudice.

Formal Analogies with Architettura Parametrica in Moretti's oeuvre

The formal, methodological, and mathematical inconsistencies identified during the analysis of the exhibition architectures partially support the idea that Moretti was inclined to adapt his theories to suit practical architectural design. Building on this observation, a comparison between the exhibition's outcomes and Luigi Moretti's professional work becomes essential. The aim is to explore the negotiation between the theory of Architettura Parametrica and its application in Moretti's practice.

The search for forms shaped by the exhibition's knowledge (or that anticipated it) should focus again on Moretti's "architectures for large numbers". In this theme, he challenged the repetition of architectural forms based on established practices, thus anticipating a cornerstone of his Architettura Parametrica. To highlight the connections between Architettura Parametrica and the exhibition's results, the discussion follows the exhibition's sequence rather than chronological order: football stadiums M and N, swimming stadiums A and B, tennis stadium, and cinema hall.

As early as the preliminary designs for the Olympic Stadium at *Foro Italico* in 1937, Moretti recognised that a simple ellipsoid was not the most efficient shape for optimising visibility for football, as shown in the sketches in Figure 3.10. Formal analogies with stadium M are evident in the various design alternatives where Moretti sketched the stadium's perimeter. Here, Moretti also anticipated the concepts of "equipotential" architectural lines, distinct from the visibility curves of stadiums M and N, likely linked more to seating arrangements than visibility. Notably, Moretti would later propose using visibility curves to organise seating. However, these insights were gradually downplayed and largely absent in the final Olympic Stadium proposal and the built project.

The Olympic Stadium insights may have been preceded by experiments for Mussolini's *Piazzale delle Adunate* (discussed in Chapter 2, see Figure 2.1) where the form of the crowd – intended as the shape assumed spontaneously by an arrangement of people – defined the architectural form, rather than a focus on optimising visibility. However, recalling the ideas behind stadium N, this square dedicated to military rallies anticipated some visibility-related concepts well before IRMOU's establishment. Its general shape seems to be informed by the need to increase the stand's surface at the optimal angle $\vartheta \cong 35°$, frequently referenced in the exhibition's stadiums. The result is a form favouring oblique views of events, much like the stands of stadium N.

More than 20 years passed before the visibility concepts outlined in those juvenile experiences were used again for a large-scale project. The *Fondo Luigi Moretti* at the Central Italian State Archive holds sketches and preliminary designs for a "Stadium Project according to the principles of Architettura Parametrica"[40] dated 1960. This proposal echoes the ideas behind the football stadiums presented at the exhibition. In a sketch (see Figure 3.11A), two focal points and a viewing angle of approximately 35° are graphically represented. This sketch, though the *Archivio Centrale dello Stato* dating raises some doubts due to its similarities with Figure 3.10, is particularly valuable as it offers a graphical key to understanding the equations and analyses underpinning the exhibition projects. Once again, the final design tempers the bold initial concepts, presenting a sort of tapering similar to the exhibition on only three sides (Figure 3.11D).

Additional football stadium projects illustrate the relationship between the "preforma" referenced by Moretti in his theoretical writing[41] and the actual architectural form. In some cases, the exhibition's insights appear less evident. For the 1960 proposal to expand and renovate Rome's Olympic Stadium the designed form tapers at two angles (see Figure 3.11E). This seems inconsistent with the angle that defined optimal visibility for stadium N and good visibility for stadium M. However, considering the athletics track, which distorts the field's viewing angles and was absent in the exhibition's architecture, the insights of Architettura Parametrica are not contradicted. More importantly,

Architettura Parametrica: In Practice 97

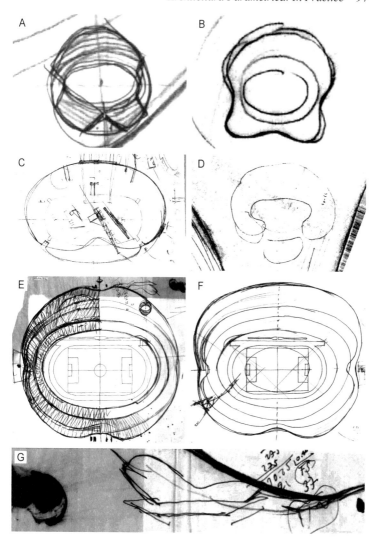

Figure 3.10 Luigi Moretti, preliminary sketches for the Olympic Stadium, Rome, 1937–1940. Note a sketch (G) resembling the elevation of football stadium N. Credits: ACSLM [auth. 650/2025], project 62, [A, E, and G] 37/48/53OR; [B and F] 37/48/54OR; [C] 37/48/31OR; [D] 37/48/30OR.

98 *Decoding Luigi Moretti's Architettura Parametrica*

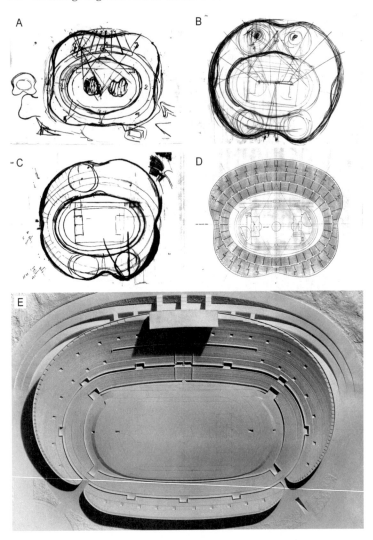

Figure 3.11 [A, B, C, and D]: Luigi Moretti, stadium project according to the principles of Architettura Parametrica, 1960. [E]: Luigi Moretti, model for the Olympic Stadium renovation, Rome, 1960. Credits: ACSLM [auth. 650/2025], project 165, [A] 60/200a/3OR, [B] 60/200a/2OR, [C] 60/200a/4OR, [D] 60/200a/7. Project 164, [E] F3078.

in this proposal, the urban context of the *Foro Italico* likely played a more significant morphogenetic role than the visibility studies.

The projects discussed so far do not yet reflect one of the exhibition's boldest insights: eliminating stands along the short side of the field, where Moretti calculated the lowest visibility quality. This omission is understandable, as it challenges not only a form but also a cultural aspect. In Italy, this part of the field, known as the "Curva", is strongly tied to football culture and often hosts the most passionate fans. Perhaps for this reason, Moretti questioned this part of the stadium in a project outside Italy, intended for broader sporting use rather than football alone. The numerous design alternatives for the Tehran Olympic complex stadiums showcase the insights of Architettura Parametrica, exploring various formal solutions derived from its established ideas on visibility. In the proposals for a 65,000-seat stadium, Moretti bravely eliminated the stands along one short side (see Figure 3.12), effectively hybridising the insights of stadiums M and N. Interestingly, in the project reports,[42] Moretti stated that the optimal viewing angle is primarily reserved for television broadcasts – a declaration seemingly aimed at maximising visibility for the largest possible audience.

Moving to the insights from swimming stadiums A and B, the projects linked to the forms of the exhibition are fewer than those for football. Moretti's only swimming stadium designs appear in his various proposals for the unbuilt Olympic complex in Tehran. The French typewritten project reports reveal that these swimming stadium designs were inspired by Architettura Parametrica. Moretti writes:

[In the swimming stadiums] the entirely new shape of the two 'cavea' is particularly interesting, as it adheres to the principles of Architettura Parametrica: in other words, the seating arrangement is calculated based on the shortest distance between the spectator and the main points of interest on the performance plan.[43]

A fairly simplified description, probably intended more to convince the client of the project's scientific basis rather than to convey the complexity of the exhibition's mathematical models. Once Moretti's parametric vision for the Tehran complex is acknowledged, it becomes necessary to consider it not as a single Architettura Parametrica project, but as a particular "structure and sequence of spaces", recalling the title of a famous article on *Spazio*. In this article, Moreti said that "there is, however, one expressive aspect that summarizes with such notable latitude the fact of architecture […] I refer to the internal and empty space of architecture".[44] The Tehran complex, with its various design alternatives, appears as a sequence of open-air urban voids, a certain kind of *urban rooms* (see Figure 3.13). Spatial solutions featured in *Spazio*, such as the double colonnade of the "pecile" at Hadrian's Villa, the shifts in Michelangelo and Antonio da Sangallo the Younger's Palazzo Farnese, or the visual fields of Mies van der Rohe's Tugendhat House, seem to have influenced Moretti's Tehran designs. These and other solutions are reinterpreted to create urban

100 *Decoding Luigi Moretti's Architettura Parametrica*

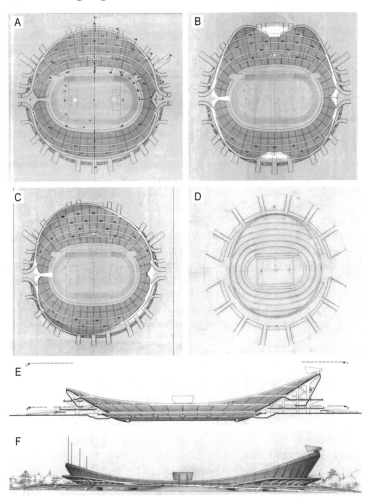

Figure 3.12 Luigi Moretti, early explorations and design proposals for the stadiums of the Tehran Olympic Complex, 1966. [A, B, C and D] Stadium for 65,000 spectators. [E and F] Stadium for 100,000 spectators. Credits: ACSLM [auth. 650/2025], project 222, [A] 66/248/11, [B] 66/248/12, [C] 66/248/13, [D] 66/248/124, [E] 66/248/120, [F] 66/248/118.

voids punctuated by parametric anomalies – open, enclosed, or semi-enclosed spaces. This unbuilt complex defines a fascinating page of architecture that deserves deeper exploration than the brief suggestions made here.

The Tehran experience, which will be explored further, highlights the importance of synoptic and comparative evaluation of different design alternatives in Moretti's working method. However, this comparison during the formal exploration phase can also be approached by "stress-testing" a design intuition. A series of sketches, from both the Olympic Stadium and the Tehran complex (see Figure 3.14), illustrates this process. The ideas and forms of stadium N are clearly recognisable in the site plan as well as in the section. This also confirms that the "pre-forma latissima" – central to the theory of Architettura Parametrica – requires a process of refinement, development, and perfection through architectural design.

Returning to the theme of formal analogies in swimming stadiums, the cited parametric *ensembles* of the Tehran complex (see Figure 3.13) show how Moretti incorporated analytical knowledge – gained from Architettura Parametrica experiences supported by IRMOU – into the exploratory phases of a project, using intuitive and qualitative approaches. With minimal strokes in his drawings, Moretti demonstrated that his swimming stadiums are far from traditional: no stands on the short sides, where visual appeal is minimal, and asymmetry along the transverse axis to better view swimmers' finishes. However, these stadiums differ from the exhibition, as they include diving facilities alongside the pool. Therefore, the forms of the exhibition could not be directly transposed to the Tehran complex, as the diving area disrupts and redistributes visual quality. Additionally, the stands are symmetrically arranged along the pool's longitudinal axis, unlike the exhibition's swimming stadium model. The exhibition's complex mathematical modelling is absent from the Tehran complex's archival documents. Yet, the complex embodies a parametric spirit. That is not solely because Moretti admitted it, but because every graphic element in the stadium stands, even at 1:5000 scale, challenges the naïve repetition of tradition-driven forms.

It is challenging to replicate this discussion on the tennis stadium's forms for two reasons: the previously discussed inconsistencies in its mathematical model and the presence of only one design proposal for this type of stadium in Luigi Moretti's body of work. Within the Tehran complex, Moretti explored the theme of tennis, proposing a perfectly circular structure with no resemblance to the stadium presented at the exhibition. Compared to the exhibition stadium, this design seems counterintuitive as it maximises visibility along the long sides while reducing it at oblique angles. This stadium reflects a different negotiation between theory and practice in Moretti's approach to Architettura Parametrica: here the opportunities of the architectural form prevailed over the demands of scientific reasoning. The composition of the Tehran complex, as evidenced by the numerous design alternatives

102 *Decoding Luigi Moretti's Architettura Parametrica*

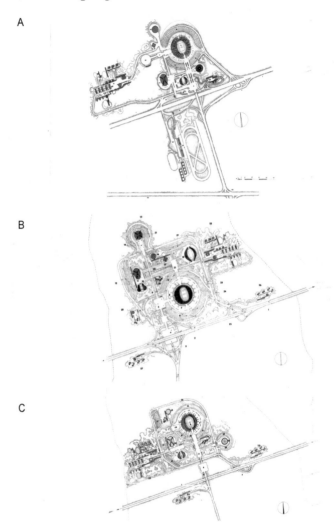

Figure 3.13 Luigi Moretti, proposals for the Tehran Olympic Complex masterplan, 1966. Credits: ACSLM [auth. 650/2025], project 222, [A] 66/248/32, [B] 66/248/114, [C] 66/248/1.

Architettura Parametrica: In Practice 103

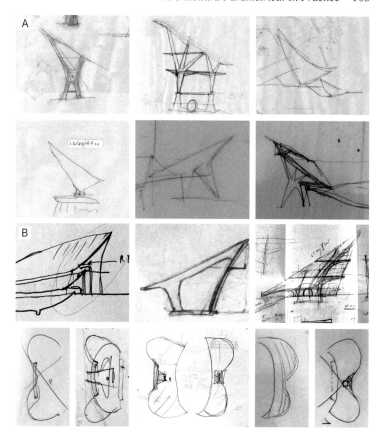

Figure 3.14 Luigi Moretti, juvenile and mature explorations of "architecture for large numbers" morphologies. Top: sketches for the Olympic Stadium project in Rome, 1937–1940. Bottom: sketches for the stadiums of the Olympic complex in Tehran, 1966. Credits: ACSLM [auth. 650/2025], project 62, [A] 37/48/53OR, 37/48/51OR, 37/48/44OR, 37/48/21OR; folder n. 27 [B].

(see Figure 3.13), for Moretti required a pure circle rather than the sculptural forms of Architettura Parametrica.

Moving to analogies with the cinema hall, the spectator's characteristics, their position, and the observed phenomenon are significantly different from the previously discussed stadiums. Luigi Moretti's 1957 *Aviorama* patent has different analogies with that of the Exhibition. *Aviorama* is described as a "device for filming and projecting cinema on a horizontal screen or on a horizontal screen combined with variously inclined flat or curved surfaces".[45] For

104 *Decoding Luigi Moretti's Architettura Parametrica*

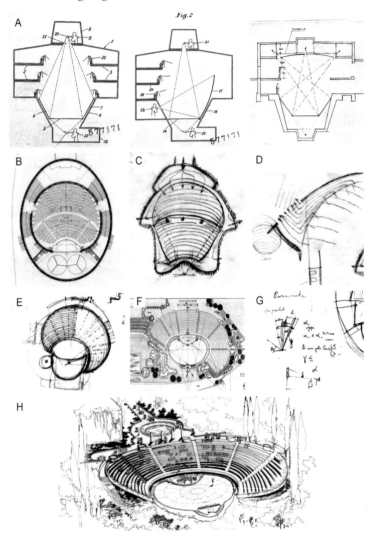

Figure 3.15 Luigi Moretti, research on visibility, space and form. Patent "Aviorama" [A, ACSLM, folder n. 40]; Proposal for GIL Theatre in Piacenza, 1933–1935 [B, ACSLM, project 49, 41/131/9]; Visibility and flow studies for Gran Teatro EUR, Rome, 1938–1942 [C and D, ACSLM, project 76, 38/82/4OR]; Visibility studies and an excerpt for a "parametric analysis of the classroom" for the Dance Academy, Rome, 1950–1969 [F and H, ACSLM, project 227, 50/155e/9, 50/115E/8. No archival code for E and G]. Credits: ACSLM [auth. 650/2025].

an architectural scholar, this patent appears as a combinatorial study of the relationships between a spectator and a screen (Figure 3.15A). A study, therefore, rooted in Architettura Parametrica. Like the stadiums' designs, *Aviorama* viewing modes are counterintuitive and challenge the sterile repetition of traditional models. However, the patent documents lack planimetric drawings, making it difficult to compare them with the exhibition's cinema hall.

The insights of the cinema hall can also be applied to both indoor and outdoor theatres. Once again, even in pre-World War II projects, the idea that optimising visibility could shape architectural form can be found in several of Moretti's projects. One design alternative for the GIL Theatre in Piacenza (1932–1933), the preliminary sketches for the *Gran Teatro EUR* (1938–1942), and the multiple alternatives for the outdoor theatre of the Dance Academy in Rome (1950–1969) all feature shapes remarkably similar to the cinema hall presented at the Architettura Parametrica exhibition (see Figure 3.15). In a sketch of the Dance Academy, Moretti goes so far as to sketch a cryptic "parametric analysis of the classroom" (Figure 3.15G). Additionally, there is a clear morphological congruence between the visibility curves of the cinema and the seating arrangements in these projects. Once again, Moretti's designs reveal the seeds of Architettura Parametrica, expressed through the adoption of forms whose efficiency is verified via analytical methods, or, especially in his early works, as insights into how to orient the form in relation to the visibility problem.

The discussion in this section may have disappointed those expecting to find the adoption of mathematical modelling in Moretti's professional practice. While no traces of these models were found, the mindset they instilled in Moretti was identified. The formal analogies outlined demonstrate that Architettura Parametrica can be translated into professional practice by relegating the equations and analyses discussed earlier in this chapter to the background, while consistently recalling the synthetic knowledge gained through them.

Methodological analogies with Architettura Parametrica in Moretti's oeuvre

The discussion on formal analogies was crucial for a first proof of Moretti's repeated attempts to apply Architettura Parametrica in professional practice. However, Moretti may have introduced themes of Architettura Parametrica that are distant from any formal concerns. To confirm this, it is necessary to explore Moretti's extensive work, focusing on the tools and cultural framework of Architettura Parametrica rather than the forms it produced in the exhibition. To do this, we must primarily examine Moretti's early design phases to identify methods that shape the design process, characterised by the absence of bias and the adoption of a scientific mindset.

This paragraph explores Architettura Parametrica from a methodological perspective, focusing on the set of tools and mindset repeatedly emphasised by Moretti: attention to visibility issues, the introduction of operational research tools, problem abstraction, and the development of various analytical campaigns. Once again, a thematic approach is favoured over a purely chronological sequence. The aim is to present a broad overview of the diverse design methods and tools in Moretti's oeuvre, shaped and guided by the theories of Architettura Parametrica.

The operational diagram of Villa Borghese parking

To challenge certain preconceptions about Architettura Parametrica, this discussion begins with a project that moves away from using mathematical equations to shape architectural form, as proposed in the exhibition. The *Villa Borghese* parking structure (1966) is ideal for this purpose, particularly due to a diagram in which other authors have already seen "a foreshadowing of a strictly parametric approach to function".[46] This diagram, given its symbolic nature, appears to present an "algorithmic" approach to architectural design, resembling a flowchart. However, mathematically, it is more accurately defined as graph – a structure that models relationships between objects rather than a sequence of actions. This distinction is crucial: while an algorithm solves problems, a graph represents or models them. This fundamental difference highlights a significant gap between Moretti's conception of Architettura Parametrica and contemporary parametricism.

Moretti proposed a dual model, described by him as "a serial scheme of operations for the underground parking at the [*Villa Borghese*] and, in general, for a multi-level or single-level parkings" (see Figure 3.16). The model represents both a general and a specific structure, making the operational scheme a true *objectile*, from which an infinite number of possible parking layouts can be derived. It also exemplifies the structure → form process theorised by Moretti in his previously discussed article on *Spazio*.[47] However, viewed through the lens of operational research, this scheme becomes a framework for testing various design alternatives related to entrance and exit placements, traffic directions, lane sizes, and carriageway numbers, as confirmed by Moretti's handwritten notes. Moretti's design approach was radical and pervasive, envisioning the structure of the parking ticket, the automation of various control and management operations, and much more. The operational diagram is highly detailed yet still allows for a "halo of indeterminacy", giving the architect freedom to operate without disregarding analytical findings. Thus, the *Villa Borghese* operational scheme is not a fixed form but rather guides and contains formal suggestions, defining a domain within which to operate. This domain expands or contracts depending on the accuracy of the preliminary design studies.

This interpretation of the parking diagram clarifies that Moretti's Architettura Parametrica can emerge even without the use of mathematical equations or design algorithms. This project also reveals how Moretti approaches

Architettura Parametrica: In Practice 107

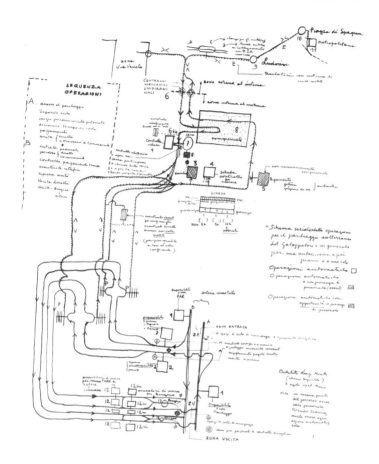

Figure 3.16 Luigi Moretti, Operational scheme of Villa Borghese underground parking, Rome, 1966. Credits: ACSLM [auth. 650/2025], project 226, 65/251/1OR.

design problems from multiple, sometimes divergent, perspectives. The *Villa Borghese* parking design employs an exceptionally broad and varied range of preliminary analyses. These analyses are now considered essential for tackling a complex challenge like a parking facility of such a vast scale that it engages with urban design. But in Moretti's working context, they were highly innovative. During the competition phase, Moretti, through IRMOU, conducted an extensive campaign of observation, analysis, interviews, and general data collection focused on the proximity of the building site. As noted in various correspondences, this effort led Moretti to the belief that "no other competitor approached the subject with such seriousness".[48] These preparatory investigations included traffic studies at key areas along the project perimeter. The analysis was intertwined with the *Study for mapping the traffic currents along Corso d'Italia*,[49] carried out by IRMOU and focusing on a major road adjacent to the parking facility. In this study, IRMOU compiled detailed observation sheets, recording vehicle origins and destinations at various intersections along *Corso d'Italia*, transit times, peak hours, and other traffic data. Alongside these quantitative analyses, IRMOU also proposed qualitative data collection, including informal interviews and a carefully designed questionnaire. The questionnaire covered a range of topics, from identifying optimal locations for underpasses to graphically mapping movement patterns. The goal of this investigation was to inform the project's earliest and most critical design decisions, such as the placement of entrances and exits, circulation and distribution schemes, lane dimensions and numbers, analytically. Ultimately, this study provided the foundational data for developing the previously discussed operational scheme.

The extensive and detailed analytical documents lead to concise conclusions that bear proto-design guidelines, allowing for multiple architectural forms and solutions. However, the rigorous analyses conducted by Moretti through IRMOU not only enable a comprehensive understanding of general problems but also facilitate the resolution of local issues. This is exemplified by the study on the "cost-effectiveness criterion for a continuous right-turn lane at a controlled intersection and its application to a concrete case"[50] whose diagrams were later exhibited in the 1960 Architettura Parametrica exhibition. In this study, the concrete case refers to an intersection near the road adjacent to the parking facility, where prior traffic analyses had already been conducted. A full exegesis of this complex study falls outside the scope of this research, but referencing it is relevant to illustrate how Architettura Parametrica provided Moretti with the tools to analyse – or, in this case, to delegate the analysis of – technical challenges inevitably encountered in architectural projects, whether on a small or large scale. The cultural significance of these analyses is encapsulated in the words with which the study's author, Dario Fürst, concludes his research:

> We allow ourselves to conclude that often modest tools, both mathematical and technical, are sufficient, provided they are applied with a certain rigor, to guide possible alternative arrangements of urban traffic without necessarily turning road users into test subjects.[51]

Moretti as an urbanist and urban designer

To continue demonstrating the validity and relevance of Architettura Parametrica, it is necessary to ask whether it remains applicable when the project output may take on a more programmatic rather than formal nature, as in territorial, urban, or city design and planning. The answer is obviously affirmative, considering the full title of the 1960 Triennale event was *Exhibition of Parametric Architecture and of Mathematical and Operational Research in Town-Planning*. Moretti was also involved in the journal *Informazioni Urbanistica*,[52] which explored the link between operational research, urban design, and territorial planning. This relation between Moretti and urban design is both intriguing and underexplored, confirming the existence of a *Moretti Urbanista*, as titled in an article by Pietro Samberi.[53] Moretti engaged in various urban design projects, from major developments like Rome's Olympic Village to master plans of different scales. In one of them, the development plan for the town of Tagliacozzo (1968), he aimed to provide, as he wrote in his report, "a set of easily accessible data for the Municipality to ensure control over assumptions, allowing timely updates based on key parameters".[54] He expressed his intent to "proceed within an operational methodology, extensively using mathematical analysis and forecasting systems", and to develop "an iterative process based on global parameters and indices that, albeit indirectly, reflect Tagliacozzo's reality and nature".[55] The plan's methodological framework includes operational schemes and decision flowcharts indicating "control magnitudes" and "validity control parameters" which require a "study of dependencies" and many other references to operational research.[56] In fact, building a "model of reality",[57] as Moretti called it in those methodological notes, necessitates a mathematical approach closely linked to the operational research of Architettura Parametrica.

The Tagliacozzo experience consolidated the value of the Architettura Parametrica framework, even when the design output concerns territorial governance and urban planning rather than architectural design. But Moretti also undertook a far greater urban challenge in the early 1960s: Rome's development plan. Of particular relevance to this research is the study commissioned by the Automobile Club of Rome and conducted by IRMOU, titled *Plan for Investigation and Studies on Parking and Traffic in the Urban Area of Rome*.[58] These documents are of particular interest as they extensively discuss the purpose, nature, role, objectives, and tools of such a large-scale study. As a result, this and other studies under Moretti's direction go beyond data collection and analysis, renewing the role of scientific methods in architectural design. This approach strengthens – and perhaps redefines – Moretti's analytical lexicon: "O & D (Origin and Destination) surveys", "sampling analysis", "quantitative analysis", "direct and indirect surveys", and "determination of maximum tolerable loads" are just some of the study's methods and objectives. At the same time, the study remains pragmatic and context-aware, designed "to avoid requiring extensive and costly surveys", at least in its early exploratory phases. Remarkably, these pages even anticipate the concept of "user pre-information", now central to smart cities, which aims to provide real-time data on urban spaces and dynamics. This study led to Moretti's involvement in the ambitious work of Rome's *Commission of Inquiry on Traffic*, whose activity was particularly intense in 1963.[59] He actively participated in this commission, defending IRMOU's studies and demonstrating continuity with the urban experiments previously showcased at the Architettura Parametrica exhibition.

This urban and technical dimension of Architettura Parametrica also shaped Moretti's aesthetic landscape through the inherent formal power of some of his graphical representations. A striking example is the scheme of "main desire lines exceeding 3,000 crossings" (see Figure 3.17A), developed with the *Istituto di Calcolo delle Probabilità – Centro per la Ricerca Operativa e Sperimentale*[60] of Rome University. This scheme offered a novel interpretation of Rome's urban form, revealing crucial yet complex relationships and providing a foundation for political decisions on the city's development.

The analyses carried out by IRMOU for the 1966 Tehran Olympic complex proposal share the same spirit with the previously discussed urban experiences. In this project, however, the studies focused on materialising architectural forms for a large-scale urban project rather than defining programmatic and political actions in a territorial planning context. For different transport modes – buses, private cars, and taxis – IRMOU calculated key travel times to reach the Olympic forum, comparing this data for the current state, as well as a first and a second expansion of the complex. These and many other analyses aimed to define key design parameters, such as access strategies to the Olympic complex, but above all, its overall dimensioning. Even today, designing an Olympic complex remains an exceptional challenge, with few case studies available to derive sizing data and strategic design insights. When considering the political dimension inherent in a project of this scale, the need to apply Architettura Parametrica's principles to guide both the project's critical early decisions and its subsequent evolution becomes evident. This need underpins and justifies Moretti's rejection of traditional, established forms in his designs.

The issues of ethics and labour organisation

In various writings and speeches discussed in Chapter 2, Moretti elevated the consideration of ethical factors in architectural design to a methodological principle. His ethics do not focus on contemporary architectural concerns such as the climate crisis but rather it emphasise social issues and the optimal use of resources in design, construction, and architectural management. As the Tehran project is deeply rooted in the culture of Architettura Parametrica – both in its forms and in the technical framework it employed – some of Moretti's notes can be reinterpreted as key methodological principles. In a document titled *Relation réservée à l'attention de Monsieur l'Architecte Badie et concernant le "Parc Farah"*,[61] Moretti made a passionate plea to reconsider the park's conception. In this report, Moretti appears particularly diplomatic, but in his notes on the design boards, he offers an unfiltered opinion:

> The current garden design is outdated and ineffective. It was created based on (supposed) aesthetic criteria, with a series of avenues and inaccessible

Architettura Parametrica: In Practice 111

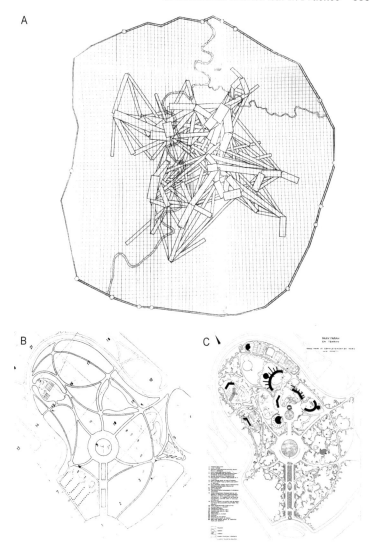

Figure 3.17 Top: Example of an analytical output with strong aesthetic potential compiled as part of the traffic investigation in Rome. With "Istituto di Calcolo delle Probabilità – Centro per la Ricerca Operativa e Sperimentale" of Rome University, desire lines of the city of Rome. Credits: ACSLM [auth. 650/2025], folder n. 50. Bottom: Existing proposal for Farah Park [A] and urban re-design by Luigi Moretti [B], Tehran, 1966. Credits: ACSLM [auth. 650/2025], [A] folder n. 50, [B-C] project 223, 66/249/1, 66/249/2.

green spaces that discourage people from stopping and using it as a meeting place, a shelter, or, above all, an educational and recreational space for young people. The aim is to radically transform the park's concept, making it, as the new ethical approach to public works demands, a park dedicated to youth, particularly children and adolescents, following principles and guidelines of social protection […].[62]

This quote highlights how the cultural dimension of Architettura Parametrica can guide design unfolding, even without relying on the technical framework discussed so far. The ethical aspect translates into a new programme for the park, now featuring an "open-air library", a "modern primary school for experimenting with new educational methods", a "specialised medical monitoring centre for children aged 5 to 10", a "refectory", and a "didactic museum […] with a strictly scientific character".[63] Moreover, the specific case of Farah Park helps dispel the widespread misconception that the cultural or technical principles of Architettura Parametrica cannot engage in dialogue with projects following more traditional approaches: Moretti's proposal preserved the monumental and celebratory value of the original design (see Figure 3.17B) while layering a new vision onto it (see Figure 3.17C). At the same time, it rebalanced the project, introducing the human scale through various volumes that define dynamic spatial sequences. In this project, Architettura Parametrica sheds its technical dimension and boldly challenges the uninspired design of a *jardin à la française* – or, as Moretti might say, a design conceived in an improvised manner.

Moretti extended the ethical rigour of design to both the execution and management of a project, considering it a professional practice. Pierluigi Borlenghi – one of Moretti's collaborators who, along with Lucio Causa and Giovanni Quadarella, inherited his studio after his death – recalls:

Today, large firms—the ones designing skyscrapers in India—consist of two to three hundred people. We, at Studio Moretti, with one head, three sub-heads, and eight draftsmen based in Rome, have designed and built: Montreal tower, Watergate, Villa Borghese's parking, the "metropolitana" bridge with Silvano Zorzi, Rome's Olympic village, Olgiata complex […]. Now, doing all this with a small studio means working, not twenty-six but certainly twenty-two hours a day.[64]

Moretti's immersion in the culture of operational research gave him the tools to manage this situation. Knowledge of tools and methodologies such as network scheduling and the Critical Path Method provided him with key strategies to optimise his studio's workflow. Numerous documents attest that Moretti's organisation was not rigid but rather scientific. Handwritten notes by Moretti and typewritten documents outline various methods for breaking down and structuring the activities required to develop an architectural project.

Each architectural design task is assigned one or more responsible persons, a timeframe for execution and verification, and, most importantly, its relationships with other tasks. Notes preserved at the *Fondo Luigi Moretti* even explain PERT (Program Evaluation and Review Technique) logic, which Moretti used to organise activities for the design of the Montreal Tower during his absences.[65] This approach is particularly relevant for researchers in architectural design for several reasons. It enables an enquiry into the operational practices of design, specifically the organisation of work required to produce a project. Moreover, it highlights Moretti's unique and somewhat isolated position within the Italian context, which remained largely reluctant to adopt this Anglo-Saxon work methodology, closely linked to operational research. But above all, it is yet another operation that enabled Moretti to uncover further implicit relationships in architecture.

Insights at the architectural scale

If we set aside the issue of architecture for large numbers, the urban scale, and the investigations associated with these dimensions, identifying Moretti's work that aligns with the methodological principles of Architettura Parametrica becomes more challenging, but not impossible. It is clear, for example, that the experiences discussed in the second part of this chapter, such as the Tehran complex, assume the adoption of Architettura Parametrica's methods, not just its forms. It is worth recalling that in Chapter 2 the origins of Architettura Parametrica were identified in projects such as the *Piazzale dell'Adunate*, the *Piazzale dell'Impero* at the *Foro Italico*, or the design process for Olympic Stadium in which Moretti planned to solve the visibility problem algebraically.[66] Although these projects were useful in outlining the evolution of Moretti's design approach, which he would later develop in his mature writings on Architettura Parametrica, they appear less relevant to the objectives of this section.

Based on the author's research into the vast Luigi Moretti archive preserved at the Central State Archive of Italy, it is essential to acknowledge the absence of projects that replicate the analytical approach showcased in the Architettura Parametrica exhibition. These shortcomings are balanced by Moretti's consistent focus on geometry as one of the essential tools for defining the relational structures of his spaces. When combined with his studies on visibility – not as a means of verifying an architectural solution but as a driver of its morphogenesis – it becomes possible to identify certain projects that are methodologically aligned with Architettura Parametrica. Among these, the unbuilt *Chiesa del Concilio Santa Maria Mater Ecclesiae* (1970) and the built Fiuggi Bonifacio VII Baths (1963–1970) can be cited. The latter has already been extensively discussed with Roberta Lucente in a study that introduced the issue of the distance between theory and practice in Moretti's work.[67]

Several documents, reports, and sketches of the *Chiesa del Concilio* demonstrate Moretti's ability to use algebraic and analytical geometry as a tool to control complex architectural forms. In a precious sketch of this church (see Figure 3.18A), geometry serves both as a design driver and as the medium for verifying and validating the project. Here, there are no fitness functions to optimise, yet this sketch helps support the thesis of Moretti's direct involvement in constructing the exhibition's equations. The mathematical structures Moretti used to geometrise the visibility problems of the exhibition's architectures are not far from those used to shape the architectural forms of this church. The numerous project documents suggest that the entire volume is constructed through a sequence of operations based on a key parameter: the "angle of maximum light opening in relation to a spontaneous act of prayer" set by Moretti at 40°[68] (Figure 3.18B). In the board on "studies on the determination of parameters defining a church space consonant with the renewed religious spirit illuminated by the Second Vatican Council"[69] many of the cultural references of both Moretti and Architettura Parametrica emerge. These include optimal viewing angles, "light spaces and their sequence", the "psychological sequence of 'pressures' and 'releases' generated by structural masses" and a "structural diagram of an abstract continuous surface without mundane construction references".[70] Additionally, in the referenced sketch, Moretti derived all fundamental dimensions using an algebraic approach. This implies that, theoretically, by adjusting the optimal prayer angle – set at 40° – all related project dimensions can be determined through a sequence of algebraic operations.

This sequence of operations, combined with the desire to achieve specific spatial effects outlined in Moretti's notes, gave the project a "semantic law", an "inner fabric" capable of unfolding it. This aspect is clarified in notes where Moretti reflected on the nature of this project:

> Naturally, form in itself can have full value even without an inner fabric determining it, or rather, if it is not conceived simultaneously with a fabric that governs it. That is, whether or not a perfectly developed form has a semantic structure that defines it and makes it a chosen one among a defined 'group' of semantics.[71]

A concept that may be read as an anticipation of the successful union between architecture and the *objectile*.[72]

Another of Moretti's projects with an explicit declaration of its parametric nature is the Corso Italia complex in Milan (1949–1956). In the pages of *Spazio*, it is described as an architecture with a "strictly parametric approach, proceeding from the determined series of spatial constraints in which it is designed".[73] This text, attributed to Moretti, explains that its parametric approach stems from meticulous studies on the flexibility of use and commercial value, combined with a form researched through a combinatorial investigation. As the text explains, Moretti systematically explored the possible configurations of building masses, service ducting, volumetric recesses, and window placements (Figure 3.19A). A meticulous process of continuous

Architettura Parametrica: In Practice 115

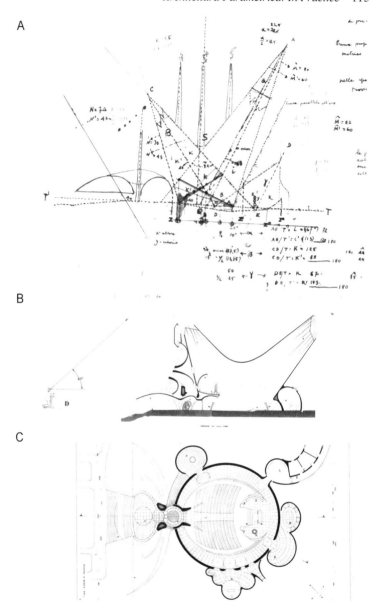

Figure 3.18 Luigi Moretti, geometric-algebraic studies and a proposal for the Chiesa del Concilio Santa Maria Mater Ecclesiae, Rome, 1970. Credits: AC-SLM [auth. 650/2025], project 252, [A] 70/275/32or, [B] 70/275/63, [C] 70/275/56.

refinement of architectural form, revealing, for example, how Moretti's volumetric exploration in the Watergate (1961–1970) can be interpreted as a combinatorial exploration with a parametric approach (Figure 3.19B). Even without drawings or sketches to confirm *Spazio's* claims, we can argue that Moretti viewed the extensive exploration of design alternatives derived from a single architectural idea as a more informal application of Architettura Parametrica. It is essential to highlight that, in this case, the scientific aspect of Architettura Parametrica is manifested in the precise definition and evaluation of functions capable of providing feedback on a design solution's quality and, consequently, guiding the evolution of the project.

In the vast body of Moretti's work, the Fiuggi Baths stands out as one of the most promising projects for exploring the themes of Architettura Parametrica.[74] Despite the presence of large-span and form-resistant structures – themes often linked, along with form-finding, to the early foundations of the parametric approach by multiple authors[75] – archival documents on this project contain no explicit references to Architettura Parametrica. This absence suggests a different methodological stance by Moretti, characterised by a synthetic and qualitative application of the knowledge he gained from decades of research on visibility and optics. In the Baths, the optimisation of viewing angles is applied informally to shape the project's sections – or more precisely, the sequence of spaces that define the design.[76] Beyond the theme of visibility, the parametric nature of this project emerges from its exceptional function, for which established design solutions are difficult to identify or apply. The primary treatment at the Fiuggi Baths consists of drinking large quantities of spring water throughout the day. The impact of this treatment on the architectural programme is unusual, ranging from complex restrooms and service area sizing to the need for a variety of activities during long treatment sessions. Although no archival documents confirm this, interviews[77] indicate Moretti's commitment to correctly dimensioning the project through an approach driven by scientific rigour. This may be Moretti's most ambiguous project when analysing his Architettura Parametrica. Yet, at the same time, it is the project that best illustrates the necessary ambiguity required to translate Architettura Parametrica from theory into design practice.

It is necessary to conclude this section by noting Moretti's unfinished Architettura Parametrica research. In various venues, he repeatedly announced he was working or intended to work on studies he would not complete, or for which no trace exists in his publications or the consulted archives.[78] The 1960 catalogue states that Moretti "laid down the spatial analysis of certain characteristic problems (theatre, stadium, underground railway station, distribution of areas for recreational and sporting services and installations, etc.) by following logical-mathematical methods and he invented".[79] The only underground railway project by Moretti is the "Central section of the Termini – Risorgimento metro" in Rome (1965). This project came after the catalogue claim, and the preserved documentation shows no resemblances with

Architettura Parametrica: In Practice 117

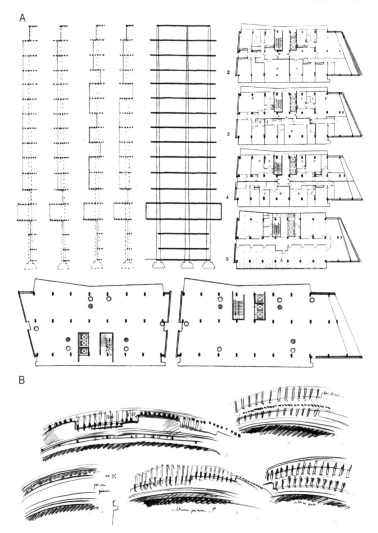

Figure 3.19 Luigi Moretti, combinatorial research inspired by Architettura Parametrica. Top: abacus of variations in fixtures, volumes, facilities in the Corso Italia complex, Milan, 1949 – 1956. Bottom: studies on variations in the façades of the Watergate complex, Washington, 1949 – 1956. Credits: [A] "Ricerche di Architettura. Sulla flessibilità di funzione di un complesso immobiliare urbano", Spazio a 3, no. 6 (—1951–1952). [B] ACSLM [auth. 650/2025], project 174, 61/210/29OR.

Architettura Parametrica.[80] Later, in *l'Architecture D'Aujourd'hui*, Moretti outlined both completed and planned research. He wrote that he had "structured, using logical-mathematical methods, the possible classes of housing forms [...] in the context of an urban space".[81] In this article, he also stated his work on a method "to define the structures of territorial master plans not through drawing, but by establishing quantified and directional guidelines derived from logical-mathematical calculation and from processing the significant matrices of each space of interest within the territory to be developed".[82] Another research focus claimed concerns defining "methods for indicating the 'optimum' service circuits, based on settlement needs and the matrix of places".[83] However, as widely noted, Moretti acknowledged that in his built works, he applied only the basic principles of Architettura Parametrica. Still, he pointed to a specific, completed project where he was actively implementing its principles. Moretti wrote: "For urban planning, particularly for the new residential district for employees (in the EUR area of Rome) nearing completion, I have begun applying some broad and elementary rules of the new methodology".[84] The district he referred to is clearly INCIS Decima (1960), yet its ACSLM documentation, along with studies by other authors, reveals no influences of Architettura Parametrica. Notably, his article in *Moebius* ends with: "In the next issue, a series of deductions on the principles of A.P. [*Architettura Parametrica*] outlined above will follow, concerning, among other things, architectural (and general artistic) criticism and a 'general parametric theory' in comparison with 'informatics'".[85] However, the following year's *Moebius* indexes contains no record of this research.

Beyond these projects and research, some of Moretti's works suggest the underlying principles of Architettura Parametrica (Figure 3.20). Most notably, the previously mentioned Fiuggi Baths feature morphologies that hint at his engagement with form-finding. The interplay of form, construction, and structural intuition invites a "parametric" reading of many of his projects, both built and unbuilt: the daring canopy for *Società Anonima Pellami* (1955–1956), the force-driven shell structures in his Viterbo Baths proposal (1955–1956), the parallel between visibility function plots from the exhibition and the contour lines in his Tevere Bridge proposal (1959), the large-span experimentation in his Olympic Village Church proposal (1966, Rome), the free-form geometries in his *Chiesa del Divino Amore* proposal (1970, Rome), and the structural and spatial virtuosity in his Tabgha Sanctuary proposal (1967). These are some of the key themes that require further research to outline additional methodological, instrumental, and technical exemplifications of Moretti's Architettura Parametrica.

In contrast to studies that have relegated Architettura Parametrica to a mere theoretical notion with no real impact on Moretti's design practice, this chapter's final section demonstrates how its tools, culture, and framework have actively guided several of his works. From the geometric-algebraic control of complex morphologies to territorial planning, from organising the design process to solving specific technical issues, from the informal use of scientific

Architettura Parametrica: In Practice 119

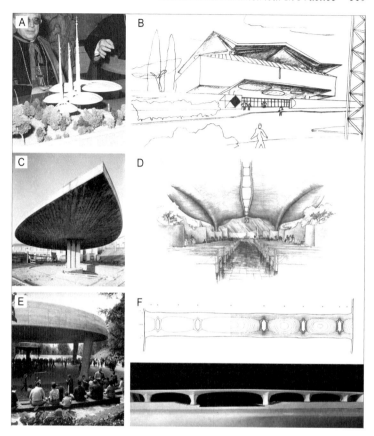

Figure 3.20 Luigi Moretti's projects that hint at the adoption of form-finding techniques: [A] Tabgha Sanctuary proposal, 1967; [B] Viterbo's Baths proposal, 1955–1956; [C] Società Anonima Pellami's canopy, Induno Olona, 1955–1956; [D] Chiesa del Divino Amore proposal, Roma, 1970; [E] Fiuggi Baths, 1963–1970, [F] Tevere's bridge proposal, Rome, 1959. Credits: ACSLM [auth. 650/2025], [A] project 232, F0002; [B] project 252, 53/159/23OR; [C] project 130, F0591; [D] project 251, 70/274/13BIS; [E] project 212, F0231; [F] project 153, 58/180/13, F0028.

insights to the gathering of data that inform design, and, above all, through the continuous questioning of established design practices. The *praxis* of Architettura Parametrica is evident in the rigour with which Moretti explored design alternatives, in his adoption of morphologies whose effectiveness he had previously tested, and in the ongoing negotiation he established between theory and design practice. Moretti's Architettura Parametrica does not necessarily rely on computational structures nor digital models to inform design practice. Rather, it emerges through a mindset rooted in scientific and ethical rigour, revealing its true essence beyond technology.

Notes

1 See Chapter 2, section "The juvenile period".
2 See the Italian preliminary typescript for the article: Luigi Moretti, "Architecture 1965: Évolution ou Révolution. Réponses au Questionnaire", *L'Architecture d'Aujourd'hui* no. 119 (1965): 48–51. For the typescript: Rome, Archivio Centrale dello Stato – Fondo Luigi Moretti (ACSLM), folder 44.
3 Cfr. Annalisa Viati Navone, "Un nuovo linguaggio per il pensiero architettonico". Ricerca operativa e architettura parametrica", in *Luigi Moretti: Razionalismo e trasgressività tra barocco e informale*, eds. Bruno Reichlin and Letizia Tedeschi (Milan: Electa, 2010), 408–419; Bruno Zevi, "Cervelli Elettronici? No macchine calcolatrici", *L'architettura. Cronache e storia* 62 (1960): 508–509 and many others.
4 Those mathematical models are exposed in Luigi Moretti and IRMOU, eds., *Mostra di architettura parametrica e di ricerca matematica e operativa nell'urbanistica* (Milan: Arti Grafiche Crespi, 1960). In the English version, Moretti is listed as the sole author: Luigi Moretti, *Exhibition of Parametric Architecture and of Mathematical and Operational Research in Town-Planning* (Rome: Istituto nazionale di ricerca matematica e operativa per l'urbanistica, 1960); Luigi Moretti, "Ricerca matematica in architettura e urbanistica" [Mathematical research in architecture and urbanism], *Moebius* IV, no. 1 (1971): 30–53. A synthesis is provided in Franco Ventriglia, "Luigi Moretti e la ricerca di un ordine oggettivo", *Rassegna dei Lavori Pubblici*, n. 11 (1960).
5 Luigi Moretti, "Forma come Struttura", *Spazio*, estratti, 1957. Already published as "Structure comme forme", *United States Lines Paris Review* 1 (1954). Republished as "Form as Structure", *Arena* (June 1967). Republished by Bucci and Mulazzani, and Viati Navone and Morel Journel.
6 See Chapter 2, paragraph "The juvenile period".
7 Moretti, "Forma come Struttura".
8 Paolo Portoghesi, Luigi Moretti, Sergio Musmeci, Armando Plebo, and Bruno Zevi, *Structures, Mathèmatiques, Architecture Contemporaine* [Debate transcript], 23 November 1964. ACSLM, folder 42.
9 Moretti, "Forma come Struttura".
10 For studies of Moretti equations with computational approaches: Fabio Bianconi, Marco Filippucci, Alessandro Buffi, and Luisa Vitali, "Morphological and Visual Optimization in Stadium Design: A Digital Reinterpretation of Luigi Moretti's Stadiums", *Architectural Science Review* 63, no. 2 (2020): 194–209; Piermaria Caponi, Fabio Cutroni, and Landolf Rhode-Barbarigos, "Revisiting the 'M Stadium' Project by Luigi Moretti: A Forgotten Model of Parametric Architecture", in *Proceedings of the IASS Annual Symposium 2019–Structural Membranes 2019*, eds., Carlos Lázaro, Kai-Uwe Bletzinger, and Eugenio Oñate (Madrid: IASS, 2019), 1–10; Caterina Palestini and Alessandro Basso, "Parametric Architecture and Representation, the Experiments of Luigi Moretti", in *Graphic Imprints: The Influence of Representation and Ideation Tools in Architecture*, ed. Carlos L. Marcos (Cham: Springer, 2019), 183–198.
11 Greg Lynn, ed., *Archaeology of the Digital* (Berlin: Sternberg Press, 2013).
12 Alexander R. Galloway, *Uncomputable: Play and Politics in the Long Digital Age* (London: Verso, 2021).

13 With a focus on swimming stadiums, this approach was anticipated in Giuseppe Canestrino, "Luigi Moretti's Formalised Methods and His Use of Mathematics in the Design Process of Architettura Parametrica's Swimming Stadiums", *Nexus Network Journal* 27 (2025 [Published online 2024]): 119–137.
14 Wolfgang Ernst, *Digital Memory and the Archive* (Minneapolis: University of Minnesota Press, 2013), 195.
15 This and the next quotations in this paragraph refer to the Italian version of the exhibition catalogue. This version is translated to better explain some mathematical aspects. Cfr. Moretti and IRMOU, eds., *Mostra di architettura parametrica*.
16 Moretti and IRMOU, eds., *Mostra di architettura parametrica*.
17 Moretti, "Ricerca matematica in architettura".
18 Luigi Moretti, *Dati parametrici per la piscina*, typescript (no data). ACSLM, folder 50.
19 The W function is written in explicit terms only for this case. In subsequent cases, this step is omitted to avoid burdening the reading.
20 See note 10.
21 Moretti and IRMOU, eds., *Mostra di architettura parametrica*.
22 Ventriglia, "Luigi Moretti e la ricerca di un ordine oggettivo".
23 The draft is kept in ACSLM, folder 51.
24 Moretti and IRMOU, eds., *Mostra di architettura parametrica*.
25 Moretti and IRMOU, eds., *Mostra di architettura parametrica*.
26 Moretti, "Ricerca matematica in architettura".
27 Edward Harrington Lockwood, *A Book of Curves* (Cambridge: Cambridge University Press, 1961).
28 Moretti, "Ricerca matematica in architettura".
29 Moretti and IRMOU, eds., *Mostra di architettura parametrica*.
30 Moretti and IRMOU, eds., *Mostra di architettura parametrica*.
31 This insight, along with other suggestions on mathematical modelling, was proposed in an email exchange by Professor Amadeo Monreal Pujadas, with whom I shared data on Moretti's stadiums during a research period at *Universitat Politècnica de Catalunya* in Barcelona.
32 Moretti and IRMOU, eds., *Mostra di architettura parametrica*.
33 Moretti and IRMOU, eds., *Mostra di architettura parametrica*.
34 As this chapter concerns architectural design rather than mathematics, the "atan2" function is used to streamline the analytical derivation of function W, despite its introduction in Fortran in 1961. The standard "arctangent" function can be used with appropriate adjustments to correct sign errors.
35 See https://en.wikipedia.org/wiki/Polar_coordinate_system#Circle
36 Luigi Moretti, "Articolo dell'Arch. Moretti scritto per 'Civiltà delle Macchine'" [Article by Arch. Moretti written for 'Civiltà delle Macchine'] [typewritten draft]. ACLSM, folder 49.
37 See Chapter 2, paragraph "Formalised approaches".
38 Moretti, "Ricerca matematica in architettura".
39 Christopher Alexander, *Notes on the Synthesis of Form* (Cambridge: Harvard University Press, 1964), 6.
40 ACSLM, "Progetto di uno stadio secondo i canoni dell'architettura parametrica", project 165. See folder 27.
41 Luigi Moretti, "Struttura come Forma", *Spazio* a 3, no. 6 (1951-1952): 21–30, 110.
42 ACSLM, "Progetto per lo stadio e del complesso olimpico a Teheran (Iran)", project 222.
43 Luigi Moretti, "Forum Olimpicum de Teheran par la haute initiative de son excellence", report (no data). ACSLM, folder 27.
44 Luigi Moretti, "Strutture e sequenzi di spazi", *Spazio* no. 7 (1952–1953): 9–20, 107–108.

45 Luigi Moretti, *Aviorama* [italian patent], n. 143320 (1957).
46 Viati Navone, "Ricerca operativa e architettura parametrica".
47 Moretti, "Struttura come Forma".
48 ACSLM, folder 27. See the correspondence with Ing. Mario Balzarini.
49 IRMOU, ed., *Studio per il rilevamento delle correnti di traffico interessanti per il corso d'Italia* (no data). ACSLM, folder 49.
50 Dario Fürst and IRMOU, *Criterio di convenienza d'una corsia per svolta continua a destra nel caso d'incrocio controllato e applicazione ad un caso concreto* (no data). ACSLM, folder 49.
51 Fürst and IRMOU, *Criterio di convenienza d'una corsia per svolta continua a destra nel caso d'incrocio controllato e applicazione ad un caso concreto.*
52 See Chapter 2, note 117.
53 Pietro Samperi, "Moretti Urbanista", in *Luigi Moretti. Architetto del Novecento*, eds. Corrado Bozzoni, Daniela Fonti, and Alessandra Muntoni (Rome: Gangemi, 2011), 75–82.
54 Luigi Moretti, *Piano Regolatore Generale del comune di Tagliacozzo* [typewritten general report] (no data), page A.1. In Archivio di Deposito del Comune di Tagliacozzo. For an in-depth study: Patrizia Montuori, "Dalla ricerca operativa alla prassi urbanistica: il Piano Regolatore Generale del Comune di Tagliacozzo di Luigi Moretti", in *Moretti. Architetto del Novecento*, 449–456.
55 Moretti, *Piano Regolatore Generale del comune di Tagliacozzo,* page B.1.
56 Moretti, *Piano Regolatore Generale del comune di Tagliacozzo,* TAV.1.
57 Moretti, *Piano Regolatore Generale del comune di Tagliacozzo.*
58 The study involved «members of the IRMOU scientific committee Prof. Bruno De Finetti, Prof. Dario Fürst, Dr. Anna Cuzzer, Dr. Giovanni Cordella and Arch. Luigi Moretti, president of the Institute». IRMOU, *Piano di indagini e studi per i parcheggi e la circolazione a Roma.* ACSLM, folder 49.
59 To further this research: ACSLM, folder 50.
60 Traduction: "Institute of Probability Calculus – Centre for Operational and Experimental Research".
61 ACSLM, folder 27.
62 ACSLM, "Parco Farah, giardini reali, a Teheran (Iran)", project 223, 66/249/1OR.
63 See note 61.
64 Filiz Sönmez and Federico Iemmola, "Intervista a Pierluigi Borlenghi su Luigi Moretti". https://www.archphoto.it/archivio/archives/1689
65 See ACSLM, folder 40.
66 See Chapter 2, note 19.
67 Roberta Lucente and Giuseppe Canestrino, "Distance between Theory and Practice in a Project by Luigi Moretti. Parametric Architecture's First Theorist", *The Journal of Architecture* 28, no. 5 (2023): 749–777. https://doi.org/10.1080/13602365.2023.2251029
68 ACSLM, "Progetto della chiesa del Concilio - S. Maria Mater Ecclesiae - Roma", project 252, 70/275/54.
69 ACSLM, project 252, 70/275/54.
70 ACSLM, project 252, 70/275/54.
71 ACSLM, project 252, 70/275/3OR.
72 See Chapter 4.
73 "Ricerche di Architettura. Sulla flessibilità di funzione di un complesso immobiliare urbano", *Spazio* a 3, no. 6 (1951–1952). For attribution, see Chapter 2, note 44.
74 Cfr. Lucente and Canestrino, "Distance between Theory and Practice".
75 Cfr. Giuseppe Canestrino, *La concezione parametrica dell'Architettura* [The parametric conception of Architecture] (Siracusa: LetteraVentidue 2024), 129–149.
76 This hypothesis of the unfolding mechanism underlying the Fiuggi Baths has been extensively investigated in Lucente and Canestrino, "Distance between Theory and Practice".

77 Sönmez and Iemmola, "Intervista a Pierluigi Borlenghi".
78 This book's research is primarily based on documentation from the Luigi Moretti archive at the *Archivio Centrale dello Stato* in Italy. Additionally, inventories from various collections of mathematician Bruno de Finetti were consulted. For future research, the *Archivio Moretti-Magnifico*, recently incorporated into the collections of the *Museo Nazionale delle Arti del XXI Secolo* in Rome, is recommended.
79 Moretti, *Exhibition of Parametric Architecture,* 8.
80 ACSLM, "Tronco centrale della metropolitana Termini - Risorgimento, Roma", project 218.
81 Moretti, "Réponses au Questionnaire" [preliminary typescript].
82 Moretti, "Réponses au Questionnaire".
83 Moretti, "Réponses au Questionnaire".
84 Moretti, "Réponses au Questionnaire".
85 Moretti, "Ricerca matematica in architettura".

4 Foresights and topicality of Architettura Parametrica

The analysis of Moretti's theories on Architettura Parametrica in Chapter 2, along with the extensive study of his parametric approach in Chapter 3, leads to a clear conclusion: Moretti did not strictly practise an early form of computational design. Nevertheless, Architettura Parametrica exhibits several proximities with computational approaches to design. It is important, first of all, to reflect on how these proximities can be discussed. Patrick Schumacher identified the seeds of computational thinking in Frei Paul Otto's work.[1] However, despite Otto's design processes not being founded on digital tools, Schumacher's research approach does not seem replicable in updating Moretti's legacy. The retrospective construction of a cultural lineage for parametric design – exemplified by Mark Burry's studies of Gaudí's form-finding[2] – cannot be merely extended to Moretti. Furthermore, applying the mathematical modelling methods today behind Moretti's "architectures for large numbers" would be reductive, as they represent only a basic step in computational design.

This chapter shifts this perspective: discussing Architettura Parametrica and the computational conception of design is meaningful because the former anticipated many principles that now underpin the latter – sometimes intuitively and qualitatively, other times with rigour. More importantly, Architettura Parametrica is a theoretical framework that, if updated, continues to offer valuable insights for contemporary design challenges. However, analysing Moretti's computational dimension requires a different approach from that used to discuss the work of other digital architecture pioneers, such as Charles Eastman, Christopher Alexander, Cedric Price, Nicholas Negroponte, and the MIT Architecture Machine Group.[3] In the work of these figures, themes such as architectural semiology, the relationship with history and tradition, and the role of the architect as an intellectual were marginal. Instead, these themes were fundamental in shaping Moretti's Architettura Parametrica.

For these reasons, it is more fruitful to explore the cultural principles of the computational conception that Moretti anticipated, rather than focusing on technical principles and tools – though these will still be discussed. It should be noted, however, that such technical principles and tools were anticipated far more clearly by other authors, including Frazer, Negroponte, Eastman, and many other pioneers of digital architecture. With a similar approach, Architettura Parametrica becomes useful not through its application, but by updating it and drawing new visions to tackle contemporary complexities from it.

Continuities and ruptures with contemporary computational design

In order to discuss the parallels and disjunctions between Architettura Parametrica and contemporary computational design, it is first necessary to clarify Moretti's relationship with computers and emerging digital technologies. Several scholars and Moretti himself have noted that during the 1960 *Exhibition of Parametric Architecture*, he used an IBM 610 computer not only to solve various problems but, more importantly, to demonstrate how modifying certain parameters affected those problems in real-time.[4] The previous chapter discussed how the computer's limitations influenced Moretti's design methods for the exhibition's architectures. However, in the exhibition, the computer served additional purposes. According to the exhibition catalogue, the problems prepared for resolution with the IBM 610 electronic computer were:

- Tabulation of a particular function (visibility)[5]

- Problem concerning the best emplacement (residences, industries, and schools etc.).

- Linear scheduling[6]

- Lösch's problem[7]

- Inversion of a matrix

- War operative research problem.[8,9]

A dedicated section of the catalogue lists several areas where the computer could be applied for operational research:

ARCHITECTURE: for the numerical solution of problems arising from spatial and functional inter-relations.

TOWN-PLANNING: to deal quantitatively with mathematical problems (from linear planning to the tabulation of functions) in which specific town-planning questions are concerned.

TRAFFIC: for the automatic analysis of the elements forming traffic in order to permit the application of scientific programs thanks to its excellent coordination.

CALCULATION OF STRUCTURES: for planning by means of mathematical models.[10]

On a practical level, Moretti sees the computer as a means to automate the resolution of recurring mathematical problems, not as a tool for delegating part of the creative process. Moretti's problems are mathematically "well-defined" problems, and therefore different from the "ill-defined" problems that today are tackled with computational approaches.[11] Moretti used the computer to solve problems with clearly stated goals, specific constraints, and a definitive solution path that makes it easier to solve them systematically. Instead, today, we use computational approaches to solve problems with unclear goals, ambiguous constraints, and no definitive solution path, which require interpretation and creativity in addressing them. Leaving aside the "architectures for large numbers", Moretti's problems typically have a single solution rather than a range of possibilities to evaluate optimal performance. His use of emerging digital techniques reflected a computerised approach rather than a truly computational one.[12] This highlights a key difference from experiments like those of the Architecture Machine Group,[13] where the computer often ventured into the creative domain. Yet, Moretti actively defended the computer both from those who saw it as a threat to creativity and from those who refused to embrace new scientific tools in architecture.[14] This stance reflects his confidence in the computer and parallels the criticism faced by Negroponte.

Rather than using the computer in a strictly computational sense, Moretti believed that architects should adopt its way of thinking. His approach to solving mathematical problems with the IBM 610 reveals an interesting parallel with the design processes of Architettura Parametrica. Moretti began by defining a design problem and analysing it with a scientific mindset. He then progressively reduced the range of possible variations, a method that closely mirrors how a computer iteratively solves optimisation problems. On this point, he wrote:

> Such a process is, in fact, a sequence of logical loops that spiral progressively tighter and more precise. This spiral form of reasoning was introduced to us by computers through the development of logical and mathematical calculations. It has now become an integral part of contemporary thought, fundamentally different from the classical approach, which derives a linear series of solutions and considerations from a fixed, unchanging premise.[15]

Moretti revisited this idea when he integrated the computer with logic-mathematics and operational research as a tool for defining the parameters shaping a design problem. More specifically, he assigned computers a unique role "for their ability to express, through self-correcting cyclical series, the probable solutions of parameter values and their relationships".[16]

Everything discussed so far makes it clear that the most significant aspect of Moretti's relationship with the computer lies in the ways of thinking it promotes. This is evident in a typescript by Moretti, where, while discussing Greek spatiality, he stated: "the basic 'computer program' of the impulses they introduced into space—the environment in which their communities lived—was the colonnade, with its precise rhythm of light and shadow, its ordered sequence of polished, radiant, and solid material, and its deep, dark voids".[17] This passage confirms that Moretti saw the computer not just as a tool but, perhaps more importantly, as a source of conceptual metaphors. His contribution to computational thinking development lay more in his theoretical positions than in his actual use of the computer. In practice, his engagement with the computer was explicitly documented only in the 1960 exhibition. Other sources provide only brief hints, for example, an article mentions the use of computers to manage the complex and evolving floor plans of the Watergate complex.[18] Once again, the approach described for Watergate appears closer to computerisation than to true computational design.

It is more appropriate, then, to focus on Moretti's theoretical positions rather than on his limited practical experience with the computer. In his essays, he moved beyond the constraints of a still rudimentary digital technology, yet he intuitively grasped its potential. If we examine where other scholars have identified the roots of computational thinking in architecture,[19] several key concepts emerge. These same ideas should also be explored in Moretti's theoretical work: optimisation, biological analogy, data excess, complexity, and the concept of the *objectile*.

The *objectile*, in particular, was not only anticipated by Moretti but also thoroughly explored and elevated to a design metaphor. He developed this concept well before Deleuze and Cache. The term *objectile,* as used by Gilles Deleuze,[20] refers to a concept that challenges the traditional understanding of objects as fixed, stable entities. The *objectile* emphasises processes of variation, becoming, and transformation. It suggests that objects are not static but are constantly shaped by forces, conditions, and contexts, making them fluid and dynamic. The *objectile* refers to a state of things "where fluctuation of the norm replaces the permanence of a law; where the object assumes a place in a continuum by variation".[21] First and foremost, it is important to recall that Deleuze defines the *objectile* immediately after referencing a concept where Leibniz "posits the idea of families of curves depending upon one or several parameters".[22] A concept that, when translated into architecture, defines "an open-ended notation which allows for infinite parametric variations".[23]

This idea of a fluctuating notation that solidifies into an object when external conditions are introduced closely parallels how Moretti conceptualised *structure* as a generative design mechanism. As discussed extensively in Chapter 2, Moretti assigned a mathematical meaning to *structure*, defining it as the set of relationships that describe an object. According to him, a "complex of relations that constitutes the *structure*, understood in logical-mathematical terms alone and independently from the concrete value of the use of adjectives, constitutes and defines the subject"[24] – much like the *objectile*. However, *structure* and the *objectile* are fundamentally different. Moretti's *structure* is more useful for understanding a design problem, while

Deleuze's *objectile* better explains how an object can vary within a broader family of forms. More importantly, Moretti's *structure* has a specific goal: its determination must oscillate until it reaches a balance between form and function – both understood as a complex set of parameters that an architectural solution must satisfy. This aspect is not central to Deleuze's *objectile* nor to the studies later developed by Cache.[25]

The metaphors used to clarify and develop these concepts differ significantly. While Deleuze relied on Leibniz's mathematics, Moretti not only referenced Évariste Galois' mathematics but also introduced a biological analogy. Moretti wrote:

> From a certain perspective, the expressive modes of the same structure could be infinite. Within certain limits, structures could materialize in different forms and expressions while remaining identical, just as it occurs in nature in countless ways among animals, plants, and humans.[26]

Moretti integrated several images from D'Arcy Thompson to illustrate his articles (see Figure 4.1). This reference was ahead of its time, as the morphogenetic ideas in D'Arcy Thompson's *On Growth and Form* "would have a deep and long-standing influence on contemporary digital architects" as Bottazzi acknowledges.[27] In *Forma come Struttura*, D'Arcy Thompson's work is merely a source of inspiration. However, in a caption on *Moebius*, this biological analogy was explored in greater depth:

> The introduction of specific numerical values for the assigned parameters corresponds to a particularization of the geometry of form, meaning the introduction of projective and metric properties. From the perspective of "related form", the structures of the two fish are identical, as are those of the various pelvic bones. (In the Cartesian reference system, a typical representative of the *Deodonti* family is depicted. In the reference system proposed by Prof. D'Arcy Thompson—featuring vertical coordinates, concentric circles, horizontal lines, and a system of hyperbolas—the reproduction of an *Orthagoriscus* or sunfish can be observed [...]).[28]

Moretti did not view biology and natural phenomena as preferred sources of design solutions, unlike Buckminster Fuller and Frei Otto.[29] He also did not use biomimicry to transfer its "self-organising" properties into architecture, as Schumacher does for Parametricism, frequently referencing Frei Otto.[30] Moretti briefly suggested organising urban settlements through "a natural process indicated by biology".[31] However, he did not develop the idea further. He also hinted at a formal biological analogy to convey the ideas behind his swimming stadium A (see Figure 3.6). But most important, Moretti used D'Arcy Thompson's concept of "related form"[32] to explain that a single *structure* could take multiple forms and determinations. He also suggests that one

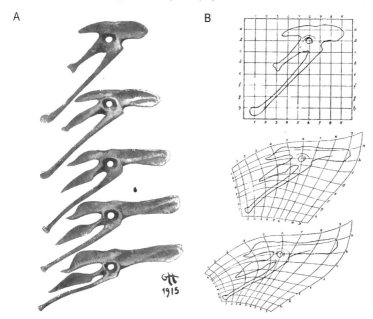

Figure 4.1 [A] Example of D'Arcy Wentworth Thompson's images used by Luigi di Moretti to illustrate his ideas and articles. Moretti used elaborations of Archaeopteryx and Apatornis in "Structure comme forme" (1954), in the English and Italian versions of the exhibition catalogue on Architettura Parametrica (1960), and in "Ricerca matematica in architettura e urbanistica" (1971). [B] Coordinate network of transitions from Archaeopteryx's pelvis to Apatornis' pelvis. Credits: D'Arcy Wentworth Thompson, On growth and form (Cambridge: University Press, 1917), 757, 759, 760.

form can transform into another through a continuous process that preserves topological properties, anticipating key ideas of the Digital Turn. Greg Lynn, for example, explores D'Arcy Thompson's transformations, noting that he "provides perhaps the first geometric description of variable deformation as an instance of discontinuous morphological development".[33] D'Arcy Thompson's transformations are fluid and continuous, yet they do not alter the underlying relationships and laws that generate them. Lynn connected these ideas to architectures like the *Peter Lewis House* (1989–1995) by Frank Gehry with Philip Johnson.[34] This confirms that Moretti's ideas implicitly contain the concept of the *objectile*, which later became central to the Digital Turn and remains relevant in contemporary architectural design.

The idea that a single *structure* can generate multiple forms raises the question of how to identify or choose a design solution. However, for Moretti, defining a specific form was not always necessary, especially in urban design. In this context, he argued that a project guided by Architettura Parametrica did not need to result in a fixed form – nor, more precisely, in a graphical representation conceived as the physical organisation of a plan. Instead, design could lead to "a planning process not immediately expressed graphically, but identified numerically and through its connections".[35] For Moretti, large-scale design could – and should – be carried out by defining a dynamic model shaped by the relationships between the parameters describing a territory. In his rudimentary digital approach, this model assumed the form of relational matrices, mapping the various phenomena influencing the design process. This anticipated several contemporary design trends. It reflects key principles of Open Source Architecture, as described by Carlo Ratti,[36] particularly the idea of a model as a participatory platform shaped by an interdisciplinary team. It also introduces the concept of a model that continuously integrates updated data to define a problem, an active model that evolves as new data emerges, as proposed by Ratti and Matthew Claudel.[37] Additionally, Moretti envisioned providing citizens with real-time information about urban spaces and events, anticipating the "user pre-information"[38] concept that is now central to smart cities. Moretti explored how data could shape both the city's form and its perception, particularly in relation to traffic, a key focus of IRMOU's research. The 1960 catalogue proposes that "a network of streets does not determine "one" traffic structure but can receive "n" coordinated structures, different and varying".[39] An exhibition example illustrated how different traffic parameters at an intersection can generate 108 regulation patterns, which can be adjusted automatically through continuous traffic data monitoring. Beyond these practical applications, this work introduced an essential architectural principle: the "open-ended" project, a concept now central to many digital approaches in architecture. On a theoretical level, Moretti also conceived the dematerialisation of traffic through information technologies. By connecting citizens, these technologies would reduce the need for physical travel. He speaks of "a connected house, in a topology defined by its very reason for being, in vital symbiosis with the city's spaces and services".[40]

During his last years, Moretti witnessed an exponential increase in data that could be used to guide design. This anticipated an issue that today challenges the ontology of architecture, that is, the "data deluge".[41] Moretti repeatedly stressed the need to distinguish useful data from useless data, warning that "if introduced into our operations, they may not only yield nothing but also cause severe distortions in judgment and confusion".[42] Moretti also foresaw that an excess of data inevitably introduces a probabilistic dimension into design.[43] He wrote:

> For useful data, we must assess whether their information is sufficient or not and determine their level of uncertainty. This requires establishing a hierarchy of uncertainty and evaluating the probability levels of

our reasoning, where these data are involved. Consequently, we must also estimate the probability levels of the conclusions derived from that reasoning.[44]

For large-scale urban design, this envisions a true *data-driven design*, where Moretti used data as "generative elements providing concrete and justified indications".[45] This reflects a recurring principle in his theories: the scientific approach is the only way to manage the growing complexity of architectural design. He argued that design had become so intricate that "the parameters representing it have now reached such a number and level of complexity that they can no longer be managed through approximation, nor inferred by extrapolating from even the recent past".[46] This complexity is not entirely accidental. Moretti, in fact, believed that one of the missions of Architettura Parametrica was precisely to unveil and articulate the complexity inherent in design.

This excess of complexity introduced another challenge in design methods: selecting a specific solution from the multiple possible determinations of a *structure*. Moretti saw this as an opportunity to introduce a subjective and creative dimension within design. Architettura Parametrica pushes the designer to move between "the spaces left open by parametric functions, however complete, allowing for a justified degree of decision-making freedom or the interpretation and selection of probabilistic margins left by rigorous solutions".[47] Moretti, thus, introduced a concept borrowed from operational research: optimisation.[48] Moretti elevated it to an ethical principle, arguing that a solution should not only meet all imposed constraints but also optimise the project's measurable performance. In doing so, he anticipated what is now known in computational design as the "fitness function". A fitness function evaluates and assigns a numerical score to potential solutions to a design problem, reflecting how well each solution meets the desired criteria or solves the problem. It "computes the desirability of any given state and expresses that desirability as a single number".[49] In contemporary computational design, fitness functions serve as a compass, guiding the search for an optimal solution. For Moretti, instead, they were scientific instruments meant to constrain decision-making freedom and minimise improvisation in the design process.

Moretti was well aware of the concept of optimisation. In the catalogue, he wrote that linear scheduling allows one to "obtain the maximum attainment of a target compatibly with certain conditions that are imposed because of objective needs or that are assumed as exigencies that must be respected without fail".[50] During the 1970s, this aspect of optimisation was explored by other digital pioneers, such as Eric Teicholz or Charles Eastman. Unlike Moretti, they developed practical methods and tools for specific areas of architectural design, such as layout planning.[51] However, we must question Moretti's cultural understanding of optimisation and his pursuit of the "optimum", a term he used, for example, in *l'Architecture d'Aujourd'hui* questionnaire.[52] A bold interpretation suggests that Moretti's view on optimisation was captured in a note where he described how architect Guido Figus synthesised solutions for his reinforced concrete shells, balancing form, function, and structure. For Moretti, optimisation could be seen as "an excited and hypersensitive exploration within the realm of a category of structures, searching for that kind of magical point capable of fixing a structure into the permanence of a form; of sublimating matter into a form abstracted from everything".[53] Moretti's concept of optimisation deserves to be reintroduced at the centre of architectural debate. Even today, it offers valuable insights into the technicist tendencies of computational architecture.

Architettura Parametrica between AI and Parametricism

A scholar exploring the relationship between architecture and mathematics is inevitably called to address how their research connects to contemporary developments in AI. I think that it is incorrect to speak of Moretti's Architettura Parametrica as a conscious anticipation of AI. I also believe that Moretti's predictions and forecasting were far from foreseeing developments such as neural networks, and, as far as I know, he was not aware of the pioneering studies on artificial intelligence, although he had some suggestions from cybernetics.[54] However, it could still be argued that Moretti's studies provide critical, cultural and theoretical elements to govern various ramifications of contemporary AI. Once again, this chapter positions Architettura Parametrica as a theoretical framework that offers valuable insights for managing certain contemporary shifts in architectural design. Remarkably, Architettura Parametrica had already addressed several challenges that now define the relationship between AI and architectural design.[55] These include the data deluge, the adoption of black-box models, the problem of over-choice, excessive complexity, and the risks of introducing an unstable technology into a millennia-old discipline like architecture. Moreover, the theories of Architettura Parametrica offer insights into challenges that Moretti had not foreseen, such as AI model biases and the hype culture surrounding AI.

Beyond the differences between Architettura Parametrica and Parametricism discussed in the introduction and in Chapter 1, it is possible to identify clearer points of contact between these two theories. Those connections have been acknowledged by Patrik Schumacher who argues that Moretti's vision for architectural design is only now being fully realised.[56] Schumacher also attributes Moretti's ability to anticipate the future with his engagement with the most innovative intellectual and scientific trends of his time. Architettura Parametrica and Parametricism provide theoretical foundations for architectural design that differ to some extent. Schumacher's approach is more systematic and structured, while Moretti's approach appears more fragmented. However, a consistent part of both theories is fundamentally rooted in technological innovation. They do not simply introduce new technologies into architecture; they absorb and transform them into cultural principles. Their strongest points of convergence lie in a fascination with computers, optimisation, and the scientific approach.

A still underexplored aspect is the role that the psychology of form played in the development of these two theories. Authors such as Bucci[57] and Reichlin[58] have highlighted Moretti's interest in "systematic studies on visual thinking".[59] In particular, Bucci traces Moretti's intellectual influences through the bibliography of his articles in *Spazio* and the books preserved in his personal library. Bucci writes: "this points to an aspect in Moretti's studies, descendant from the theory of Gestalt, that involves a part of American artistic and architectural culture. Rudolf Arnheim's contributions to the psychology of form, Ernst Gombrich's interest on the origins of artistic form, and Konrad Lorenz's research on visual perception, published in the volume edited by Lancelot Law Whyte and developed by the respective authors in other important studies, had a decisive impact on the successive theoretical nodes confronted by Moretti. Above all, it is the distinction between 'structure,' 'form,' and 'image' discussed in *Aspects of Form* that intrigued the architect".[60] The last volume cited by Bucci was written by Arnheim, whose connection to Moretti has been thoroughly examined by Viati Navone.[61] Studies like Hermann Weyl's *Symmetry*, reviewed in *Spazio*,[62] provided insights into the geometric foundations of various scientific principles, reigniting Moretti's interest in mathematics. Meanwhile, Arnheim's research introduced Moretti to the complexities of form perception, a central theme in his writings, such as *The Value of Moldings*.[63] All this leads Moretti, in an essay that does not explicitly concern Architettura Parametrica, to assert:

> The colours of the house should be controlled and arranged, making them adaptable while considering their psychological impact. The choice of materials should account for tactile pleasantness and surface qualities, whether glossy or matte under light. Natural and artificial lighting should be adjustable in both intensity and colour tone.[64]

A similar network of references is also present in Schumacher's theories. More specifically, he asserts that the role of architecture is "to give form to function" and that "theoretical resources that contribute to this enhancement are brought to bear: network theory, Gestalt theory and semiology".[65] In *The Autopoiesis of Architecture*, Schumacher dedicates entire sections to Gestalt theory, stating that one of the core principles of Parametricism, "parametric figuration", is directly inspired by Gestalt psychology.[66] Although Schumacher's discussion of Gestalt theory draws on different authors – Max Wertheimer, Kurt Koffka, and Wolfgang Köhler[67] – than those referenced by Moretti, there is a clear continuity in how Architettura Parametrica and Parametricism engage with these concepts.

But perhaps more than their similarities, it is their differences that offer the most valuable insights when comparing Schumacher's and Moretti's thinking. The most significant distinction lies in their approach to architectural language. Schumacher advocated for a design language shaped by digital software exploration, embracing forms such as blobs and splines. Moretti, instead, advocated for a design approach free from predetermined forms, emphasising the need to start each project with a fresh and unbiased perspective. Yet, despite this divergence, there is a key analogy in how both authors navigate form. Moretti draws on D'Arcy Thompson's idea of a fluid transition between "related form".[68] Similarly, Schumacher's design process emphasises the "parametric malleability"[69] of form. This concept suggests that certain forms can continuously adjust in response to evolving stimuli. However, Moretti and Schumacher approach "form's malleability" in different ways. For Moretti, it arose organically from analysing internal interdependencies within his *structure*. For Schumacher, it resulted from the active intensification of these interdependencies, deliberately shaped by the designer.[70] Finally, their theories stem from fundamentally different motivations. In his manifesto, Schumacher stated: "Parametricism emerges from the creative exploitation of parametric design systems in view of articulating increasingly complex social processes".[71] Moretti's Architettura Parametrica did not emerge from technical exploration but rather from a rupture with tradition, which, in his view, had never applied the necessary scientific rigour to design.

This final aspect is crucial today. Architettura Parametrica is a theoretical framework that originates from an internal reflection within architecture itself, only later establishing a relationship with technology. Beyond Moretti's foresight, this principle has allowed it to remain relevant despite the profound technological revolutions that have reshaped architectural design. Architettura Parametrica continues to offer key principles for both understanding and guiding diverse design narratives.

Notes

1 Patrik Schumacher, *The Autopoiesis of Architecture. Volume 2: A New Agenda for Architecture* (Chichester: Wiley, 2012), 680.
2 Mark Burry, "Antonì Gaudí and Frei Otto: Essential Precursors of the Parametricism Manifesto", *AD – Architectural Design*, 86, no. 240 (2016): 30–35.
3 See Chapter 1, note 4.
4 Moretti writes: "Certain of these structures, by means of a 610 IBM computer, could change the forms in which they were projected, based on certain conditions, or parameters, that the observer could choose to select". Luigi Moretti, "Ricerca matematica in architettura e urbanistica" [Mathematical research in architecture and urbanism]. *Moebius* IV, no. 1 (1971): 30–53. Cfr. Anna Cuzzer, Giovanni Cordella, Cristoforo Sergio Bertuglia, "Testimonianza. Ricordi dell'IRMOU" [Witness. Memories of the IRMOU], in *Luigi Moretti: Razionalismo e trasgressività tra barocco e informale* [Luigi Moretti: Rationalism and Transgressiveness between Baroque and Informal], eds. Bruno Reichlin and Letizia Tedeschi (Milan: Electa, 2010), 421–427.

Foresights and Topicality of Architettura Parametrica 135

5 The catalogue discusses the tabulated visibility function for one of the two football stadiums (it is not specified whether it is the N or M stadium).
6 The problem addresses the optimal investment coordination in the construction of houses, schools, and hospitals.
7 In urban planning, the Loch problem solves the rational location of residential and production centres.
8 The problem addresses the identification of the optimal firing angle for an explosive device.
9 Luigi Moretti, *Exhibition of Parametric Architecture and of Mathematical and Operational Research in Town-Planning* (Rome: Istituto nazionale di ricerca matematica e operativa per l'urbanistica, 1960), 66–67.
10 Moretti, *Exhibition of Parametric Architecture*, 66.
11 For a discussion of the mathematical nature of architectural problems: Giuseppe Canestrino, "Considerations on Optimization as an Architectural Design Tool", *Nexus Network Journal* 23 (2021): 919–931.
12 One of the most revealing discussions of the nature of computation and how it differs from computerisation in architecture can be found in Kostas Terzidis, Algorithmic Architecture (Oxford: Architectural Press, 2006).
13 Nicholas Negroponte, *The Architecture Machine: Toward a More Human Environment* (Cambridge: MIT Press, 1970); Nicholas Negroponte, *Soft Architecture Machines* (Cambridge: MIT Press, 1976).
14 Moretti, "Ricerca matematica in architettura".
15 Luigi Moretti, "Strumentazione scientifica per l'urbanistica" [debate transcript], *Giornata di studio sul tema Cultura e realizzazioni urbanistiche: convergenze e divergenze,* Fondazione Aldo della Rocca (Rome: CNR, 16 December 1965). Republished in Gabriele Esposito De Vita, ed., *Luigi Moretti e la Fondazione della Rocca. Urbanistica e Ricerca Operativa* (Rome: GB Editoria, 2009).
16 Moretti, "Ricerca matematica in architettura".
17 Luigi Moretti, *Vita di un congegno* [typewritten draft for an article for "Balamundi"]. ACSLM, folder 47.
18 "Designers Throw Curves to a Computer", *Engineering News-Record*, 3 June 1965, 24.
19 See Chapter 1, note 4.
20 Gilles Deleuze, *The Fold: Leibniz and the Baroque* (London: The Athlone Press Ltd., 1993), 18–20.
21 Deleuze, *The Fold*, 19.
22 Deleuze, *The Fold*, 18.
23 Mario Carpo, ed., *The Digital Turn in Architecture 1992–2012* (Chichester: Wiley, 2012), 146. The quote is retrieved from the new introduction to the section "Topological Architecture (1998–2003)".
24 Luigi Moretti, "Struttura come Forma", *Spazio* a 3, no. 6 (1951-1952): 21–30, 110.
25 Cfr. Stephen Perrella, "Bernard Cache/Objectile, Topological Architecture and the Ambiguous Sign", in *Hypersurface Architecture*, ed. Stephen Perrella, *AD – Architectura Design* 68, no. 5–6 (1998): 66–69; Bernard Cache, *Earth Moves: The Furnishing of Territories* (Cambridge, MA: MIT Press, 1995), 87–100; Bernard Cache, *Objectile* (Montreal: Canadian Centre for Architecture, 2015).
26 Luigi Moretti, "Forma come Struttura", *Spazio*, estratti, 1957. Already published as "Structure comme forme", *United States Lines Paris Review* 1 (1954). Republished as "Form as Structure", *Arena* (June 1967). Republished by Bucci and Mulazzani and Viati Navone and Morel Journel.
27 Roberto Bottazzi, *Digital Architecture beyond Computers: Fragments of a Cultural History of Computational Design* (London: Bloomsbury Visual Art, 2018), 181.
28 Moretti, "Ricerca matematica in architettura".

29 Daniel López-Pérez, *Pattern-Thinking: R. Buckminster Fuller* (Zurich: Lars Müller Publishers, 2020).
30 Frei Paul Otto and Berthold Burkhardt, *Occupying and Connecting* (Stuttgart: Edition Axel Menges, 2008).
31 See the Italian preliminary typescript for the article: Luigi Moretti, "Architecture 1965: Évolution ou Révolution. Réponses au Questionnaire", *L'Architecture d'Aujourd'hui*, no. 119 (1965): 8–51. For the typescript: Rome, Archivio Centrale dello Stato – Fondo Luigi Moretti (ACSLM), folder 44.
32 D'Arcy Wentworth Thompson, "On the Theory of Transformations, or the Comparison of Related Forms", in *On Growth and Form,* D'Arcy Wentworth Thompson (Cambridge: University Press, 1945), 719–777.
33 Greg Lynn, "Architectural Curvilinearity: The Folded, the Pliant, and the Supple", in *Folding in Architecture,* ed. Greg Lynn, *AD Profile* 102, *AD – Architectural Design* 63 (March–April 1993): 8–15.
34 Cfr. Greg Lynn, ed., *Frank Gehry: Lewis Residence* (Montreal: Canadian Centre for Architecture, 2014).
35 Moretti, "Strumentazione scientifica per l'urbanistica".
36 Carlo Ratti and Matthew Claudel, *Open Source Architecture* (London: Thames & Hudson, 2015). See also Antoine Picon and Wendy W. Fok, eds., *Digital Property: Open-Source Architecture, AD – Architectural Design* 86, no. 5 (2016).
37 Carlo Ratti and Matthew Claudel, *The City of Tomorrow: Sensors, Networks, Hackers, and the Future of Urban Life* (New Haven: Yale University Press, 2016).
38 This concept is investigated in numerous documents related to IRMOU's study plan on traffic phenomena in the city of Rome. See ACSLM, folder 50.
39 Moretti, *Exhibition of Parametric Architecture,* 48.
40 Luigi Moretti, brief text published in a brochure for "Balamundi". ACSLM, folder 47.
41 Cfr. Giuseppe Canestrino, "Architecture's 'Recording Deluge': The Nexus between Architectural Design, AI, and Data Harvesting", *The Plan Journal* 8, no. 2 (2023): 283–301.
42 Moretti, "Strumentazione scientifica per l'urbanistica".
43 Cfr. Canestrino, "Architecture's 'Recording Deluge'".
44 Moretti, "Strumentazione scientifica per l'urbanistica".
45 Moretti, "Strumentazione scientifica per l'urbanistica".
46 Moretti, "Strumentazione scientifica per l'urbanistica".
47 Moretti, "Réponses au Questionnaire" [preliminary typescript].
48 Giuseppe Canestrino, "Considerations on Optimization as an Architectural Design Tool", *Nexus Network Journal* 23 (2021): 919–931.
49 For definitions and explanations from the developer of a software that has democratised optimisation in architectural design, see David Rutten, "Galapagos: On the Logic and Limitations of Generic Solvers", *AD – Architectural Design* 83, no. 2 (2013): 132–135.
50 Moretti, *Exhibition of Parametric Architecture,* 50.
51 For an analysis of the evolution of computational applications in layout planning and their contemporary potential: Giuseppe Canestrino, Laura Greco, Francesco Spada, and Roberta Lucente, "Generating Architectural Plans with Evolutionary Multiobjective Optimization Algorithms: A Benchmark Case with an Existing Construction System", in *Transformative Design – Proceedings of the XXIV International Conference of the Iberoamerican Society of Digital Graphics – Sigradi 2020*, eds. Natalia Builes Escobar and David A. Torreblanca-Díaz (São Paulo: Blucher, 2020), 149–156.
52 Moretti, "Réponses au Questionnaire" [preliminary typescript].
53 Moretti, "Struttura come Forma".
54 See Chapter 1, note 13 for Moretti references to the work of Norbert Wiener.

55 Several of these issues posed by recent AI developments in architecture have been addressed in Canestrino, "Architecture's 'Recording Deluge'"; Neil Leach, *Architecture in the Age of Artificial Intelligence: An Introduction to AI for Architects* (London: Bloomsbury Visual Arts, 2022); Phillip Bernstein, *Machine Learning: Architecture in the Age of Artificial Intelligence* (London: RIBA Publishing, 2022); Stanislas Chaillou, *Artificial Intelligence and Architecture: From Research to Practice* (Basel: Birkhäuser, 2022); Matias del Campo, ed., *Artificial Intelligence in Architecture*, special issue, *Architectural Design* 94, no. 3 (May/June 2024); Matias del Campo and Neil Leach, eds., *Machine Hallucinations: Architecture and Artificial Intelligence*, special issue, *Architectural Design* 92, no. 3 (2022).
56 Patrick Schumacher, "From Parametric Architecture to Parameters of Social: Interview by Zaira Magliozzi", *AR Magazine* a LV, no. 125/126 (2021), 440–455.
57 Federico Bucci, "Painted Words", in *Luigi Moretti: Works and Writings*, eds. Federico Bucci and Marco Mulazzani (New York: Princeton Architectural Press, 2002), 136–155.
58 Bruno Reichlin, "Figure della spazialità", in *Luigi Moretti: Razionalismo e trasgressività tra barocco e informale* [Luigi Moretti: Rationalism and Transgressiveness between Baroque and Informal], eds. Bruno Reichlin and Letizia Tedeschi (Milan: Electa, 2010), 19–59.
59 Federico Bucci, "Automorfismi e 'unità di linguaggio': la teoria architettonica di Luigi Moretti" [Automorphisms and "Unity of Language": The Architectural Theory of Luigi Moretti], *Studi e ricerche di storia dell'architettura* 10 (2021): 108–122.
60 Bucci, "Painted Words".
61 Annalisa Viati Navone, *La Saracena di Luigi Moretti fra Suggestioni Mediterranee, Barocche e Informali* (Cinisello Balsamo and Mendrisio: Silvana; Mendrisio Academy Press, 2012), 270–275.
62 Bucci, "Painted Words", 148. For the review, see *Spazio* no. 7 (1952–1953): 97.
63 See, for example, the mathematical modelling of *Palazzo Ossoli*, discussed in Chapter 2, section "Moretti's mathematical conception of architecture".
64 Moretti, "Balamundi".
65 Schumacher, *The Autopoiesis of Architecture. Volume 2*, 2.
66 Schumacher, *The Autopoiesis of Architecture. Volume 2*, 165–167; Patrik Schumacher, *Parametricism as Style – Parametricist Manifesto*, 2008. https://patrikschumacher.com/parametricism-as-style-parametricist-manifesto. Presented and discussed at the Dark Side Club, 11th Architecture Biennale, Venice 2008.
67 Schumacher, *The Autopoiesis of Architecture. Volume 2*, 153–165.
68 Cfr. Thompson, "On the Theory of Transformations".
69 Schumacher, *The Autopoiesis of Architecture. Volume 2*, 654–656.
70 Schumacher, *The Autopoiesis of Architecture. Volume 2*, 655.
71 Schumacher, *Parametricist Manifesto*.

Conclusions

After that there will, I hope, be people who will find profit in deciphering all this mess.[1]

The theories, methods, tools, and outcomes of Luigi Moretti's Architettura Parametrica have been alternately demonised, criticised, rediscovered, mystified, and mythologised. Yet they have rarely been examined as a distinct design stance – one where fertile theoretical explorations were paired with pioneering design experiments. Moretti engaged Architettura Parametrica in a critical and inventive dialogue with cultural contexts that were alien to architecture at the time. It was not a sudden intuition, but rather a slow, laborious, and deeply informed stratification of knowledge. Through what Franco Purini describes as an "alchemical transmutation",[2] Moretti transformed a multitude of influences into a design attitude perfectly suited to his architectural vision. An architectural vision where formalism – both personal and collective – is not rejected outright but continuously questioned and constrained by a scientific design approach. This scientific rigour progressively narrowed the exploratory range of formalism, steering design towards continuous refinement. Perfection, as Moretti acknowledged, is a theoretical horizon where one reaches "immutable, fixed forms" if there is the "absolute precision of the parameters and the functions that link them".[3] Architettura Parametrica anticipated the need for computational design because of how Moretti complexified the design problem. Moretti strived to expose the full complexity of architectural design understanding and practice. The myriad parameters he tried to take into account generated infinite permutations that, in theory, only a computer could resolve. In practice, however, his approach was different. Though immersed in scientific culture, he often tackled design problems with a humanistic sensibility. Sometimes, logical synthesis prevailed; in other cases, a combinatory method; elsewhere, an intuitive approach. He bended forms to technical constraints while simultaneously shaping technique through formal intuition.

The unfolding of Architettura Parametrica is a type of entelechy – from the Greek *entelekheia* – a term Moretti himself introduced, drawing from medieval philosophical thought.[4] In this perspective, Architettura Parametrica permits the realisation of the inherent potential of a design that responds to an architectural problem. As the design evolves, it gradually reveals its inner logic, guiding the spaces and forms towards their "complete" state. Architettura Parametrica is a way to facilitate this process as it fulfils what was always potential. It is a narrative through which the design achieves its fullest expression, aligning functional, aesthetic, and experiential dimensions into a unified manifestation of its original potential. This unfolding is made possible by an architect who, with great humility, subordinated personal formal desires to the guidance – whether precise or approximate – offered by multiple disciplines, from biology to computer science.

This book has explored the varying degrees of "completeness" in the entelechy of Architettura Parametrica, from intuitive early experiments to the demanding challenges of professional practice. Architettura Parametrica emerged as something more than a "marvellous toy", as some of IRMOU's collaborators defined it.[5] Moretti's experience offers a unique perspective on the evolving relationship between architecture and digital technologies, with a precise focus on early computational practices. His pioneering design applications are significant for their visionary methodology rather than for advancements in tools and techniques they introduced. Flaws and limitations surfaced in the most rigorous test of his Architettura Parametrica: the mathematical models of the 1960 exhibition, "architectures for large numbers" designed almost like laboratory experiments. Yet, for an architectural scholar and practitioner, this does not diminish the validity of his theoretical framework; rather, it humanises it and highlights its flexibility. Moretti negotiated between the utopian ambitions of his theory and the practical demands of design, achieving a delicate balance. This negotiation allowed him to attain a higher architectural quality – one that could not be reached through mere technical refinement alone. By mediating between theory and practice, he ensured that theory remained relevant rather than abstract while providing practice with the necessary rigour. In doing so, Moretti anticipated contemporary computational approaches that do not passively submit to technology but instead carefully regulate its role in shaping the unfolding of the design process.

Moretti's work reminds us that architecture employs mathematics – or rather, multiple forms of mathematics. He constructed design narratives by drawing on arithmetic, geometry, algebra, calculus and "folds", computer science, and both abstract and practical mathematical approaches. This book has shown that Moretti did not merely use mathematics; he absorbed its values, conventions, and cultural and methodological sensitivities. More than simply using the computer, he adopted its metaphors and ways of thinking. In doing so, he anticipated one of the possible – and perhaps most widespread – ways of integrating advanced computational techniques into architectural design. In *Formulations*, Andrew Witt suggests several reasons why architects are drawn to mathematical models. One is mathematics' ability to provide formal vocabularies derived from logical necessity.[6] When explored through the right lenses, these vocabularies offer boundless formal inventiveness, grounded in a clear epistemological framework. For Moretti, mathematics, computers, and computation had both procedural and aesthetic functions. This duality – between process and formal exploration, between technique and the visions it inspires – remains highly relevant in the contemporary relationship between architecture and digital tools.

Moretti's work also demonstrates that architecture may do more than merely employ mathematics. His architecture feeds on the distilled essence of mathematics. His engagement with Évariste Galois' theories parallels Gilles Deleuze's relationship with Leibniz. Both Moretti and Deleuze established a cultural alliance with a mathematician, extracting a vision of the world – or perhaps a conceptual landscape – from their work. With some boldness, one might argue that Moretti's theoretical framework could have stood alongside Deleuze's as the foundation of the Digital Turn, leading to a "Digital Turn Autre", echoing Michel Tapié's *Art Autre* or Moretti's *Architettura Altra*.[7] This provocation implies that any attempt to reinterpret and update Moretti's Architettura Parametrica inevitably leads to an architecture that rejects gratuitous formalism in favour of forms progressively shaped by scientific inquiry, guided by rigour and ethics. That is because Architettura Parametrica promotes formal exploration in domains revealed by mathematical analysis, rejecting both "unrestrained eclecticism" and the "chaotic chatter of forms".[8] In Moretti's words, Architettura Parametrica addresses "a serious phenomenon, because if all forms are valid, then one begins to suspect their general invalidity!".[9]

Moretti's writings, models, and professional applications show how Architettura Parametrica emerged from an era marked by deep cultural debates and limited – or completely absent – computational resources. As the Digital Turn and its aftermath continue to push architecture along an accelerating technological path, Moretti's Architettura Parametrica provides a valuable counterpoint: it underscores that the purpose of advanced methodologies and tools must ultimately be tested against the human values at the core of architectural practice. This is not an easy task today, nor was it for Moretti. As Moretti said – referencing Michelangelo's words on a drawing of *Pietà for Vittoria Colonna* – "one does not know how much blood it costs"[10] to realise his vision of architecture.

Notes

1 Évariste Galois, *Testamentary Letter to Auguste Chevalier*, May 29, 1832, Bibliothèque nationale de France, Département des manuscrits, NAF 3414, fol. 48r–49v.
2 Franco Purini, *La misura italiana dell'architettura* (Rome-Bari: Laterza, 2008), 30.
3 Luigi Moretti, "Ricerca matematica in architettura e urbanistica" [Mathematical research in architecture and urbanism], *Moebius* IV, no. 1 (1971): 30–53.
4 Moretti, "Ricerca matematica in architettura e urbanistica", 30–53.

Conclusions 141

5 Anna Cuzzer, Giovanni Cordella, Cristoforo Sergio Bertuglia, "Testimonianza. Ricordi dell'IRMOU" [Witness. Memories of IRMOU], in *Luigi Moretti: Razionalismo e trasgressività tra barocco e informale* [Luigi Moretti: Rationalism and Transgressiveness between Baroque and Informal], eds. Bruno Reichlin and Letizia Tedeschi (Milan: Electa, 2010), 421–427.
6 Cfr. Andrew Witt, "The Architectural Uses of Mathematical Things", in *Formulations* (Cambridge: MIT Press, 2021), 97–99.
7 Moretti uses this expression in Paolo Portoghesi, Luigi Moretti, Sergio Musmeci, Armando Plebo, and Bruno Zevi, *Structures, Mathèmatiques, Architecture Contemporaine* [Debate transcript], 23 November 1964. ACSLM, folder 42.
8 *Structures, Mathèmatiques, Architecture Contemporaine*.
9 Luigi Moretti, *Architecture italienne: linéaments structuraux de son évolution* [typewritten debate transcript], ACSLM, folder 46. Reprinted in Annalisa Viati Navone and Guillemette Morel Journel, *Luigi Moretti: Structure et espace* (Paris: Éditions de la Villette, 2024), 181–191.
10 Moretti, *Architecture italienne*, 181–191. Moretti refers to a drawing of the *Pietà per Vittoria Colonna* in which Michelangelo wrote "Non vi si pensa quanto sangue costa". This phrase also appears in Dante Alighieri's *Divina Commedia, Paradiso, Canto XXIX*.

Bibliography

"Designers Throw Curves to a Computer." *Engineering News-Record*, June 3, 1965, 24.

"Parametrica Architettura" [*Parametric Architecture*]. In *Dizionario Enciclopedico di Architettura e Urbanistica* [*Encyclopaedic Dictionary of Architecture and Urban Design*], edited by Paolo Portoghesi, 377. Rome: Istituto Editoriale Romano, 1968.

"Ricerche di Architettura. Sulla flessibilità di funzione di un complesso immobiliare urbano" [*Architectural Research: On the Flexibility of Function in an Urban Real Estate Complex*]. *Spazio* a 3, no. 6 (1951–1952).

Alexander, Christopher. *Notes on the Synthesis of Form*. Cambridge: Harvard University Press, 1964.

Andriani, Carmen, Massimiliano Fuksas, Michelangelo Lupone, Franco Purini, Livio Sacchi, and Antonino Saggio. "Videointerviste." In *Lo spazio digitale dell'architettura italiana* [*The Digital Space of Italian Architecture*], edited by Maurizio Unali, 73–91. Rome: Edizioni Kappa, 2006.

Argan, Giulio Carlo, Luigi Moretti, Raffaello Morghen, and Adalberto Pazzini. "Coincidenze e Relazioni delle Espressioni Culturali" [Debate Transcript]. *Civiltà delle Macchine*, a XIII, no. 4 (1965): 37–47.

Baffa Rivolta, Matilde, and Augusto Rossari, eds. *Alexander Klein: Lo Studio delle Piante e la Progettazione degli Spazi negli Alloggi Minimi: Scritti e Progetti dal 1906 al 1957*. Milan: Mazzotta, 1975.

Benadusi, Lorenzo. "Il mito della scienza" [*The Myth of Science*]. In *Scienze e cultura dell'Italia unita* [*Science and Culture in Unified Italy*], edited by Francesco Cassata and Claudio Pogliano, 157–176. Turin: Einaudi, 2011.

Bernstein, Phillip. *Machine Learning: Architecture in the Age of Artificial Intelligence*. London: RIBA Publishing, 2022.

Bettini, Virginio, Siro Lombardini, Luigi Moretti, and Pietro Prini. "Tecnologia e problema ecologico" [*Technology and the Ecological Problem*]. *Civiltà delle Macchine* a XX, no. 3–4 (1972): 19–38.

Bianconi, Fabio, Marco Filippucci, Alessandro Buffi, and Luisa Vitali. "Morphological and Visual Optimization in Stadium Design: A Digital Reinterpretation of Luigi Moretti's Stadiums." *Architectural Science Review* 63, no. 2 (2020): 194–209.

Bonelli, Renato. *moretti*. Rome: Editalia, 1975.

Bottazzi, Roberto. *Digital Architecture Beyond Computers: Fragments of a Cultural History of Computational Design*. London: Bloomsbury Visual Art, 2018.

Bucci, Federico. "Automorfismi e 'unità di linguaggio': La teoria architettonica di Luigi Moretti" [*Automorphisms and 'Unity of Language': The Architectural Theory of Luigi Moretti*]. *Studi e ricerche di storia dell'architettura* 10 (2021): 108–122.

Bucci, Federico. *FORM, STRUCTURE, SPACE: Notes on Luigi Moretti's Architectural Theory*. Matosinhos: AMAG, 2021.

Bucci, Federico, and Marco Mulazzani. *Luigi Moretti: Opere e scritti*. Milan: Electa, 2000. Republished as *Luigi Moretti: Works and Writings*. New York: Princeton Architectural Press, 2002.

Burry, Mark. "Antonì Gaudí and Frei Otto: Essential Precursors of the Parametricism Manifesto." *AD – Architectural Design* 86, no. 240 (2016): 30–35.

Buzzati, Dino. "Grideremo 'GOL!' da un'ala di farfalla. Che cos'è l'Architettura Parametrica" [*We Will Shout 'GOL!' from a Butterfly Wing: What Is Parametric Architecture*]. *Corriere della Sera*, October 19, 1960, 5.

Cache, Bernard. *Earth Moves: The Furnishing of Territories*. Cambridge: MIT Press, 1995.

Cache, Bernard. *Objectile*. Montreal: Canadian Centre for Architecture, 2015.

Canestrino, Giuseppe. "Considerations on Optimization as an Architectural Design Tool." *Nexus Network Journal* 23 (2021): 919–931. https://doi.org/10.1007/s00004-021-00563-y

Canestrino, Giuseppe. "Architecture's 'Recording Deluge': The Nexus between Architectural Design, AI, and Data Harvesting." *The Plan Journal* 8, no. 2 (2023): 283–301 https://doi.org/10.15274/tpj.2023.08.02.4.

Canestrino, Giuseppe. *La concezione parametrica dell'Architettura* [*The Parametric Conception of Architecture*]. Siracusa: LetteraVentidue, 2024.

Canestrino, Giuseppe. "Luigi Moretti's Formalised Methods and His Use of Mathematics in the Design Process of Architettura Parametrica's Swimming Stadiums." *Nexus Network Journal* 27 (2025 [Published online 2024]): 119–137. https://doi.org/10.1007/s00004-024-00784-x

Canestrino, Giuseppe, Laura Greco, Francesco Spada, and Roberta Lucente. "Generating Architectural Plans with Evolutionary Multiobjective Optimization Algorithms: A Benchmark Case with an Existing Construction System." In *Transformative Design – Proceedings of the XXIV International Conference of the Iberoamerican Society of Digital Graphics – Sigradi 2020*, edited by Natalia Builes Escobar and David A. Torreblanca-Díaz, 149–156. São Paulo: Blucher, 2020.

Caponi, Piermaria, Fabio Cutroni, and Landolf Rhode-Barbarigos. "Revisiting the 'M Stadium' Project by Luigi Moretti: A Forgotten Model of Parametric Architecture." In *Proceedings of the IASS Annual Symposium 2019–Structural Membranes 2019*, edited by Carlos Lázaro, Kai-Uwe Bletzinger, and Eugenio Oñate, 1–10. Madrid: IASS, 2019.

Cardoso Llach, Daniel. *Builders of the Vision: Software and the Imagination of Design*. New York and London: Routledge, 2015.

Carpo, Mario, ed. *The Digital Turn in Architecture 1992–2012*. Chichester: Wiley, 2012.

Carpo, Mario. "Parametric Notations: The Birth of the Non-Standard." *Architectural Design* 86, no. 2 (2016): 24–29.

Carpo, Mario. "A Short but Believable History of the Digital Turn in Architecture." *e-flux* 03 (2023). https://www.e-flux.com/architecture/chronograms/528659/a-short-but-believable-history-of-the-digital-turn-in-architecture/

Carpo, Mario. *Beyond Digital: Design and Automation at the End of Modernity.* Cambridge: MIT Press, 2023.

Chaillou, Stanislas. *Artificial Intelligence and Architecture: From Research to Practice.* Basel: Birkhäuser, 2022.

Chermayeff, Serge, and Christopher Alexander. *Community and Privacy: Toward a New Architecture of Humanism.* New York: Doubleday & Company, 1963.

Ciribini, Giuseppe. "Prefazione." In *Il Componenting: Catalogo della mostra.* Bologna: Edizione E.A. Fiere di Bologna, 1968.

Ciribini, Giuseppe. "Dal 'performance design' alla strategia dei componenti" [*From 'Performance Design' to Component Strategy*]. *Casabella* 33, no. 342 (November 1969): 40–44.

Claypool, Mollie. *The Digital in Architecture: Then, Now and in the Future.* Copenhagen: SPACE10, 2019. https://discovery.ucl.ac.uk/id/eprint/10116421/

Croce, Benedetto. *Indagini su Hegel e schiarimenti filosofici* [*Investigations into Hegel and Philosophical Clarifications*]. Bari: Laterza, 1952.

Cuzzer, Anna, Giovanni Cordella, and Cristoforo Sergio Bertuglia. "Testimonianza. Ricordi dell'IRMOU" [Witness. Memories of the IRMOU]. In *Luigi Moretti: Razionalismo e trasgressività tra barocco e informale* [Luigi Moretti: Rationalism and Transgressiveness between Baroque and Informal], edited by Bruno Reichlin and Letizia Tedeschi, 421–427. Milan: Electa, 2010.

D'Amelio, Maria Grazia, and Tommaso Magnifico. "Luigi Moretti's Project for the Foro Mussolini." *AR Magazine* a LV, no. 125–126 (2021): 184–205.

De Landa, Manuel. "Deleuze and the Use of the Genetic Algorithm in Architecture." *AD – Architectural Design* 72, no. 1 (2002): 9–13.

De Luca, Francesco, and Marco Nardini. *Dietro le quinte: Tecniche d'avanguardia nella progettazione contemporanea.* Turin: Testo & Immagine, 2003. Originally published as *Behind the Scenes: Avant-Garde Techniques of Contemporary Design.* Basel: Birkhäuser, 2002.

del Campo, Matias, and Neil Leach, eds. "Machine Hallucinations: Architecture and Artificial Intelligence." Special issue, *Architectural Design* 92, no. 3 (2022).

del Campo, Matias, ed. *Artificial Intelligence in Architecture.* Special issue, *Architectural Design* 94, no. 3 (2024).

Deleuze, Gilles. *The Fold: Leibniz and the Baroque.* London: The Athlone Press Ltd., 1993.

Deleuze, Gilles, and Félix Guattari. *What Is Philosophy?* London: Verso, 1994.

Eisenman, Peter. "Profiles of Text. Luigi Moretti, Casa 'Il Girasole,' 1947–50." In *Ten Canonical Buildings 1950–2000*, 26–48. New York: Rizzoli, 2008.

Eisenman, Peter, with Elisa Iturbe. *Lateness.* Princeton: Princeton University Press, 2020.

Ernst, Wolfgang. *Digital Memory and the Archive.* Minneapolis: University of Minnesota Press, 2013.

Foti, Massimo, and Mario Zaffagnini. *La sfida elettronica: Realtà e prospettive nell'uso del computer in architettura.* Bologna: STEB, 1969.

Fox, Michael, and Bradley Bell. *The Evolution of Computation in Architecture.* New York: Routledge, 2024.

Frampton, Kenneth. Introduction to Luigi Moretti, "The Values of Profiles. Structures and Sequences of Spaces." *Oppositions* 4 (1974): 109–139. With translation and additional introduction by Thomas Stevens.

Frazer, John. "The Architectural Relevance of Cybernetics." *Systems Research* 10, no. 3 (1993): 43–48.
Frazer, John. "Parametric Computation: History and Future." *Architectural Design* 86, no. 2 (2016): 18–23.
Friedman, Yona. *Toward a Scientific Architecture*. Cambridge: MIT Press, 1975.
Fürst, Dario, and IRMOU. *Criterio di convenienza d'una corsia per svolta continua a destra nel caso d'incrocio controllato e applicazione ad un caso concreto* [cost-effectiveness criterion for a continuous right-turn lane at a controlled intersection and its application to a concrete case]. No date. ACSLM, folder 49.
Galilei, Galileo. *Concerning Two New Sciences – The Second Day*. Ed. Naz., vol. VIII, 169–170.
Galloway, Alexander R. *Uncomputable: Play and Politics in the Long Digital Age*. London: Verso, 2021.
Galois, Évariste. *Testamentary Letter to Auguste Chevalier*, May 29, 1832. Bibliothèque nationale de France, Département des manuscrits, NAF 3414, fol. 48r–49v.
Giangrande, Alessandro, and Elena Mortola. "Il computer: Un aiuto nel processo creativo del progettista" [The Computer: An Aid in the Designer's Creative Process]. In *Architettura & Computer*, edited by Maria Zevi, 67–83. Rome: Bulzoni Editore, 1972.
Goodhouse, Andrew, ed. *When Is the Digital in Architecture?* Montreal: Canadian Centre for Architecture; Cambridge: MIT Press, 2017.
Gramsci, Antonio. "Argomenti di cultura. Logica formale e mentalità scientifica" [Topics of Culture: Formal Logic and Scientific Mentality]. In *I Quaderni del Carcere*, quaderno 17(IV), §52 (I) (1933–1935). https://quadernidelcarcere.wordpress.com/2015/02/19/argomenti-di-cultura-logica-formale-e-mentalita-scientifica/
Gramsci, Antonio. "Note di cultura italiana" [Notes on Italian Culture]. In *I Quaderni del Carcere* [*Prison Notebooks*], quaderno 14(I), §38 (1933–1935). https://quadernidelcarcere.wordpress.com/2014/12/07/note-di-cultura-italiana/
Greco, Antonella, Giorgio Muratore, and Francesco Perego. *Foro Italico. Manifesto per un'architettura*. Milan: CLEAR, 1999.
Imperiale, Alice. "An 'Other' Aesthetic: Moretti's Parametric Architecture." *LOG* 44 (2018): 71–82.
IRMOU, ed. *Studio per il rilevamento delle correnti di traffico interessanti per il corso d'Italia* [*Study for the Survey of Traffic Flows Affecting Corso d'Italia*]. No date. ACSLM, folder 49.
IRMOU. *Piano di indagini e studi per i parcheggi e la circolazione a Roma* [*Plan for Surveys and Studies on Parking and Traffic Circulation in Rome*]. No date. ACSLM, folder 49.
Jencks, Charles. *Architecture 2000: Predictions and Methods*. London: Studio Vista Limited, 1971.
Leach, Neil. *Architecture in the Age of Artificial Intelligence: An Introduction to AI for Architects*. London: Bloomsbury Visual Arts, 2022.
Lockwood, Edward Harrington. *A Book of Curves*. Cambridge: Cambridge University Press, 1961.
López-Pérez, Daniel. *Pattern-Thinking: R. Buckminster Fuller*. Zurich: Lars Müller Publishers, 2020.
Lucente, Roberta. *Il progetto come fonte, come metodo, come prassi* [*The Project as Source, as Method, as Practice*]. Rome: Aracne, 2014.

Lucente, Roberta, and Giuseppe Canestrino. "Distance between Theory and Practice in a Project by Luigi Moretti, Parametric Architecture's First Theorist." *The Journal of Architecture* 28, no. 5 (2023): 749–777. https://doi.org/10.1080/13602365.2023.2251029

Lynn, Greg. "Architectural Curvilinearity: The Folded, the Pliant, and the Supple." In *Folding in Architecture*, edited by Greg Lynn, *AD Profile* 102, *AD – Architectural Design* 63 (March–April 1993): 8–15.

Lynn, Greg, ed. *Archaeology of the Digital*. Berlin: Sternberg Press, 2013.

Lynn, Greg, ed. *Frank Gehry: Lewis Residence*. Montreal: Canadian Centre for Architecture, 2014.

Magnifico, Tommaso. "Luigi Moretti: Being in the Clearing of the World." *AR Magazine* a LV, no. 125–126 (2021): 46–67.

Maraghini Garrone, Chiara. *TABULA RASA: La storia dell'ICAR di Michel Tapié de Céleyran*. Turin: Paola Caramella Editore, 2020.

Maranelli, Francesco. "The Arrival of the Information Model, 1969: The New International Building Industrialization Frontier and Italy's 'Electronic Challenge.'" In *Construction Matters: Proceedings of the 8th International Congress on Construction History*, edited by Stefan Holzer, Silke Langenberg, Clemens Knobling, and Orkun Kasap, 48–55. Zurich: vdf Hochschulverlag, 2024.

Marconi, Plinio. "Il Piazzale dell'Impero al Foro Mussolini in Roma." *Architettura* 20, no. 9–10 (September–October 1941): 347–359.

Massad, Fredy, and Alicia Guerrero Yeste. "Talking about the Revolution: Interview to Antonino Saggio." *Il Progetto*, no. 9 (2001). http://www.arc1.uniroma1.it/saggio/rivoluzioneinformatica/Interviste/Btwm/Interview.html

Montuori, Patrizia. "Dalla ricerca operativa alla prassi urbanistica: il Piano Regolatore Generale del Comune di Tagliacozzo di Luigi Moretti" [*From Operational Research to Urban Planning Practice: Luigi Moretti's General Plan of the Municipality of Tagliacozzo*]. In *Luigi Moretti. Architetto del Novecento*, edited by Corrado Bozzoni, Daniela Fonti, and Alessandra Muntoni, 449–456. Rome: Gangemi, 2011.

Morel Journel, Guillemette. "Lire et faire lire une pensée atypique. Les textes de Luigi Moretti" [*Read and Let Others Read an Atypical Thought: The Texts of Luigi Moretti*]. In *Moretti: Structure et espace*, edited by Annalisa Viati Navone and Guillemette Morel Journel, 35–53. Paris: Éditions de la Villette, 2024.

Moretti, Luigi. "Articolo dell'Arch. Moretti scritto per *Civiltà delle Macchine*" [*Article by Arch. Moretti Written for Civiltà delle Macchine*]. Typewritten draft. No date. ACSLM, folder 49.

Moretti, Luigi. *Dati parametrici per la piscina* [*Parametric Data for the Swimming Pool*]. Typescript, no date. ACSLM, folder 50.

Moretti, Luigi. *Forum Olimpicum de Teheran par la haute initiative de son excellence* [*Olympic Forum of Tehran by the High Initiative of His Excellency*]. Report, no date. ACSLM, folder 27.

Moretti, Luigi. *Piano Regolatore Generale del Comune di Tagliacozzo*. Typewritten general report, no date. In Archivio di Deposito del Comune di Tagliacozzo.

Moretti, Luigi. *Vita di un congegno* [*Life of a Device*]. Typewritten draft for an article for *Balamundi*, no date. ACSLM, folder 47.

Moretti, Luigi. *Architettura a parametri limitati, 1925–1945*. Published in Tommaso Magnifico et al., eds., *Luigi Moretti: The Form, Structure and Poetic of Modernity*, *AR Magazine* no. 125–126 (special issue, 2021): 70–89. https://www.architettiroma.it/ar-web/ar-magazine-125-126/

Moretti, Luigi. "Giotto Architetto". *Quadrivio*, no. 9 (7 March 1937). Republished in *Luigi Moretti: Works and Writings; Luigi Moretti: Structure et espace*.
Moretti, Luigi. "Eclettismo e unità di linguaggio." *Spazio* a 1, no. 1 (1950): 5–7. Republished in *Luigi Moretti: Works and Writings; Luigi Moretti: Structure et espace; Luigi Moretti: Lessons of SPAZIO*.
Moretti, Luigi. "Genesi di forme dalla figura umana." *Spazio* a 1, no. 2 (1950): 5. Republished in *Luigi Moretti: Works and Writings; Luigi Moretti: Structure et espace; Luigi Moretti: Lessons of SPAZIO*.
Moretti, Luigi. "Struttura come Forma." *Spazio* a 3, no. 6 (1951–1952): 21–30, 110. Republished in *Luigi Moretti: Works and Writings; Luigi Moretti: Structure et espace; Luigi Moretti: Lessons of SPAZIO*.
Moretti, Luigi. "Valori della modanatura" [The Values of Moulding]. *Spazio* a 3, no. 6 (1951–1952): 5–12, 112. Republished in *Luigi Moretti: Works and Writings; Luigi Moretti: Structure et espace; Luigi Moretti: Lessons of SPAZIO*.
Moretti, Luigi. "Strutture e sequenze di spazi." *Spazio* no. 7 (1952–1953): 9–20, 107–108. Republished in *Luigi Moretti: Works and Writings; Luigi Moretti: Structure et espace; Luigi Moretti: Lessons of SPAZIO*.
Moretti, Luigi. "Forma come Struttura". *Spazio*, estratti, 1957. Originally published as "Structure comme forme," *United States Lines Paris Review* 1 (1954). Republished as "Form as Structure," *Arena* (June 1967). Republished in *Luigi Moretti: Works and Writings; Luigi Moretti: Structure et espace*.
Moretti, Luigi. *Aviorama* [Italian Patent], no. 143320 (1957).
Moretti, Luigi, and IRMOU, eds. *Mostra di architettura parametrica e di ricerca matematica e operativa nell'urbanistica*. Milan: Arti Grafiche Crespi, 1960.
Moretti, Luigi. *Exhibition of Parametric Architecture and of Mathematical and Operational Research in Town-Planning*. Rome: Istituto Nazionale di Ricerca Matematica e Operativa per l'Urbanistica, 1960.
Moretti, Luigi. "Spazi-luce nell'architettura religiosa" [*Light-Spaces in Religious Architecture*]. In *Atti della IX Settimana di Arte Sacra*. Rome: Tipografia Poliglotta Vaticana, 1961.
Moretti, Luigi. *Strutture di Insiemi* [*Structures of Sets*], 1962. Reprinted in *Opera Aperta*, a. I, no. 3–4 (1965): 100–104. Republished in *Luigi Moretti: Works and Writings; Luigi Moretti: Structure et espace*.
Moretti, Luigi. "Finalità e mezzi della Riforma Urbanistica" [*Purposes and Tools of the Urban Planning Agenda*]. Debate transcript, April 23, 1963. Published in *I quaderni del π*, no. 6 (1964).
Moretti, Luigi. *Il significato attuale della dizione architettura* [*The Current Meaning of the Term Architecture*]. Debate transcript, Accademia di San Luca, April 16, 1964. Republished in *Moretti visto da Moretti* [Moretti Seen by Moretti]. Rome: Palombi, 2007.
Moretti, Luigi, and Michel Tapié. *Le Baroque Généralisé: Manifeste du Baroque Ensebliste*. Turin: Edizioni del Dioscuro, 1965.
Moretti, Luigi. *Italian Preliminary Typescript of "Architecture 1965: Évolution ou Révolution. Réponses au Questionnaire"* [Architecture 1965: Evolution or Revolution. Responses to the Questionnaire]. *L'Architecture d'Aujourd'hui*, no. 119 (1965): 48–51. ACSLM, folder 44.
Moretti, Luigi. "Alcune considerazioni sulla programmazione scientifica nel campo dell'urbanistica" [*Some Considerations on Scientific Programming in Urban Design*]. Relazione al 3° convegno INARCH su "I problemi dello sviluppo di Roma", February 20, 1965.

Moretti, Luigi. "Annotazioni sul barocco" [Notes on the Baroque]. In *Le Baroque Généralisé: Manifeste du Baroque Ensebliste*, edited by Luigi Moretti and Michel Tapié. Turin: Edizioni del Dioscuro, 1965.

Moretti, Luigi. "Strumentazione scientifica per l'urbanistica" [*Scientific Instrumentation for Urban Planning*]. Debate transcript, *Giornata di studio sul tema Cultura e realizzazioni urbanistiche: convergenze e divergenze*, Fondazione Aldo della Rocca (Rome: CNR, December 16, 1965). Republished in Gabriele Esposito De Vita, ed., *Luigi Moretti e la Fondazione della Rocca. Urbanistica e Ricerca Operativa* (Rome: GB Editoria, 2009).

Moretti, Luigi. *Architecture italienne: Linéaments structuraux de son évolution* [*Italian Architecture: Structural Lineaments of Its Evolution*], 1967. Typewritten debate transcript. ACSLM, folder 46. Republished in: *Luigi Moretti: Structure et espace.*

Moretti, Luigi. "Forma come Struttura". Debate transcript, exhibition *Le Corbusier e le nuove tecniche del costruire*. Rome: Galleria Nazionale d'Arte Moderna, April 20, 1969.

Moretti, Luigi. "Ricerca matematica in architettura e urbanistica" [*Mathematical Research in Architecture and Urbanism*]. *Moebius* IV, no. 1 (1971): 30–53. Republished in *Luigi Moretti: Works and Writings; Luigi Moretti: Lessons of SPAZIO.*

Moretti, Luigi. "Ultime testimonianze di Giuseppe Vaccaro." *L'architettura. Cronache e storia* a XVIII, no. 3 (1972): 146–161.

Morse, Philip M. *Methods of Operations Research*. London: Chapman and Hall, 1951.

Musmeci, Sergio. "Il calcolo elettronico e la creazione di nuove forme strutturali" [*Electronic Calculation and the Creation of New Structural Forms*]. In *Architettura & Computer*, edited by Maria Zevi, 147–166. Rome: Bulzoni Editore, 1972.

Negroponte, Nicholas. *The Architecture Machine: Toward a More Human Environment*. Cambridge: MIT Press, 1970.

Negroponte, Nicholas. *Soft Architecture Machines*. Cambridge: MIT Press, 1976.

Neumann, Peter M. *The Mathematical Writings of Évariste Galois*. Zurich: European Mathematical Society, 2011.

Nicoloso, Paolo. *Gli architetti di Mussolini*. Milan: Franco Angeli, 1999.

Otto, Frei Paul, and Berthold Burkhardt. *Occupying and Connecting*. Stuttgart: Edition Axel Menges, 2008.

Palestini, Caterina, and Alessandro Basso. "Parametric Architecture and Representation: The Experiments of Luigi Moretti." In *Graphic Imprints: The Influence of Representation and Ideation Tools in Architecture*, edited by Carlos L. Marcos, 183–198. Cham: Springer, 2019.

Pask, Gordon. "The Architectural Relevance of Cybernetics." *Architectural Design* 39, no. 9 (1969): 494–496.

Pellicani, Luciano, and Elio Cadelo. *Contro la modernità: Le radici della cultura antiscientifica in Italia* [*Against Modernity: The Roots of Anti-Scientific Culture in Italy*]. Soveria Mannelli: Rubbettino, 2013.

Perrella, Stephen. "Bernard Cache/Objectile, Topological Architecture and the Ambiguous Sign." In *Hypersurface Architecture*, edited by Stephen Perrella, *AD – Architectural Design* 68, no. 5–6 (1998): 66–69.

Picon, Antoine. *Digital Culture in Architecture: An Introduction for the Design Professions*. Basel: Birkhäuser Architecture, 2010.

Picon, Antoine, and Wendy W. Fok, eds. *Digital Property: Open-Source Architecture. AD – Architectural Design* 86, no. 5 (2016).

Bibliography 149

Portoghesi, Paolo, Luigi Moretti, Sergio Musmeci, Armando Plebo, and Bruno Zevi. "Structures, Mathèmatiques, Architecture Contemporaine" [Debate Transcript]. 23 November 1964, in Rome. ACSLM, folder 42.

Purini, Franco. *La misura italiana dell'architettura*. Rome-Bari: Laterza, 2008.

Purini, Franco. "A Journey around Digital." *Metamorfosi* no. 9–10 (2021): 12–23.

Quaroni, Ludovico. "Il computer, mito e speranza dell'architetto" [*The Computer, Myth and Hope of the Architect*]. In *Architettura & Computer*, edited by Maria Zevi, 207–216. Rome: Bulzoni Editore, 1972.

Ratti, Carlo, and Matthew Claudel. *Open Source Architecture*. London: Thames & Hudson, 2015.

Ratti, Carlo, and Matthew Claudel. *The City of Tomorrow: Sensors, Networks, Hackers, and the Future of Urban Life*. New Haven: Yale University Press, 2016.

Reichlin, Bruno. "Figure della spazialità." In *Luigi Moretti: Razionalismo e trasgressività tra barocco e informale* [*Luigi Moretti: Rationalism and Transgressiveness between Baroque and Informal*], edited by Bruno Reichlin and Letizia Tedeschi, 19–59. Milan: Electa, 2010.

Ribichini, Luca, Tommaso Magnifico, and Flavio Mangione. "The Imperial Theatre by Luigi Moretti: The Importance of Drawing in the Concept of Space." *Disegnare Idee Immagini* 46, no. 1 (2013): 30–41.

Rostagni, Cecilia. *Luigi Moretti 1907–1973*. Milan: Electa, 2008.

Rutten, David. "Galapagos: On the Logic and Limitations of Generic Solvers." *AD – Architectural Design* 83, no. 2 (2013): 132–135.

Saggio, Antonino. *Thoughts on a Paradigm Shift: The IT Revolution in Architecture*. Rome: Vita Nostra Edizioni, 2020.

Samperi, Pietro. "Moretti Urbanista." In *Luigi Moretti. Architetto del Novecento*, edited by Corrado Bozzoni, Daniela Fonti, and Alessandra Muntoni, 75–82. Rome: Gangemi, 2011.

Schneider, Philip, and Teresa Fankhänel. "Architectural Software Timeline." In *The Architecture Machine: The Role of Computers in Architecture*, edited by Teresa Fankhänel and Andres Lepik, 226–237. Basel: Birkhäuser, 2020.

Schumacher, Patrik. *Parametricism as Style – Parametricist Manifesto*. 2008. https://patrikschumacher.com/parametricism-as-style-parametricist-manifesto. Presented and discussed at the Dark Side Club, 11th Architecture Biennale, Venice, 2008.

Schumacher, Patrik. *The Autopoiesis of Architecture. Volume 2: A New Agenda for Architecture*. Chichester: Wiley, 2012.

Schumacher, Patrick. "From Parametric Architecture to Parameters of Social: Interview by Zaira Magliozzi." *AR Magazine* 125/126 (2021): 440–455.

Severati, Carlo. "Il computer e il ruolo del designer" [The Computer and the Designer's Role]. In *Architettura & Computer*, edited by Maria Zevi, 217–219. Rome: Bulzoni Editore, 1972.

Sönmez, Filiz, and Federico Iemmola. "Intervista a Pierluigi Borlenghi su Luigi Moretti." https://www.archphoto.it/archivio/archives/1689

Steenson, Molly Wright. *Architectural Intelligence: How Designers and Architects Created the Digital Landscape*. Cambridge: MIT Press, 2017.

Tafuri, Manfredo. *Utopia, Design, and Capitalist Development*. Cambridge: MIT Press, 1976. Originally published as *Progetto e utopia: Architettura e sviluppo capitalistico*. Bari: Laterza, 1973.

Tafuri, Manfredo. *Architettura italiana 1944–1981*. Turin: Einaudi, 1982.

150 Bibliography

Tapié, Michel. "Devenir d'un art 'autre'" [Becoming of an 'Other' Art]. *United States Lines Paris Review*, July 1954.

Tapié, Michel. "Overture." In *Le Baroque Généralisé: Manifeste du Baroque Ensembliste*, edited by Luigi Moretti and Michel Tapié. Turin: Edizioni del Dioscuro, 1965.

Tapié, Michel. "D'un ordre autre dans le baroque ensembliste" [Of Another Order in Ensembliste Baroque]. *Opera Aperta*, a I, no. 3–4 (1965): 97–99.

Tedeschi, Letizia. "Algoritmie spaziali. Gli artisti, la rivista *Spazio* e Luigi Moretti (1950–1953)" [Spatial Algorithms: The Artists, the Journal "Spazio," and Luigi Moretti (1950–1953)]. In *Luigi Moretti: Razionalismo e trasgressività tra barocco e informale* [Luigi Moretti: Rationalism and Transgressiveness between Baroque and Informal], edited by Bruno Reichlin and Letizia Tedeschi, 136–177. Milan: Electa, 2010.

Terzidis, Kostas. *Algorithmic Architecture*. Oxford: Architectural Press, 2006.

Thompson, D'Arcy Wentworth. *On Growth and Form*. Cambridge: University Press, 1917.

Vardouli, Theodora, and Olga Touloumi, eds. *Computer Architectures: Constructing the Common Ground*. New York and London: Routledge, 2019.

Ventriglia, Franco. "Luigi Moretti e la ricerca di un ordine oggettivo." *Rassegna dei Lavori Pubblici*, no. 11 (1960).

Venturi, Robert. *Complexity and Contradiction in Architecture*. 2nd ed. New York: Museum of Modern Art, 1977. First published 1966.

Viati Navone, Annalisa. "'Un nuovo linguaggio per il pensiero architettonico'. Ricerca operativa e architettura parametrica." In *Luigi Moretti: Razionalismo e trasgressività tra barocco e informale* [Luigi Moretti: Rationalism and Transgressiveness between Baroque and Informal], edited by Bruno Reichlin and Letizia Tedeschi, 408–419. Milan: Electa, 2010.

Viati Navone. "Annalisa." *La Saracena di Luigi Moretti fra Suggestioni Mediterranee, Barocche e Informali*. Cinisello Balsamo and Mendrisio: Silvana; Mendrisio Academy Press, 2012.

Viati Navone, Annalisa. "The Baroque under the Light of the Taccuino: An Intellectual Trajectory Constructed a Posteriori." *AR Magazine* a LV, no. 125–126 (2021): 220–237.

Wiener, Norbert. *Cybernetics: Or Control and Communication in the Animal and the Machine*. 2nd ed. Cambridge, MA: MIT Press, 1961. First published 1948.

Wigley, Mark. "The Drawing that Ate Architecture." Jencks Foundation (2023). https://www.jencksfoundation.org/explore/text/the-drawing-that-ate-architecture

Witt, Andrew. "The Architectural Uses of Mathematical Things." In *Formulations*, 97–99. Cambridge: MIT Press, 2021.

Yiannoudes, Socrates. *Architecture in Digital Culture: Machines, Networks and Computation*. New York: Routledge, 2022.

Zevi, Bruno. "Luigi Moretti double-face. Ambizione contro ingegno." *L'Espresso*, 17 February 1957. Reprinted in Bruno Zevi, *Cronache di Architettura*, n. 145. Bari: Laterza, 1975.

Zevi, Bruno. "Cervelli Elettronici? No, macchine calcolatrici" [*Electronic Brains? No, Calculating Machines*]. *L'architettura. Cronache e storia* 62 (1960): 508–509.

Zevi, Bruno. "La scomparsa di Luigi Moretti. Computer inceppato dal dannunzianesimo" [*The Passing of Luigi Moretti: Computer Jammed by D'Annunzianism*].

L'Espresso, 29 July 1973. Reprinted in Bruno Zevi, *Cronache di architettura*, n. 130. Bari: Laterza, 1975.
Zevi, Bruno. *The Modern Language of Architecture*. Translated edition. Seattle: University of Washington Press, 1978. Originally published as *Il linguaggio moderno dell'architettura*. Turin: Einaudi, 1973.
Zevi, Maria, ed. *Architettura & Computer*. Rome: Bulzoni Editore, 1972.

Luigi Moretti's Referenced projects

The dates and the names listed are taken from the Fondo Luigi Moretti – Archivio Centrale dello Stato Italiano catalogue.

1933–1935. *P.N.F. New G.I.L. House – Project for a theater and offices*. Piacenza [project 49].
1936. *Fencing Academy at Foro Mussolini* [also known as Casa delle Armi]. Rome [project 55].
1936. *Piazzale delle Adunate*. Rome [project 59].
1937. *Piazzale dell'Impero*. Rome [project 71].
1937–1940. *Olympic Stadium project and construction up to the second tier of stands*. Rome [project 62].
1938–1942. *Grande teatro at the Universal Exposition*. Rome [project 76].
1947–1950. *House known as Il Girasole*. Rome [project 110].
1949–1956. *Building complex for offices and residences in Corso Italia and Via Rugabella*. Milan [project 121].
1950–1969. *Project for the new headquarters of the Dance Academy*. Rome [project 117].
1953–1960. *Project for the development of the new thermal baths*. Viterbo [project 122].
1955–1956. *Offices and equipment for the supervision and support of the workers of Società anonima Pellami (Comacini)*. Induno Olona [project 130].
1959. *Competition for a bridge on the Tiber*. Rome [project 153].
1960. *Expansion and renovation of the Olympic Stadium*. Rome [project 164].
1960. *IRMOU Architettura Parametrica exhibition at the 12th Triennale*. Milan [project 162].
1960. *Project for a stadium according to parametric architecture principles*. No place mentioned [project 165].
1961–1970. *Watergate Residential District*. Washington [project 174].
1965. *Central section of the Termini–Risorgimento metro line*. Rome [project 218].
1965. *Renovation of the Bonifacio VIII Springs thermal complex*. Fiuggi [project 212].
1966. *Underground parking at Villa Borghese*. Rome [project 226].
1966. *Farah Park, Royal Gardens*. Tehran [project 223].
1966. *Project for the stadium and the Olympic complex*. Tehran [project 222].
1967. *Project for the sanctuary on Lake Tiberias*. Taghba [project 232].
1970. *Project for the Council Church – St. Mary Mater Ecclesiae*. Rome [project 252].
1970. *Project for the new Santuario del Divino Amore*. Rome [project 251].

Index

Note: Page numbers in italics refer to figures. Numbers followed by "n" denote endnote number.

Accademia di San Luca 33, 59n1
aesthetic 36, 41, 56–59, 110, 139–140; *see also* International Centre for Aesthetic Research
artificial intelligence 6, 8, 14–16, 25, 132, 137n55; AI Winter 15
Alexander, Christopher 1, 7, 15, 40, 95, 124
algorithm 3–4, 7, 9, 22, 34, 39, 62n74, 106; algorithmic art 15; algorithmic reenactment 71
Alighieri, Dante 141n10
An architecture of limited parameters 24–25, 30, 35, 40, 56
analysis 25, 27–28, 36, 44, 109, 116, 125; mathematical analysis 41, 71, 109; parametric analysis *104*, 105; statistical analysis 16; visibility analysis 67–93
angle of view 28, 78–79, 84, 90, 96, 99, 114, 116; angle camera lenses 25; optical cone 38; visual cone 27, 31, 37
Aquinas, Thomas (St.) 56
archaeology of the digital 71
architecture autre 53, 56, 140; art autre 45, 55–56, 140
architecture for large number 4, 48, 67, *103*, 113
Architecture Machine Group (MIT) 9, 124, 126
Ariosto, Ludovico 11
Arnheim, Rudolf 133
Automorphism 34–35, 39, 47, 62n72
Aviorama 103, *104*, 105

Bauhaus 42
Benevolo, Leonardo 12
Bernini, Gian Lorenzo 45
Biology 1, 4, 22, 48, 58, 128, 139; biological analogies 10, 127–128; biologist 17n13, 52; biomimicry 128
Blobs 3, 134
Bonelli, Renato 13
Borlenghi, Pierluigi 112
Borromini 24, 45
Bottazzi, Roberto 2, 6, 128
Bucci, Federico 16, 33, 39, 133
Buonarroti, Michelangelo 31, 40, 45, 99, 140, 141n10
Buzzati, Dino 25, 41

Cache, Bernard 127–128; *see also* objectile
Cantor, Georg 56
Carpo, Mario 2, 7–8, 13
Causa, Lucio 112
chain 34–35, 37–38, 53; chain-like structure 24; of differences 30, 38; minimal chains 35; of thoughts 25
Chevalier, Auguste 54
Chiesa del Concilio Santa Maria Mater Ecclesiae 113, *115*
Chiesa del Divino Amore 118, *119*
cinema hall 48, 66, 70, 73, 88–93, 103, 105
Claudel, Matthew 130
Claypool, Mollie 2, 6, 9
communication theory *see* cybernetics
componenting 12, 19n42

Index

computational 2, 6, 9, 13, 16, 22, 24, 120, 124, 125–131, 139–140; cartfacts 71; design 4, 124, 138
computer 3, 6, 8–10, 12–15, 34, 46, 52, 125–127, 133, 134n4, 139–140
cone, optical and visual *see* angle of view
Corso Italia building complex 33, 114, *117*
Critical Path Method 112
Croce, Benedetto 11
crowd shape 28, 30, 67, 96
cybernetics 6, 8–9, 13, 25, 132

Dance Academy in Rome *104*, 105
data deluge 130, 132
data-driven design 131
De Landa, Manuel 30
Deleuze, Gilles 2, 4, 10, 44, 127–128, 140; *see also* objectile
differences 34–40, 47, 49, 53
digital memory 71
digital turn 2, 7, 15, 129, 140

Eastman, Charles 124, 131
Eisenman, Peter 1, 44
emergent proprierties 42, 48
empty space 99
ensemble/ensemblisme 37, 56–57, 101
entelechy 138–139
Ernst, Wolfgang 71

fabric 54, 59, 114
Figus, Guido 8, 132
Fiuggi baths 113, 116, 118, *119*, 122n76
football stadium M 74–78, 96
football stadium N 78–81, 96, 97, 101
Forma come struttura 33–34, 39–40, 46, 53, 56–58, 67
formalised design approaches 7, 17n7, 45–53, 57
form-finding 6, 8, 10, 28, 30, 116, 118, *119*, 124
Foro Italico 1, 25–32, 70, 96, 99, 113, 145
Foti, Massimo 12, 14–15
Frampton, Kenneth 1–2, 12
Frazer, John 2–3, 5, 124
Friedman, Yona 7, 9, 18n21
Fuksas, Massimiliano 15

Fuller, Richard. Buckminster 9, 15, 128
functionalism 44; functional architecture 51, 53
Fürst, Dario 108

Galilei, Galileo 11, 24, 45
Galloway, Alexander R. 71
Galois, Évariste 11, 30, 39–40, 45, 53–57, 128, 140
Gaudí, Antoni 9, 124
Gaussian 28, 30
Gehry, Frank Owen 129
Gentile, Giovanni 11
Gestalt 133
Giangrande, Alessandro 14
GIL Theatre, Piacenza *104*, 105
Giotto di Bondone 23, 25, 45
Gombrich, Ernst 133
Gramsci, Antonio 11
Gran Teatro EUR 30, *104*, 105
Granular space and thinking 35
graph 106
Greek architecture 39; Greek spatiality 126
group 34, 42, 44, 48, 54, 56, 58; of chains 35; of difference 35, 38, 49; of semantics 114; theory 40, 52, 54–55
Guattari, Félix 44

Hadrian's Villa 73
Haldane, John 17n13
Heisenberg, Werner 35, 56
heuristic 8–9
house/housing 70, 130, 133

IBM 47; IBM 610 9, 71, 125–126, 134n4
Imperiale, Alice 56
INCIS Decima 118
industrial design 42
informal art 22, 56
informatics 118
Informazioni Urbanistiche 51, 109
International Centre for Aesthetic Research (ICAR) 22, 56–57
IRMOU 8, 10, 12, 23, 34, 45–47, 51, 70, 96, 101, 107–110, 130; IRMOU composition 63n102
isomorphism 34–35, 39
Istituto di Calcolo delle Probabilità – Centro per la Ricerca Operativa e Sperimentale 110, *111*

154 *Index*

Italian architectural design culture 10–16
Iturbe Elisa 44

Jacobs, François 17n13
Jencks, Charles 7–8, 12

Klein, Alexander 40
Koffka, Kurt 133
Köhler, Wolfgang 133

late style 44
Lawrence, Thomas Edward 11
Leibniz, Gottfried 127–128, 140
Lightpen 14
Llull, Ramon 45
Lorenz, Konrad 133
Lucente, Roberta 133
Lynn, Greg 129

Magnifico, Tommaso 31
manifesto 57, 134
mathematic, abstract 1, 36, 45, 57, 59
McLuhan, Marshall 15
Minsky, Marvin 14
moldings/Mouldings 25, 36, 133
Monreal Pujadas, Amadeo 121n31
Montreal Tower 133
Morel Journel, Guillemette 12
morphogenesis 28, 39, 113
Mortola, Elena 14
Mulazzani, Marco 16, 22
Musmeci, Sergio 12, 14, 19n45
Mussolini, Benito 33, 96; *Foro Mussolini* 26

Needham, Joseph 17n13
Negroponte, Nicholas 8–9, 14, 45, 126
neural networks 132

O & D (Origin and Destination) 109
objectile 4, 106, 114, 127–129
Olympic stadium 26–28, 96, *97*, *98*, 99, *100*, 101, *102*, *103*, 110
Open Source Architecture 130
operational research 3–4, 22, 34, 40–41, 44–48, 52, 66, 106, 109, 112–113, 125–126, 131
optimisation 4, 22, 25, 47, 57, 67, 70, 126–127, 131–133
Otto, Frei Paul 7, 9, 124

Palazzo dei Conservatori 31, 40
Palazzo Farnese 99
Palazzo Ossoli 36, *38*, 58
parameter 2, 3, 7, 9
parametricism 2–3, 6, 106, 128, 132–134
Parc Farah 110, *111*, 112
Pask, Gordon 8, 13
patent 103, *104*, 105
perception 22, 25, 30, 31, 38, 40, 58, 133
PERT (Program Evaluation and Review Technique) 113
Peruzzi, Baldassarre 36, *38*, 58
Peter Lewis House 129
Philip, Johnson 129
Piazzale dell'Impero 30, *32*, 113
Piazzale delle Adunate 27, *29*, 67, 96
Plato 56
Portoghesi, Paolo 48
Pound, Ezra 11
Price, Cedric 8, 13, 124
probability 16, 52, 56, 130–131
proto-parametric 6, 9, 11, 13–14
Purini, Franco 13, 15–16, 138

Quadarella, Giovanni 112
quantum/quantize 35, 40
Quaroni, Ludovico 13

Reichlin, Bruno 16, 133
Roisecco, Giulio 12, 19n45
Rostagni, Cecilia 16, 22, 56

Saarinen, Eero 15
Sacchi, Livio 15
Sacripanti, Maurizio 13
Saggio, Antonino 15
Sangallo, Antonio da (the Younger) 99
Schumacher, Patrik 2, 6, 124, 128, 132–134
scientific method 12, 109
scientific nationalism 11
self-organising properties 128
semantic 41, 114
Severati, Carlo 14
Sketchpad 109–130
smart city 1
Società Anonima Pellami 118, *119*
Spazio 24–25, 33–34, 36, 41, 44–47, 52, 99, 106, 114, 116, 133
Spinoza, Baruch 56
Splines 3, 134

Stock Exchange Tower *see* Montreal Tower
structure, mathematical 22, 33–48, 50, 52–55, 57, 77, 106, 114, 127–132, 134, 134n2; baroque structure 58–59
Struttura come forma 8, 33–34, 41, 57
survey 76, 109
Sutherland, Ivan 14
swimming stadium A and B 76, 78, 81–85, 95–96, 99, 101, 121n13, 128

Tabgha Sanctuary 118, *119*
Tafuri, Manfredo 1, 4n5, 13–14
Tagliacozzo 109
Tapié, Michel 22, 40, 45, 55–58, 140
Tedeschi, Letizia 16, 56
Tehran Olympic Complex 99, *100*, 101, *102*, *103*
Teicholz, Eric 131
tennis stadium 48, 85–88, 95–96, 101
Terzidis, Kostas 135n12
Tevere's Bridge 118, *119*
Thompson, D'Arcy Wentworth 11, 39, 128, *129*, 134
topology 47, 55–56, 70, 130; topological properties 129; topological thinking 30, 85
town planning 51, 125
traffic 45, 48, 51, 106, 108–109, 125, 130, 136n38

Triennale, Milan 22, 45, 48, 67, 109
Tugendhat House 99

uncertainty principle 35, 56
United States Lines Paris Review 56
urban design 48, 107–109, 130–131; urban planning 21, 23, 48, 51–52, 109, 118
Utzon, Jørn Oberg 15

Vaccaro, Giuseppe 54
Venturi, Robert 1
Viati Navone 24–25, 31
Villa Borghese 106, *107*, 112
Viterbo's Baths 118, *119*
Vitruvio 42–43

Wachsmann, Konrad 15
Watergate complex 116, *117*, 127
Wertheimer, Max 133
Weyl, Hermann 133
Whyte, Lancelot Law 133
Wiener, Norbert 8–9, 17n13
Word War II 11, 23
Wright, Frank Lloyd 11, 53

Zaffagnini, Mario 12, 14–15
Zevi, Bruno 1–2, 4, 11–13, 33, 70
Zevi, Maria 14
Zorzi, Silvano 112